8.95

PRAISE FOR *THE FIGHT FOR FREE SPEECH*

"The past greets the present in Ian Rosenberg's captivating free speech stories. These true-to-life accounts invite readers to reflect on the value of liberty and the price of freedom. Rosenberg's revealing narratives, based on ten seminal cases, are crafted with the finesse of a gifted writer combined with the acumen of a learned lawyer. Forceful yet thoughtful, credible yet concise, historical yet modern, engaging yet erudite—they all tumble together in *The Fight for Free Speech*, a mind-opening book aptly fit for our times."

Ronald K. L. Collins, editor of *First Amendment News* and co-author of *We Must Not Be Afraid to Be Free*

"Ian Rosenberg's riveting portrayal of ten of the Supreme Court's leading free speech cases is a page-turner! *The Fight for Free Speech* tells the gripping, behind-the-scenes stories of those whose visions and passion paved the way for their causes to be heard before our country's High Court."

Hon. Frederic Block, United States District Judge and author of *Crimes and Punishments: Entering the Mind of a Sentencing Judge*

"With verve and aplomb, *The Fight for Free Speech* reveals actual free speech conflicts on the ground along with the basic First Amendment law they engendered. It is a gift for citizenship."

Donald A. Downs, Alexander Meiklejohn Professor of Political Science, University of Wisconsin–Madison

"*The Fight for Free Speech* is an accessible but learned survey of the concepts upon which the Constitutional right to free speech rests. Its ten chapters weave fascinating narratives about the people who stood up for free speech and the Supreme Court Justices who have struggled to understand how and where to delineate the lines that separate this precious freedom from behavior and language that can be prohibited. Rosenberg explores and contextualizes the signature tropes of free-speech discourse including the marketplace of ideas, shouting fire in a crowded theater, rights that don't stop at the schoolhouse door, prior restraint, the right to parody, and hate speech in order to make our ongoing discourse more careful and accurate. The book is a perfect text for college courses in a variety of fields, including history, government, communication, and politics. It is also a challenging book for AP high school classes. Rosenberg beautifully combines the legal discussions with stories of contemporary examples, and leaves plenty of space to add new examples that will surely present themselves on a regular basis. It is guaranteed to start a discussion!"

Randall Iden, Faculty Director, Master of Science in Communication Program, Northwestern University

THE FIGHT FOR FREE SPEECH

TEN CASES
THAT DEFINE OUR
FIRST AMENDMENT
FREEDOMS

IAN ROSENBERG

NEW YORK UNIVERSITY PRESS
NEW YORK

NEW YORK UNIVERSITY PRESS
New York
www.nyupress.org

References to Internet websites (URLs) were accurate at the time of writing. Neither the author nor New York University Press is responsible for URLs that may have expired or changed since the manuscript was prepared.

Library of Congress Cataloging-in-Publication Data
Names: Rosenberg, Ian, author.
Title: The fight for free speech : ten cases that define our First Amendment freedoms
/ Ian Rosenberg.
Description: New York : New York University Press, 2021. |
Includes bibliographical references and index.
Identifiers: LCCN 2020015039 (print) | LCCN 2020015040 (ebook) | ISBN 9781479801565
(cloth) | ISBN 9781479801541 (ebook) | ISBN 9781479801589 (ebook)
Subjects: LCSH: Freedom of speech—United States.
Classification: LCC KF4772 .R67 2021 (print) | LCC KF4772 (ebook) | DDC 342.7308/53--dc23
LC record available at https://lccn.loc.gov/2020015039

LC ebook record available at https://lccn.loc.gov/2020015040New York University Press books
are printed on acid-free paper, and their binding materials are chosen for strength and durabil-
ity. We strive to use environmentally responsible suppliers and materials to the greatest extent
possible in publishing our books.

Manufactured in the United States of America

Book designed and typeset by Charles B. Hames

10 9 8 7 6 5 4 3 2 1

Also available as an ebook

For Caroline

The constitutional right of free expression is powerful medicine in a society as diverse and populous as ours. It is designed and intended to remove governmental restraints from the arena of public discussion, putting the decision as to what views shall be voiced largely into the hands of each of us. . . .

Justice John Marshall Harlan II, *Cohen v. California*, 1971

CONTENTS

INTRODUCTION

After the 2018 mass shooting at Marjory Stoneman Douglas High School, I was talking to my family at the dinner table about the news report I was reviewing, as part of my job as a media lawyer, on the student survivors turned activists. My children (at the time ages twelve and ten) became very serious about what would happen if they left school during the day to join the National School Walkout protests. Could they be punished? What were their rights?

Americans of all ages are confronted with increasing frequency by a barrage of free speech questions. What are libel laws, and do they need to be changed to stop the press from lying? Does Colin Kaepernick have a right to take a knee? Can *Saturday Night Live* be punished for parody? Amid these controversies, we hear free speech shouted as a rallying cry from disparate voices, liberal as well as conservative, from the Women's March to social media trolls. And while Americans are demanding free speech, they are often doing so without necessarily knowing what their rights really entail. Unfortunately, meaningful answers are out of reach unless we know what the First Amendment protects, allows, and restricts. At the same time, cutting through the misinformation and complexities surrounding Supreme Court rulings is a daunting task even for lawyers.

Yet conversations like the ones I have had with my kids have compelled me to rethink what I have learned and practiced as a First Amendment lawyer for over twenty years. Contrary to the prevailing opinion in law schools, *everyone* can have a practical working knowledge of free speech law. The trick is to ditch jargon and academic theory, and make an effort to describe how First Amendment law applies to the controversies of today. Wisdom can be condensed without being dumbed down.[1]

As a media lawyer and teacher to communications graduate students, most of my career has focused on explaining complicated legal concepts to smart people who are not lawyers. From these experiences I have distilled a wide spectrum of First Amendment law down to ten critical cases.[2] Each chapter in this book will focus on a contemporary free speech question—from student walkouts for gun safety to Samantha Bee's expletives, from Nazis marching in Charlottesville to stopping Stormy Daniels from talk-show-hopping—and then identify, unpack, and explain the key Supreme Court case that provides the answers. Together they create a practical framework for viewing where our free speech protections have come from and how they can develop in the future.

Each case also reveals the compelling story of someone who spoke out and ended up fighting for their free speech rights all the way to our nation's highest court. Equally important, the resulting Supreme Court decisions are the stories the justices tell *us* about the meaning of our Constitution and our country. These surprising and enlightening tales deserve to be known by wider audiences beyond legal circles.

In streamlining these concepts, this book deliberately sits in stark contrast to what many first-year students are taught in law school: that the law is like a "seamless web."[3] The idea is that you need to study all aspects of the law, with as many details as possible, so that the threads of each decision are woven together in a tightly knit whole that won't unravel. *The Fight for Free Speech* rejects that academic model as both misleading and impractical. This book is much more like buying a rug at Ikea. It may not be an intricately made tapestry, but it covers what you need just as well, and you can get it a lot quicker and cheaper. My hope in paring it down this way is that you will gain an awareness of your rights, whether you are an organizer planning a protest, an activist on Twitter, or simply an engaged member of your community.

Justice David Souter gave a prescient talk in 2012 where he told the story of Benjamin Franklin being asked, "shortly after the 1787 convention adjourned, what kind of government the constitution would give us if it was adopted." Franklin's wise reply was, "A republic, *if you can keep it.*" This remark is particularly imperative to remember in our modern era because, Souter cautioned, "you can't keep it in ignorance."[4] We can't hope to keep our democracy alive if citizens remain uninformed of our First Amendment rights and history.

In our current cultural landscape, where people are demanding their right to speak and be heard, *The Fight for Free Speech* is a user's guide for combating ignorance and bringing an understanding of free speech law to all. Come with me and travel through the past. We will meet the unlikely pioneers who went before us, and let their journeys illuminate our free speech freedoms today.

1 / THE WOMEN'S MARCH AND THE MARKETPLACE OF IDEAS

A wave of pink "pussyhats" was moving from the Capitol toward the White House.[1] Protestors were holding signs aloft as they participated in the Women's March of 2017. "Our Rights Are Not Up for Grabs. Neither Are We." "Our Arms Are Tired from Holding These Signs Since the 1920's." "My Nana Didn't Flee Russia for This."[2] The crowds chanted in call and response, "Tell me what democracy looks like!" "This is what democracy looks like!"

What began as a post-election Facebook post transformed into over three million women and men demonstrating across the country and the globe at over three hundred sister events. Gloria Steinem, the feminist standard-bearer and honorary chairwoman of the event, exulted to the crowds: "Thank you for understanding that sometimes we must put our bodies where our beliefs are."[3] Coming the day after the inauguration of President Trump, the march was also intentionally a protest of his election, offering a defiant rebuke of his nascent administration. Civil rights activist Angela Davis addressed the crowds in DC and set forth this mission in no uncertain terms: "The next 1,459 days of the Trump administration will be 1,459 days of resistance: resistance on the ground, resistance in the classrooms, resistance on the job, resistance in our art and in our music."[4]

Celebrities from the art and music worlds were front and center as featured speakers. Actress America Ferrera kicked things off by telling the crowd, "It's been a heart-rending time to be both a woman and an immigrant. Our dignity, our character, our rights have all been under attack."[5] Scarlett Johansson wanted everyone to "get really, really personal," and talked about visiting Planned Parenthood when she was fifteen years old, where she was treated with compassion, "no judgment," and "gentle guidance."[6]

Madonna caused controversy in some circles, as usual, in her speech that day. With her trademark mix of candor and provocation, she revealed, "Yes, I'm angry. Yes, I am outraged. Yes, I have thought an awful lot about blowing up the White House."[7] However, in her next breath she clearly rejected this notion, "But I know that this won't change anything. We cannot fall into despair. . . . We must love one another or die. I choose love."[8] The *New York Times* reported that the Secret Service had no comment on her statement, adding, "though an investigation seemed unlikely."[9] On *Fox & Friends*, former House speaker and Republican pundit Newt Gingrich would later say that Madonna "ought to be arrested."[10]

What Madonna might have been surprised to find out is that a hundred short years ago she most likely would not only have been arrested for her speech, but would have been sentenced to years of jail time. She, and all the marchers, owe their First Amendment protections to one tenacious young immigrant who set in motion the events that forever changed our relationship to free speech.

* * *

In 1913, Mollie Steimer arrived at Ellis Island at the age of sixteen.[11] Her family was fleeing Russia's virulent anti-Semitic discrimination and violence, so that she and her five brothers, as her parents put it, "would be brought up in a free country."[12]

Standing just four foot nine inches tall,[13] Steimer was later described by legendary anarchist and feminist Emma Goldman as "diminutive and quaint-looking . . . with an iron will and a tender heart."[14] She worked in a ladies' shirtwaist factory, laboring long hours to earn fifteen dollars a week to support herself and help her family.[15] "Life was hard," Steimer wrote. "Came home late, got up early. Things began to protest in me against a system of life where people who are hard workers have to struggle bitterly just to be able to exist."[16] These feelings of dissatisfaction led her to reading about anarchism, "to search for a way out."[17] Soon Steimer became deeply devoted to the anarchist ideals of communal property, collective action, and the abolition of government, and firmly believed that this new social order "would really make life worthwhile."[18]

Steimer joined up with a group of fellow Russian Jewish anarchists led by Jacob Abrams, a short man with dark eyes, long brown hair, and a thin mustache.[19] Abrams worked as a bookbinder and union leader, and Steimer said his "energetic personality . . . won my admiration immediately."[20] Abrams and Steimer, along with their working-class compatriots—the equally "tough and fanatical" Jacob Schwartz, Hyman Lachowsky (both bookbinders), and Samuel Lipman (a furrier)—regularly met clandestinely at an apartment in East Harlem. Together this group published an anarchist journal in Yiddish, first called *Der Shturm* (The Storm) and later renamed *Frayhayt* (Freedom).[21]

In August 1918, Steimer and her fellow anarchists were incensed by the news of a new mission launched as part of the United States' continuing involvement in World War I.[22] President Woodrow Wilson had just announced that he would be sending American troops to Russia.[23] The decision was supposedly made to support Czechoslovak allies in the continuing fight against Germany. However, many viewed the action as little more than a thinly disguised effort to help the "White" Russians and attack the "Red" Bolsheviks during their civil war.[24] Steimer saw it as an indefensible attempt to subvert the Russian Revolution, which she wrote would "lead to . . . the freeing of mankind."[25]

The group decided to produce two leaflets furiously denouncing Wilson and his Russian endeavor. Lipman wrote one in English and Schwartz one in Yiddish, each approximately four hundred words.[26] In their rented basement storefront on a newly purchased press they quickly printed five thousand copies of each, on thin four-by-twelve-inch pieces of paper.[27]

The English-language leaflet was titled "The Hypocrisy of the United States and Her Allies." It condemned Wilson and attacked his "shameful, cowardly silence about the intervention in Russia [which] reveals the hypocrisy of the plutocratic gang in Washington and vicinity." The document goes on to lambaste the president as "too much of a coward to come out openly and say: 'We capitalistic nations cannot afford to have a proletarian republic in Russia.'" It ends with a plea:

> Will you allow the Russian Revolution to be crushed? YOU: Yes, we mean YOU the people of America! . . . The Russian Revolution cries: "WORKERS OF THE WORLD! AWAKE! RISE! PUT DOWN YOUR ENEMY AND MINE! Yes friends, there is only one enemy of the workers of the world and that is CAPITALISM. . . . AWAKE! AWAKE, YOU WORKERS OF THE WORLD!

It was signed simply: "Revolutionists." It also has a clarifying "P.S." that adds, "It is absurd to call us pro-German. We hate and despise German militarism more than do your hypocritical tyrants."[28]

The second leaflet, in Yiddish, titled "Workers—Wake Up!!," addressed the same concerns, but in a more anguished tone and with a much more particular audience in mind. Pointedly addressing "[w]orkers in the ammunition factories," it announces that "you are producing bullets, bayonets, cannon, to murder not only the Germans, but also your dearest, best, who are in Russia and are fighting for freedom." In contrast to the vaguer advocacy of the English leaflet, this one made a specific call for action:

> Workers, our reply to the barbaric intervention has to be a general strike! An open challenge only will let the government know that not only the Russian Worker fights for freedom, but also here in America lives the spirit of revolution. Do not let the government scare you with their wild punishment in prisons, hanging and shooting. We must not and will not betray the splendid fighters of Russia. Workers, up to fight. . . . Woe unto those who will be in the way of progress. Let solidarity live![29]

This one was signed "The Rebels."

Steimer took most of the leaflets to scatter surreptitiously around the city. She threw some from Lower East Side rooftops and several people who found them were so provoked that they contacted the police.[30] A reserve squad and detectives "scoured the neighborhood in search of the perpetrators," without success.[31] Her distribution and the leaflets' words were so shocking as to make New York City headlines the next day, reporting: "Wilson Attacked in Circulars from Roofs of East Side" and "Seditious Circulars Scattered in Streets."[32]

On August 23, 1918, Steimer took another batch to the factory she worked at, and tossed several out the bathroom window.[33] Workers outside the building at 7:45 that morning looked up to see the leaflets fluttering down toward them. Although they couldn't read the Yiddish words, they went to the police, who conducted a floor by floor search of the building. With thorough detective work, they found that an employee of the American Hat Company, Hyman Rosansky, had punched in earlier than usual that day. After questioning at police headquarters, Rosansky revealed that he was scheduled to pick up more leaflets from the group that evening on East 104th Street.[34] (Steimer later described Rosansky as a "sympathizer" who "expressed a wish to participate" and that, when "caught and questioned, he gave us all out.")[35]

Staking out the rendezvous point from nearby doorways, the police ultimately nabbed Steimer and all the other group members one by one.[36] The interrogations at police headquarters ranged from civil to violent. Steimer claimed that Lachowsky, Lipman, and Schwartz were severely beaten. By early the next morning, all of them confessed to their involvement, without implicating one another.[37] The arrests of these anarchists for "attacking President Wilson and American war policy" made news.[38] The *Washington Times* called them the "Blast Group," and noted that the men "wore long hair and were heavily bearded."[39] The *New York Journal* characterized "the girl" as "defiant and of a quick and alert manner."[40]

The defendants were charged with violating the Sedition Act, enacted just three months earlier, which made almost all speech critical of the government a crime.[41] This act was an amendment to the Espionage Act of 1917, which primarily criminalized obstructing recruitment to or causing insubordination in the military.[42] Specifically, they were accused of conspiring to "unlawfully utter, print, write and publish . . . disloyal, scurrilous and abusive language" about the US government that was intended to bring it "into contempt, scorn, contumely and disrepute [and] . . . to incite, provoke and encourage resistance" to the war.[43] In addition to Steimer and her associates, more than two thousand individuals would ultimately be prosecuted under the acts, resulting in over a thousand convictions.[44]

The night before their trial, Jacob Schwartz died in the prison ward of Bellevue Hospital. An autopsy determined that pneumonia was the cause of death, but his fellow defendants vehemently rejected that conclusion and believed police brutality was to blame. His friends would place a wreath on his coffin that expressed their sentiments: "Jacob Schwartz, as the result of the Third Degree, on the night of his arrest, Aug. 23, died."[45] (During her trial testimony, the *New York Tribune* reported that Steimer "clenched her fist and almost screamed: 'I insist that Schwartz was killed by the police!'")[46] An unfinished letter Schwartz had begun before being sent to the hospital helped to cast a legendary glow over what many anarchists viewed as his martyrdom for their cause: "Farewell, comrades. When you appear before the court I will be with you no longer. Struggle without fear, fight bravely. I am sorry I have to leave you."[47]

On October 14, the anarchist speech trial began in a Manhattan federal district court (the initial trial court in the federal system). Unfortunately for the defendants, a visiting judge from Alabama named Henry DeLamar Clayton Jr. would be presiding. Clayton was racist, anti–women's suffrage, anti-immigrant, and anti-Semitic.[48] One telling example of how these prejudices were blatantly displayed during the trial occurred when Judge Clayton became frustrated with the line of questioning from the defendants' lawyer, Harry Weinberger. (Weinberger, whose parents were Hungarian Jewish immigrants, described himself as a "pugnacious little" fighter.)[49] After refusing to allow Weinberger to continue speaking, Clayton told the court, "I have tried to out-talk an Irishman, and I never can do it, and the Lord knows I can not out-talk a Jew."[50]

Clayton seemed incapable of, or unconcerned about, hiding his distaste for the immigrant defendants. During Abrams's testimony, he twice asked, "Why don't you go back to Russia?"[51] At another point with Abrams on the stand, Clayton demonstrated his unwillingness to consider the defendants as Americans. The revealing exchange is recounted in Professor Richard Polenberg's richly detailed historical study, *Fighting Faiths: The Abrams Case, the Supreme Court, and Free Speech*:

Abrams, speaking in a soft voice with a distinct Yiddish accent, was earnestly attempting to defend his anarchist beliefs. "This government was built on a revolution," Abrams said. ". . . When our forefathers of the American Revolution—" That was as far as he got. "Your what?" Judge Clayton interrupted. "My forefathers," Abrams replied. "Do you mean to refer to the fathers of this nation as your forefathers?" Clayton asked. Abrams said, "We are all a big human family," and "Those that stand for the people, I call them father." But the judge had made his point, and the jury had no doubt gotten it.[52]

Clayton's condescending treatment of Steimer was no better, but she continued to rebelliously assert her beliefs. She refused to stand when the judge entered, and the bailiff called "all rise" to no avail.[53] When questioned on whether or not she was an anarchist, Steimer pressed to define her philosophy in her own terms:

By anarchism, I understand a new social order, where no group of people shall be governed by another group of people. Individual freedom shall prevail in the full sense of the word. Private ownership shall be abolished. . . . We shall not have to struggle for our daily existence, as we do now. No one shall live on the product of others. Everyone person shall produce as much as he can and . . . receive according to his need. Instead of striving to get money, we shall strive towards educations, towards knowledge. . . . To the fulfillment of this idea I shall devote all my energy, and, if necessary, render my life for it.[54]

Weinberger made a strenuous final effort to persuade the jury to support free speech in an exhaustive two-hour closing argument.[55] He contended that the defendants were not supporting the German cause, and therefore were not encouraging resistance to the American war effort.[56] He maintained that even immigrant anarchists had "the right to question and protest against an army being sent to Russia, to fight the Bolsheviki. They had the right, not because they are American citizens, because they are not, but because they are here and free speech is guaranteed to all citizens and noncitizens."[57]

Despite Weinberger's valiant efforts, the outcome of the two-week trial was hardly in doubt. After little more than an hour, the jury returned guilty verdicts for Abrams, Lachowsky, Lipman, Rosansky, and Steimer.[58] On the day of the sentencing, the *New York Tribune* set the scene: "Mollie Steimer, a tiny person, dressed in a red Russian blouse, entered the court smiling, with flowers on her arm, which she gave to other defendants, except Rosansky, whom they ostracized because he had turned informer."[59] The United States attorney recommended leniency for Rosansky, because of his cooperation with the authorities, and he was sentenced to three years in the federal penitentiary.[60] For the men, Clayton imposed the maximum sentence of twenty years each, and he gave Steimer fifteen.[61]

As Steimer responded to her sentence, Clayton attempted to cut her off. "I'm not going to permit you to make a soap-box oration, Mollie," he scolded her, "and this is one time that you are brought in contact with the knowledge that there is some authority even over an anarchist woman."[62] Nevertheless, she persisted. "Though you have sent troops to Russia," Steimer announced to the courtroom, "though you have sent soldiers to slaughter our revolutionists, you cannot crush our revolutionary spirit."[63] The armistice bringing an end to World War I was only weeks away, but Steimer and her anarchist comrades' constitutional battle for free speech had just begun.

A year had passed since the anarchists' convictions by the time the Supreme Court heard their case in October 1919. Harry Weinberger summarized his brief in concise terms: "the point is put up . . . pretty straight as to whether or not you have the right to criticize the President and the policies of the government."[64] In his oral argument before the Court, Weinberger asserted that the freedom to speak out against the government had been protected by the framers of the constitution. Those revolutionaries viewed "the unabridgeable liberty of discussion as a natural right," and therefore, he boldly claimed, the Sedition Act was unconstitutional.[65]

Knowing that the Court had at that time never taken such an expansive view of the First Amendment, Weinberger also more pragmatically argued that there was insufficient evidence to support the jury verdict that the defendants had conspired to foster resistance to the war.[66] He reiterated the point he had made to the jury, that in calling for a munitions factory strike, the defendants were not supporting Germany, but rather seeking to defend Russia.[67] Even if some anti-war speech could constitutionally be made criminal, Weinberger maintained that this was speech of a different category. He characterized the leaflets as merely "a public discussion of a public policy in reference to a country with which we were not at war."[68]

Arguing on behalf of the government was Robert P. Stewart, who had been appointed earlier that year by President Wilson to be the first assistant attorney general in "charge of criminal matters" for the Department of Justice.[69] Stewart's main point was that the Court had upheld the constitutionality of the Espionage Act just seven months earlier in a case called *Schenck v. United States*.[70] Since the Sedition Act was an amendment to the Espionage Act and put similar limits on speech, he insisted that the *Abrams* convictions must be "equally constitutional."[71]

The *Schenck* case has been identified by University of Chicago law professor Geoffrey Stone as "the Supreme Court's first significant decision interpreting the First Amendment."[72] In *Schenck*, during the war, two leaders of the Socialist Party had been found guilty of obstructing the draft and causing insubordination in the armed forces in violation of the Espionage Act.[73] Their actions had been to print and distribute fifteen thousand leaflets attacking the draft (a "conscript is little better than a convict," it said) and urging peaceful resistance to it (such as petitioning for the repeal of the act).[74] Some of the leaflets were mailed directly to drafted men.[75] Justice Oliver Wendell Holmes,

Jr., writing for a unanimous Supreme Court, affirmed the convictions, including Schenck's ten-year sentence, in short order.[76]

The seventy-eight-year-old Justice Holmes had been born into a Boston Brahmin family (his father, a prominent physician and writer, coined the term "Brahmin" to describe New England's elite), served in the Union army during the Civil War, and was a brilliant writer.[77] He was tall and slim, dressed nattily, and sported an impressive white walrus mustache. Holmes looked and acted like a Hollywood vision of a Supreme Court justice: wise and regal. He was also an old-fashioned patriot who once said, "Damn a man who ain't for his country right or wrong."[78]

Holmes's reflexive support of the United States involvement in World War I may have influenced his decision to uphold Schenck's conviction. Deploying his signature stylish turns of phrase, Justice Holmes expounded on why the specific limits on speech in the Espionage Act did not violate the First Amendment:

> We admit that, in many places and in ordinary times, the defendants, in saying all that was said in the circular, would have been within their constitutional rights. But the character of every act depends upon the circumstances in which it is done. The most stringent protection of free speech would not protect a man in falsely shouting fire in a theatre and causing a panic.[79]

With that fiery image, Holmes brought into the public consciousness what has been called "the most well-known—yet misquoted and misused—phrase in Supreme Court history."[80] It not only justified the wartime speech limitation for Schenck, but rhetorically spoke more broadly to the idea that limits on free speech should naturally be expected in our society.

Like a zombie, Holmes's metaphor continues lumbering on to our present day, stalking free speech wherever it goes, in the guise of universally accepted wisdom.[81] People who want to restrict free speech invariably begin by saying some version of "you can't yell fire. . . ." And while the sentence as written was certainly intended to be supportive of speech restrictions, it is consistently remembered incorrectly and used indiscriminately. Limits on "shouting fire" are justified, Holmes wrote, only if they are done "*falsely*" *and* end up "causing a *panic.*" No one would ever think of punishing someone for yelling "fire" when there was actually a fire burning—in fact that person should be congratulated on potentially saving the lives of their fellow theatergoers! In addition, if there is no "panic" or harm, then any speech restriction is unnecessary, and even worse, may deter people from calling out a warning when one is needed. Both of these often-forgotten components—falsity *and* harm—are crucial to comprehending the true limits of the First Amendment and should be prerequisites in any consideration of prohibiting speech. (If you, dear reader, take away nothing else from this book, please go forth and flaunt your knowledge of how to use this adage properly from now on.)

So in *Schenck,* Holmes and the Court had decided, with seemingly little hand-wringing, that the First Amendment had no power to stop the government from imprisoning people for nonviolent speech that criticized the government.[82] Within days of that decision, the Supreme Court affirmed Espionage Act convictions in two more cases of anti-draft speech. The fact that the defendants in these cases were a presidential candidate and a newspaper publisher made no difference in their outcomes; each time, Justice Holmes delivered the opinion of the unanimous Court.[83] Given these very recent and similar precedents, Assistant Attorney General Stewart had every reason to believe that another unanimous judgment in the government's favor was sure to follow in *Abrams.* And yet, shockingly, Holmes himself was about to change course and lead the country on a new path toward a First Amendment revolution.

Seven justices on the Court had no difficulty deciding that the defendants' convictions in *Abrams* should all be upheld. However, Justice Holmes, supported by his friend Justice Louis Brandeis, was thinking differently.[84] As the majority opinion was being prepared, Holmes went to the upright desk in his home study and was about to write "twelve paragraphs that would change the history of free speech in America."[85] Immediately after finishing his dissenting opinion, Holmes wrote modestly in a letter to his friend Felix Frankfurter (the future Supreme Court justice) that he wasn't sure what he had written "*quasi in furore* [as if possessed] . . . is good enough."[86] He needn't have worried. What he wrote was so well reasoned and subversive that when he sent it around to his fellow justices for their consideration, it prompted a remarkable visit.

A week later, three justices of the Supreme Court arrived unannounced at Holmes's town house.[87] They were there to personally appeal to Holmes to reconsider his position, and join them in supporting the convictions of the anarchists and the validity of the Sedition Act. What happened next, and how they tried to convince him, is reconstructed in Professor Thomas Healy's gripping intellectual history, *The Great Dissent: How Oliver Wendell Holmes Changed His Mind— and Changed the History of Free Speech in America*:

A dissent like this, [they argued,] from a figure as venerable as Holmes, might weaken the country's resolve and give comfort to the enemy. The nation's security was at stake, the justices told Holmes. As an old soldier, he should close ranks and set aside his personal views. They even appealed to [his wife] Fanny, who nodded her head in agreement. The tone of their plea was friendly, even affectionate, and Holmes listened thoughtfully. He had always respected the institution of the Court and more than once had suppressed his own beliefs for the sake of unanimity. But this time he felt a duty to speak his mind. He told his colleagues he regretted he could not join them, and they left without pressing him further.[88]

Three days after the failed intervention, the Supreme Court's decision in *Abrams v. United States* was announced. Justice John Clarke, the most junior member of the Court, wrote the opinion for the seven-member majority, affirming the convictions. (Only Brandeis joined Holmes in dissent.)[89] Clarke dismissed what he described as the "faintly" argued First Amendment issues in a single sentence, holding that such claims had already been rejected in *Schenck*.[90] Clarke also rejected Weinberger's claim, "that the only intent of these defendants was to prevent injury to the Russian cause," writing, "Men must be held to have intended, and to be accountable for, the effects which their acts were likely to produce."[91]

After Clarke's summary of the case, Justice Holmes read his dissenting opinion from the bench to publicly emphasize how "grievously misguided" the majority opinion was in his view.[92] Holmes began by articulating a demanding test for when "the right to free speech" could be restricted: "It is only the present danger of *immediate* evil or an intent to bring it about that warrants Congress in setting a limit to the expression of opinion."[93] Emphasizing how strict this test was in application, Holmes determined that "nobody can suppose that the surreptitious publishing of a silly leaflet by an unknown man, without more, would present any immediate danger that its opinions would hinder the success of the government arms."[94]

Holmes went on to indignantly discuss the inappropriate harshness of the punishments: "In this case, sentences of twenty years' imprisonment have been imposed for the publishing of two leaflets that I believe the defendants had as much right to publish as the Government has to publish the Constitution of the United States now vainly invoked by them."[95] Additionally, he called the motivation behind the severity of the sentences into question. "The most nominal punishment seems to me all that possibly could be inflicted," Holmes opined, "unless the defendants are to be made to suffer not for what the indictment alleges, but for the creed that they avow...."[96]

For his conclusion, Holmes constructed an expansive edifice that not only provided a rationale for his opinion in *Abrams*, but also for reconsidering the meaning of the First Amendment. In a little over four hundred words, he sought to convey why speech is dangerous, what free speech can do for society, and how strenuously we must resist the impulse to punish even the speech we hate. The result is the single most important paragraph in all of First Amendment law:

Persecution for the expression of opinions seems to me perfectly logical. If you have no doubt of your premises or your power, and want a certain result with all your heart, you naturally express your wishes in law, and sweep away all opposition. To allow opposition by speech seems to indicate that you think the speech impotent, as when a man says that he has squared the circle, or that you do not care wholeheartedly for the result, or that you doubt either your power or your premises. But when men have realized that time has upset many fighting faiths, they may come to believe even more than they believe the very foundations of their own conduct that the ultimate good desired is better reached by free trade in ideas—that the best test of truth is the power of the thought to get itself accepted in the competition of the market, and that truth is the only ground upon which their wishes safely can be carried out. That, at any rate, is the theory of our Constitution. It is an experiment, as all life is an experiment. Every year, if not every day, we have to wager our salvation upon some prophecy based upon imperfect knowledge. While that experiment is part of our system, I think that we should be eternally vigilant against attempts to check the expression of opinions that we loathe and believe to be fraught with death, unless they so imminently threaten immediate interference with the lawful and pressing purposes of the law that an immediate check is required to save the country. . . . Only the emergency that makes it immediately dangerous to leave the correction of evil counsels to time warrants making any exception to the sweeping command, "Congress shall make no law . . . abridging the freedom of speech."[97]

The impact of these words over time is hard to overstate. It would become "the most quoted paragraph ever written about the freedom of speech."[98] Even more meaningfully, it marked a turning point in recognizing the power of the First Amendment.[99] This new vision of the First Amendment eloquently articulated why the government should be constitutionally prohibited from punishing Americans for their speech, simply because the government opposed or feared the ideas in that speech.[100] It also placed dissenting voices at the center, not the margins, of First Amendment protection, even during wartime.[101]

As noted dissenter Justice Ruth Bader Ginsburg has described, since a dissent does not decide a case or create a rule of law, one of its primary purposes is for "appealing to the intelligence of a future day."[102] The *Abrams* dissent certainly achieved this goal, but it also did something more. Harvard Law Professor Mark Tushnet has written that a truly great dissent is one in which "its vision of democracy and the Constitution and its rhetoric themselves contributed to making its doctrine seem correct."[103] Holmes's words measure up to that rare distinction: they not only spoke to the future, they transformed it.

Central to this new free speech perspective was the metaphor Holmes conjured up that became known as the "marketplace of ideas." Although Holmes himself never used that term, it nevertheless captures the spirit of this unique justification for free speech.[104] Holmes turns to the chaos and cacophony of the market place to convey the connection between America's democratic capitalism and the value of searching for truth in a forum where the government cannot exclude critical voices from the public debate.[105] It also seems possible that Holmes strategically chose an economic symbol to make his revolutionary defense of anti-capitalist speech more persuasive to his conservative contemporaries.[106]

While celebrating the theoretical potential for the marketplace of ideas to encourage openness to a wide variety of speech, we should not, however, fail to recognize the substantial body of academic critique that has challenged the marketplace of ideas theory. Much of this discussion centers around the question of: who is truly heard in the marketplace? If women, minorities, and poor people are not granted equal opportunity to enter the market, how can their voices participate in the competition for truth? As University of Hawaii at Manoa professor of law emeritus, and a leading expert on antidiscrimination law and critical race theory, Charles R. Lawrence III puts it, "We must eschew abstractions of first amendment theory that proceed without attention to the dysfunction in the marketplace of ideas created by racism and unequal access to that market."[107] Even when access issues are addressed, feminist legal pioneer Professor Catharine A. MacKinnon further calls into question whether disenfranchised groups ever really benefit from the marketplace forum:

> Think about whether the speech of the Nazis has historically en-hanced the speech of the Jews. Has the speech of the Klan expanded the speech of Blacks? Has the so-called speech of pornographers en-larged the speech of women? In this context, apply to what they call the marketplace of ideas the question . . . : Is there a relationship be-tween our poverty in speech and their wealth?[108]

In addition to these equity concerns, the prospect of a market lead-ing to truth is hard for many consumers to swallow. The free market may be an effective economic system, but how does a mechanism de-signed to enable selling act as a model to facilitate truth seeking? The influence of money and advertising dollars in a market-based system also raises real concerns about truth resulting from a process in which wealth buys you a bigger and better megaphone.[109]

Mark Twain is credited with saying that "a lie can travel around the world and back while the truth is still lacing up its boots."[110] And that perception is supercharged in today's social media–paced world, in which the truth can be swamped under a tweet storm of instant falsehoods. There are those who would argue that whatever value the marketplace metaphor had in the past, it is becoming quickly outmoded in our internet age.[111]

All of these powerful critiques provide revealing insights into American society and justify ongoing debate. At the same time, in order to have any kind of meaningful discussion about free speech today it remains necessary to engage with Holmes' enduring marketplace conception. Grappling with the marketplace of ideas is vital for both those who seek to support our country's current approach to free speech and for those who wish to change it.[112]

Putting metaphor and theory aside, how did the *Abrams* dissent practically change the law regarding advocacy of illegal action? The short answer to this complex question is that it didn't—at least not for a long time. It took more than a decade until the Supreme Court struck down a speech-restricting statute as unconstitutional on First Amendment grounds.[113] And it was not until fifty years after *Abrams*, in a case called *Brandenburg v. Ohio*, that a version of the test Holmes and Brandeis suggested in their dissent fully evolved into its modern and lasting form. The *Brandenburg* holding states that "the constitutional guarantees of free speech and free press do not permit a State to forbid or proscribe advocacy of the use of force or of law violation except where such advocacy is directed to inciting or producing imminent lawless action and is likely to incite or produce such action."[114] In other words, only speech advocating illegal conduct that is directed and likely to trigger imminent illegal action is not protected by the First Amendment, and therefore can be prohibited. This progression, from punishment of speech about criminal conduct to robust protections for such speech, is directly attributable to Holmes's decision to change his mind in *Abrams*.[115]

The remarkable evolution of First Amendment rights from virtually nonexistent to possessing superhero-like strength demonstrates our country's common law judicial system in action. The "common law" means law that comes from judicial interpretation and decisions, rather than legislative statutes. Each decision builds on the next, with courts abiding by the past decisions (often called precedents) of the courts above them in their system.

Holmes literally wrote the book on this subject. His groundbreaking classic *The Common Law*, published in 1881 as he turned forty, begins by declaring, "The life of the law has not been logic; it has been experience."[116] What Holmes meant by this was that the common law is not focused on mathematical precision, but rather develops over time as society changes, based in large part on the experiences of judges and the parties before them. Whether you find this process an inspiring one of messily evolving liberty or look with cynicism at its often-lurching inconsistency, the *Abrams* case and its influence reflect the common law nature of our system for good and ill. And in doing so it provides an origin story that is indispensable to understanding the First Amendment today.

* * *

While it's all well and good to talk about the triumph of First Amendment values over a half century, what did the Abrams decision mean at the time for the anarchists? It meant they went to prison. The Supreme Court majority, despite the protestations of Holmes and Brandeis, had rejected the defendants' claims and so the convictions stood. By December 1919, Abrams, Lipman, Lachowsky, and Steimer had all begun serving their terms of fifteen to twenty years.[117] They would remain incarcerated for the next two years, until the tireless lobbying efforts of their lawyer Weinberger were finally successful. He was able to get the new administration of President Warren Harding to commute their sentences on the condition that they be "at once deported to Russia, never to return."[118]

Steimer initially refused to accept an amnesty deal. "I don't want to be deported. I don't want to be pardoned," she told the authorities. "You sentenced me; when all political prisoners will be freed, I will be freed."[119] But she later said she was ultimately prevailed upon to go along with the plan "when I was told that the boys are . . . only waiting for me."[120]

On November 23, 1921, Abrams, Lachowsky, Lipman, and Steimer were ready to depart to Russia from a pier in South Brooklyn aboard the SS *Esthonia*.[121] The group had mixed emotions as they prepared to leave their loved ones and America forever, to face an uncertain future. Steimer stoically told sixty friends and family that had gathered to see them off, "Good-bye, all of you. I hope that America will be freer in the future than it is today."[122]

From that time onward, their lives would be filled with even greater hardships. Persecuted and jailed in Russia for her anarchist beliefs, Steimer once again had no choice but to accept deportation. This time her only alternative was to suffer through three years of imprisonment in a gulag.[123] Lipman, who had become a Communist and a professor of economic geography, was killed in the Stalinist purges of the late 1930s.[124] And Lachowsky was most likely murdered in his native Minsk by the Nazis sometime after 1941.[125]

Abrams and Steimer separately managed to make their way to Mexico by 1942.[126] Steimer would live there for the rest of her days, never setting foot again in America, and through it all remained steadfastly committed to anarchist causes until her death in 1980.[127] When she was sixty-three, Steimer described her lifelong struggle for what they believed in: "We fought injustice in our humble way as best we could; and if the result was prison, hard labour, deportations and lots of suffering, well, this was something that every human being who fights for a better humanity has to expect."[128]

* * *

As a person who always spoke her mind and refused to accept the status quo, Steimer would likely have felt right at home with the participants of the Women's March. She may also have appreciated Madonna's fearlessness in breaking cultural norms. Madonna's remark about having "thought an awful lot about blowing up the White House" would not have shocked Steimer, although the lack of action taken against the speech might have surprised her.

The fact is that Madonna's statement would certainly be protected under the *Brandenburg* test, since it was neither "directed to inciting or producing imminent lawless action" from the crowd, nor "likely to incite or produce such action." And Steimer deserves recognition for her role in making such speech, and even more broadly speech that criticizes the government, protected under the First Amendment. On the day of her deportation nearly one hundred years ago, Mollie Steimer expressed the hope that America would be freer in the future. Her hope came to pass, and our speech is freer today than it ever would have been without her.

2 / TAKE A KNEE AND THE PLEDGE OF ALLEGIANCE

In early August 2016, Colin Kaepernick, an NFL quarterback for the San Francisco 49ers, remained seated during the playing of the national anthem and no one seemed to notice. He did it again six days later and still no one commented. Perhaps it was because Kaepernick's throwing shoulder was sore and he wasn't in uniform.[1] On August 26, the quarterback was in uniform, and this time when he stayed seated, people started to take notice.[2]

"I am not going to stand up to show pride in a flag for a country that oppresses Black people and people of color," Kaepernick told an NFL Media reporter after the game. "To me, this is bigger than football and it would be selfish on my part to look the other way. There are bodies in the street and people getting paid leave and getting away with murder."[3]

Kaepernick did not notify the team about his protest. "This is not something that I am going to run by anybody," he explained. "I am not looking for approval. I have to stand up for people that are oppressed. . . . If they take football away, my endorsements from me, I know that I stood up for what is right."[4] In response, the NFL issued a brief statement: "Players are encouraged but not required to stand during the playing of the national anthem."[5]

Two days later, Kaepernick spoke with the media and tried to provide greater context for his actions. "There is police brutality. People of color have been targeted by police," he told reporters. "So that's something that this country has to change. There's things we can do to hold them more accountable."[6] Although he was not asked to elaborate, Kaepernick was undoubtedly referring in part to the deaths just a month before of Alton Sterling and Philando Castile.[7] Both men were Black, both killed by police within one day of each other, and both of their deaths had been captured on videos shared by millions, including Kaepernick.[8] "This stand wasn't for me," he tried to make clear. "This is because I'm seeing things happen to people that don't have a voice, people that don't have a platform to talk and have their voices heard, and effect change."[9]

Among the first questions for Kaepernick from the press were what he had to say to people who saw the flag "as a symbol for the military." "I have great respect for the men and women that have fought for this country," he responded. "I have family, I have friends that have gone and fought for this country. And they fight for freedom, they fight for the people, they fight for liberty and justice, for everyone. That's not happening. People are dying in vain because this country isn't holding their end of the bargain up, as far as giving freedom and justice, liberty to everybody."[10]

A more personal military perspective on Kaepernick's actions was presented when Nate Boyer, a former Army Green Beret and Seattle Seahawks long snapper, wrote an open letter addressed to Colin for the *Army Times*. Boyer started off by describing himself as "a big fan" and acknowledged that he knew Kaepernick supports the military.[11] He went on to say that "[e]ven though my initial reaction to your protest was one of anger, I'm trying to listen to what you're saying and why you're doing it."[12]

With only two days before their next game, Kaepernick quickly reached out to Boyer and arranged for them to get together and talk.[13]

Kaepernick and Boyer, along with 49ers safety Eric Reid, met in the lobby of a Westin hotel in San Diego where the team was staying. The three of them talked for ninety minutes.[14] Reid later said that their discussion "led to the decision . . . to not sit but to take a knee, to show respect to the people that felt hurt by that action."[15] Boyer agreed that the change showed "sensitivity" and that "people take a knee to pray. In the military, we take a knee all the time . . . [it is] the classic symbol of respect in front of a brother's grave site."[16]

The next day, at their final preseason game, against the San Diego Chargers, teammates Kaepernick and Reid both took a knee during the anthem.[17] With little fanfare, the "Take a Knee" protests had begun. And it would develop into one of the most publicized and polarizing free speech controversies of the decade. Surveying a brief history of how the protests evolved provides a revealing window into the intersection of race, patriotism, and our free speech rights as Americans.[18]

That same day, at another NFL game in Oakland, Seattle Seahawks cornerback Jerry Lane sat during the anthem, saying he was "standing behind Kaepernick."[19] Soccer star Megan Rapinoe also took a knee at a United States women's national team match against Thailand. Rapinoe said afterward that her actions were "a nod to Kaepernick and everything that he's standing for right now." She added, "Being a gay American, I know what it means to look at the flag and not have it protect all of your liberties."[20]

On the opening night of the NFL's regular season, Denver Broncos linebacker Brandon Marshal took a knee during the anthem, and swiftly lost two sponsorship deals.[21] That Sunday, which coincided with the fifteenth anniversary of the 9/11 terrorist attacks, four members of the Miami Dolphins took a knee, and players on the Seahawks and Kansas City Chiefs linked arms with their teammates during the anthem.[22] At a WNBA playoff game that month, the entire Indiana Fever team took a knee together.[23]

The protests were spreading. Kaepernick's individual stance was beginning to look like it had launched a movement. Meanwhile, his football career was stalled. By March 2017, Kaepernick opted out of his contract with the 49ers and became a free agent. Any hopes that he would quickly sign with another team were slowly deflated.[24]

On the protest front, one particularly notable refusal to stand for the national anthem came the following preseason, on August 13, 2017, just days after the deadly "Unite the Right" rally in Charlottesville. Michael Bennett, defensive end for the Seattle Seahawks and a supporter of Kaepernick's, did not join his teammates in locking arms along the sideline, but instead sat down on a bench, and said the events in Charlottesville "had a lot to do with" his decision.[25] In his book, *Things That Make White People Uncomfortable,* he later divulged that at the time he was also thinking about

> the gap between what we are taught the flag represents and the lived experience of too many people. . . . By not standing, I wanted to honor the founding principles of this country—the freedom of self-expression, liberty, and the equal opportunity to pursue happiness—and challenge us to try to reach those goals. I wanted to use my platform to inspire young people to see us not just as athletes or pitchmen for products, but as changemakers.[26]

A month later, President Trump threw himself into the brewing culture war concerning the protests.[27] At a political rally in Alabama, he told a cheering crowd, "Wouldn't you love to see one of these N.F.L. owners, when somebody disrespects our flag, to say, 'Get that son of a bitch off the field right now, out, he's fired. He's fired!'"[28] The crowd enthusiastically responded with chants of "USA! USA! USA!"[29]

NFL players were more unified than ever in their outrage over Trump's insulting profanity and message. In response, Denver Broncos linebacker Von Miller was one among many who would take a knee for the first time, saying, "Me and my teammates, we felt like President Trump's speech was an assault on our most cherished right, freedom of speech."[30] That weekend, more than two hundred NFL players knelt or sat during the pregame national anthem.[31] The Associated Press calculated that meant about one in eight of the NFL players on active rosters protested.[32] The unity, however, went only so far. While a "handful" of white players participated in these protests seeking to highlight discrimination against people of color, "the vast majority of those actively protesting were Black."[33] In his insightful book *The Heritage: Black Athletes, a Divided America, and the Politics of Patriotism*, journalist Howard Bryant addresses how the Take a Knee protests exposed this striking disparity:

> Like the military, sports was also supposed to be the place where race was secondary to the battle effort, and for years, sports had profited from the gauzy little lie that teammates battled together, understood each other, lived in such close proximity that maybe the rest of the country could learn from the game's *brotherhood*. What Kaepernick revealed was that sports was no less divided along racial lines than the rest of the country, even if its workforce comprised a black majority.[34]

During this resurgence of NFL player protests, Kaepernick himself remained unemployed. In October 2017, Kaepernick filed a grievance accusing the NFL and team owners of collusion.[35] The legal filing, made under the NFL collective bargaining agreement between the league and the players' union, demanded an arbitration hearing on his claims that the owners were secretly acting together to keep him from playing.[36] The complaint contended that "NFL and NFL Team Owners have colluded to deprive Mr. Kaepernick of employment rights in retaliation for Mr. Kaepernick's leadership and advocacy for equality and social justice. . . ."[37] In plain terms, Kaepernick claimed he was being blackballed.

His celebrity attorney, Mark Geragos, made a statement that "principled and peaceful protest . . . should not be punished and athletes should not be denied employment based on partisan political provocation by the Executive Branch of our government. Such a precedent threatens all patriotic Americans and harkens back to our darkest days as a nation."[38] Kaepernick's objective, Geragos added, "has always been, and remains, to simply be treated fairly by the league he performed at the highest level for and to return to the football playing field."[39] Geragos would later also be hired by Eric Reid, Kaepernick's friend who had knelt in protest for more than an entire season. Geragos filed a similar collusion grievance against the NFL on Reid's behalf when he remained unsigned after almost two months as a free agent.[40]

As document searches and depositions of NFL commissioner Roger Goodell and "some of the most powerful owners in the league" progressed in Kaepernick's case, the NFL moved toward trying to officially change its anthem policy.[41] It is worth recognizing that standing on the field for the national anthem was not a standard practice for NFL players until 2009.[42] Even after that time, the NFL rulebook did not mention the national anthem at all, and the league's game operations manual contained only a policy statement that "all players must be on the sideline for the National Anthem . . . [and] *should* stand at attention."[43] On May 23, 2018, Goodell announced a new policy that explicitly required players to "stand and show respect for the flag and the Anthem," but stated that those who "choose not to stand . . . may stay in the locker room or in a similar location off the field until after the Anthem has been performed."[44] The next day, President Trump praised the change on *Fox & Friends* and said that "the NFL owners did the right thing," adding that players who don't stand for the anthem, "maybe they shouldn't be in the country."[45]

Regardless of whether one views the NFL policy change as a compromise or a capitulation, its impact was short-lived. Less than two months later, the NFL and the Players Association (the union for NFL athletes) issued a joint statement that the policy was on hold, after an uproar over reports that the Miami Dolphins had plans to impose as much as a four-game suspension on players who violated the policy by protesting during the anthem.[46] The policy, still too hot to handle, has remained indefinitely suspended.[47]

In criticizing the policy, Malcolm Jenkins, a safety with the Philadelphia Eagles, said that the NFL owners' decision was an attempt to "thwart the players' constitutional rights to express themselves."[48] But was that policy actually a violation of NFL players' First Amendment rights? A short, but incomplete, answer is no, because the First Amendment only applies to efforts by the *government* to restrict speech. As Erwin Chemerinsky, the dean of Berkeley Law, summarized it at the time, "Private employers can fire employees for their speech without having to worry about the First Amendment."[49]

However, the analysis of this vital question should not end there. Since the public outcry on both sides of this controversy focuses less on what the NFL *can* do, and more on what the teams *should* do as a matter of free speech values, the Supreme Court's decisions on whether Americans have a right to refrain from saying something are particularly relevant to this national debate. And although the Court has never spoken on the national anthem specifically, it has twice considered whether or not public school students could refuse to pledge allegiance to the flag—resulting in two strikingly different interpretations of our First Amendment rights.

* * *

In the fall of 1935, ten-year-old William Gobitas and his twelve-year-old sister, Lillian, were considering a decision that would change the course of their lives.[50] They lived with their family of six in a house over their father's store, Economy Grocery, in the coal mining town of Minersville, Pennsylvania.[51] Unlike 90 percent of the ten thousand residents of Minersville who were Catholic, the Gobitas family were Jehovah's Witnesses.[52]

The leader of their religion at that time, Joseph Rutherford, had given a speech on the radio encouraging Witnesses to "object and refuse to salute the flag and pledge allegiance to it."[53] Lillian later explained that Rutherford had said that Witnesses "respect the flag but that going through rituals before an image or emblems was actually idolatry. . . . Our relationship with Jehovah would strictly forbid this."[54] Both Lillian and William wanted to follow Rutherford's guidance, but Lillian wavered. "I loved school, and I was with a nice group. I was actually kind of popular. I was class president in the seventh grade and I had good grades. And I felt that, Oh, if I stop saluting the flag, I will blow all this!"[55]

On October 22, 1935, William came home from his fifth grade class and excitedly told his family, "I stopped saluting the flag! . . . The teacher tried to put up my arm, but I held on to my pocket."[56] Lillian reacted decisively. "I knew this was the moment," she said. "I did a lot of reading and checking in the Bible and I really took my own stand." The next day she went up to her teacher before class and said, "Miss Shofstal, I can't salute the flag anymore." Lillian was pleasantly surprised to receive a hug from her teacher, who told her that she respected Lillian's courage. When the moment came to recite the Pledge of Allegiance, Lillian recalled that she "didn't know whether it was right to stand up or sit down. . . . So I sat down and the whole room was aghast. After that, when I'd come to school they would throw a hail of pebbles and yell things like, Here comes Jehovah! They were just jeering at me."[57]

School officials "watched for two weeks" as the siblings refused to stand during the pledge, but their school district superintendent, Charles E. Roudabush, was furious.[58] Roudabush was known as a "relentless disciplinarian." He wanted to punish the children, but had been informed by the state's attorney general that a formal school flag-salute rule was required before he could take any disciplinary action.[59] A school board meeting was called, and their father, Walter, a popular figure in the community, spoke on his children's behalf, attempting to defend their loyalty and religious convictions. William and Lillian did not attend, but submitted handwritten letters to spell out their beliefs. William wrote, "I do not salute the flag not because I do not love my country but I love my country and I love God more and I must obey His commandments."[60] Their heartfelt pleas fell on deaf ears, and the board unanimously approved a requirement that "all teachers and pupils . . . [must] salute the flag of our country as a part of the daily exercises."[61] Roudabush immediately announced that William and Lillian were now officially expelled. As their demoralized father exited the meeting he cried out, "I'm going to take you to court for this!"[62]

Gobitas followed through on his parting words, and with the support of the Jehovah's Witnesses' national legal counsel, brought a lawsuit against the school district in the federal district court in Philadelphia.[63] Over a year had passed since the school board meeting, and in that time at least 134 students in eleven states had been expelled for abstaining from the Pledge of Allegiance because of their beliefs.[64]

As their case was being prepared, Lillian and William still needed to be educated. Initially, they were home schooled, but when Roudabush heard this, Lillian said he threatened that they "would be sent to reform school" if they were not taught by a professional teacher.[65] So the Gobitases, and several other local Jehovah's Witness families whose children had refused to pledge, set up a a makeshift school at the Jones family farm thirty miles away. Between twenty and forty students attended what was called the "Jones Kingdom School." Given the distances and the poor quality of the local roads, many of the students, including Lillian and William, had to stay at the farm during the week. The living conditions on the farm were so crowded with these new boarders that the children had to sleep three to a bed.[66]

At the bench trial, Roudabush was the school district's only witness. When questioned as to why a few children should not be allowed to refrain from saluting the flag, Roudabush responded that it would be "demoralizing to the whole group" because "the tendency would be to spread. In our mixed population where we have foreigners of every variety, it would be no time until they would form a dislike, a disregard for our flag and country."[67] The superintendent acknowledged that, although Lillian and William were "very good children," he disdainfully described their parents' views as "perverted."[68]

Walter Gobitas and his children testified about their religious faith and how it was the basis for their position on saluting the flag. William, now twelve years old, answered his lawyer's questions with maturity:

Q: Why didn't you salute the flag in the school?
A: Because it is contrary to God's law.
Q: What law of God do you believe it is contrary to?
A: In Exodus, Chapter 20, verses 4 to 7. . . .
Q: What does that say . . .
A: Here I have it: "Thou shalt not make unto thee any graven image, or any likeness of any thing that is in heaven above, or that is in the earth beneath, or that is in the water under the earth; Thou shalt not bow down thyself to them, nor serve them. . . ."[69]

In 1938, Judge Albert Maris ruled strongly in favor of the Gobitas family. In deciding *Minersville School District v. Gobitis*—at some point, the court misspelled Walter Gobitas's last name as "Gobitis" and the mistake would continue throughout their legal process all the way to the Supreme Court—Maris found that their religious liberties had in fact been infringed. He dismissed the school district's claims that the actions of "these two earnest Christian children . . . even remotely prejudice or imperil the safety, health, morals" or any other rights of their fellow students.[70] His opinion resoundingly rejected claims that it was necessary to make the pledge mandatory:

> Our country's safety surely does not depend upon the totalitarian idea of forcing all citizens into one common mold of thinking and acting or requiring them to render a lip service of loyalty in a manner which conflicts with their sincere religious convictions. Such a doctrine seems to me utterly alien to the genius and spirit of our nation and destructive of that personal liberty of which our flag itself is the symbol.[71]

The school district appealed the ruling, which caused the Witness children to remain shut out of the public schools.[72] Five months later, the US Court of Appeals for the Third Circuit unanimously affirmed the decision in favor of the Gobitases.[73] "A salute to the flag under such [compelled] circumstances," Judge William Clark held, "is an affront to the principles for which the flag stands."[74]

Undeterred, the school district made a final appeal of the decision, aided by the financial support of the American Legion and other "patriotic" organizations.[75] The Supreme Court agreed to hear the appeal, and oral argument took place on April 25, 1940. The justices' decision to take on the case was likely influenced by world events at the time. As Nazi dominance in Europe continued to expand, the crucial issues involved in *Minersville School District v. Gobitis*—liberty, loyalty, and patriotism—took on an even greater urgency.[76]

Remarkably, the Jehovah's Witnesses' religious leader, Rutherford, who had practiced law earlier in his career, argued part of the case himself before the Court.[77] The Gobitas family traveled to be in the courtroom that day, and Lillian found it "electrifying" to hear him argue on their behalf "from a Biblical standpoint."[78] The second part of the Gobitases' oral argument was presented by George Gardner, a Harvard Law professor working on behalf of the American Civil Liberties Union.[79] Gardner put forward the more conventional legal position, and focused on the religious liberty interests he advocated were protected by the First and Fourteenth Amendments.[80]

It is necessary to pause and recognize here that the First Amendment, including its free speech, free press, and religious liberties clauses—along with the rest of the Bill of Rights—was originally held to apply only to the federal government and federal laws (remember it says "*Congress* shall make no law . . ."). Over time, the Supreme Court applied most of these fundamental protections, including all of the First Amendment, to state action and state laws as well. This "incorporation doctrine" interpreted the language of the Fourteenth Amendment's Due Process Clause ("No *state* shall . . . deprive any person of life, liberty or property without due process of law") as the vehicle for applying the guarantees of these amendments as binding on the states.[81]

Back at the oral argument, things were not going well for Gardner. He was facing a barrage of questions from one of the Court's newest justices, Felix Frankfurter.[82] Frankfurter was an immigrant from Vienna, who came to this country at age twelve not speaking a word of English.[83] As a young man he attended public school on the Lower East Side and then City College. He went on to graduate from Harvard Law School, and became the first Jewish professor there, as well as a close confidant of President Franklin Roosevelt.[84] His civil libertarian pedigree was beyond reproach. Before joining the Court, he had defended the anarchists Sacco and Vanzetti, and was a cofounder of the ACLU.[85] Everything in his background should have made him a natural ally for the Gobitas children. However, any such expectations were about to be upended by the opinion he was going to write, during the same period that France was falling to the Nazis.[86]

Justice Frankfurter's opinion, on behalf of all but one member of the Court, reversed the decisions of the lower courts and ruled in favor of the school district. Frankfurter framed the issue at hand as a matter of balancing "conflicting claims of liberty and authority."[87] "Our present task," he began, "is to reconcile two rights in order to prevent either from destroying the other."[88]

For Frankfurter, the choice was clear. Religious freedom was outweighed in favor of the power of government to enforce patriotism, which Frankfurter believed was "an interest inferior to none in the hierarchy of legal values."[89] As the war in Europe threatened to engulf the world, Frankfurter thought unity was absolutely necessary to preserve freedom, declaring, "National unity is the basis of national security."[90] "The ultimate foundation of a free society is the binding tie of cohesive sentiment," he maintained, "without which there can ultimately be no liberties, civil or religious."[91]

Frankfurter not only prioritized cohesion over other values, he also prioritized the flag over other symbols. "'We live by symbols," he stated, adding, "The flag is the symbol of our national unity, transcending all internal differences, however large, within the framework of the Constitution."[92]

In what would become a hallmark of his judicial philosophy on the Court, Frankfurter closed his opinion emphasizing the need for judicial restraint.[93] "The wisdom of training children in patriotic impulses by those compulsions which necessarily pervade so much of the educational process" was not a matter, in Frankfurter's view, for the "independent judgment" of the judicial branch.[94] Even assuming the "folly" of forcing students to recite the pledge against their will, Frankfurter insisted that the courts must defer to local legislatures. To rule otherwise, he concluded, would inappropriately turn the Supreme Court into "the school board for the country."[95]

Justice Harlan Stone, a former dean of Columbia Law School and United States attorney general, was the lone dissenter. He began by focusing on the compelled nature of the speech at issue. Stone described First Amendment liberty as guaranteeing "the freedom of the individual from compulsion as to what he shall think and what he shall say."[96]

Stone found no comfort in Frankfurter's reliance on the judgment of local elected officials. Taking the long view, Stone instructed that "[h]istory teaches us that there have been but few infringements of personal liberty by the state which have not been justified, as they are here, in the name of righteousness and the public good, and few which have not been directed, as they are now, at politically helpless minorities."[97] Therefore, in Stone's view, abdicating judicial responsibility when freedoms of speech and religion were threatened would unacceptably result in the "surrender of the constitutional protection of the liberty of small minorities to the popular will."[98]

Stone acknowledged the importance of unity and patriotism to democracy, but at the same he also held firm that "[t]he Constitution expresses more than the conviction of the people that democratic processes must be preserved at all costs."[99] In contrast to Frankfurter's view that liberty sometimes must be sacrificed for security, Stone saw the Constitution differently. "It is," he urged, "an expression of faith and a command that freedom of mind and spirit must be preserved, which government must obey if it is to adhere to that justice and moderation without which no free government can exist."[100]

* * *

Lillian Gobitas was in her kitchen when she heard the news on the radio that the Supreme Court had decided her case, and that "it was against us, eight to one. Talk about a cold feeling! We absolutely did not expect that. That just set off a *wave* of persecution. It was like open season on Jehovah's Witnesses. That's when the mobs escalated."[101] Lillian's description of the violent aftermath of the *Gobitis* decision did not exaggerate what happened to her family or throughout the nation. The Gobitases' family store was threatened and then boycotted.[102] Only a week after the case was decided, the Department of Justice had received complaints of hundreds of attacks on Jehovah's Witnesses.[103] Religious bigotry mixed with paranoia about "fifth columnists" (Nazi sympathizers seeking to undermine the country from within the United States) led to horrific acts of violence across the country. In Maine, mobs set fire to a local Kingdom Hall, the Jehovah's Witnesses place of worship, dragged people from their homes, demanding they salute the flag, and assaulted them.[104] In West Virginia, Jehovah's Witnesses were "rounded up and roped like cattle" by a sheriff's deputy and forced to drink castor oil.[105] In Nebraska, a Witness was castrated.[106]

Another telling incident involved a report of four women and seven men who were being marched out of a Southern town by a crowd throwing wood, rocks, and bricks at them. When a journalist asked the sheriff what was happening in front of them, he replied, "Jehovah's Witnesses. . . . They're running 'em out of here. They're traitors—the Supreme Court says so. Ain't you heard?"[107] By the year's end, the ACLU reported almost fifteen hundred Witnesses had been persecuted in 335 separate incidents of mob violence across forty-four states.[108] This "unprecedented reaction to a Supreme Court decision" has been described as "the worst outbreak of religious persecution in the United States in the twentieth century."[109]

Over 170 newspapers denounced the *Gobitis* opinion.[110] The *New Republic*, which Frankfurter himself had cofounded, compared the Supreme Court to a German court that had punished Jehovah's Witnesses for refusing to give the Nazi salute. The editors told the majority it should "be embarrassed to know that their attitude was in substance the same as that of the German tribunal."[111] As time passed, the condemnation of the decision only continued. Victor Rotnem, who lead the Justice Department's Civil Rights Division, wrote in severe terms:

> This ugly picture of the two years following the *Gobitis* decision is an eloquent argument in support of the minority contention of Mr. Justice Stone. The placing of symbolic exercises on a higher plane than freedom of conscience has made this symbol an instrument of oppres-

sion of a religious minority. The flag has been violated by its misuse to deny the very freedoms it is intended to represent.[112]

Meanwhile the impact of the ruling spread dramatically. Within three years after the Court's ruling, about two thousand students, almost all of them Jehovah's Witnesses, in every state had been expelled for refusing to salute the flag.[113] In some cases, parents of the expelled students were then prosecuted for violating mandatory school attendance laws.[114]

As criticism of the *Gobitis* decision continued, three justices who had joined Frankfurter's opinion did an astonishing about-face. In another First Amendment case involving Jehovah's Witnesses, Justices Hugo Black, William Douglas, and Frank Murphy plainly stated in their dissent, "Since we joined in the opinion in the *Gobitis* case, we think this is an appropriate occasion to state that we now believe that it was also wrongly decided."[115] In Supreme Court terms, this was the equivalent of an engraved invitation to revisit the case. And the Jehovah's Witnesses' new national legal counsel, Hayden Covington, quickly responded by finding appealing new plaintiffs to lead just such a test case.[116]

* * *

Marie Barnett was nine years old. Raised as a Jehovah's Witness "from birth," she attended Slip Hill Grade School in West Virginia with her sister, Gathie, age eleven, and just twenty-five other students in a four-room schoolhouse.[117] "My older sister, my cousins, and I were going to school right on the edge of Charleston . . . and when the flag exercise was begun, the school didn't even have a flag," Marie recollected, "so they put up a picture of a flag. When we refused to salute it, they brought in a real flag to see if that would make any difference. We still refused."[118] Gathie wanted to make it understood that their refusal to salute was not something their parents put them up to, "it was our idea," and that her sister and she "respect the flag and what it stands for. We don't have anything against that. We just don't believe in worshipping or saluting it."[119]

The Barnett sisters' classmates started calling them names once they stopped saluting the flag. "One name they called us was 'Jap' because of the war," Gathie said.[120] After the bombing of Pearl Harbor, the country was quickly becoming swept up in fear, patriotism, and nationalistic fervor.[121]

A month after the United States entered the war, the West Virginia Board of Education passed a resolution that required teachers and students to participate in saluting the flag.[122] The language of the resolution drew directly from the *Gobitis* decision, and set forth that "refusal to salute the flag [was to] be regarded as an act of insubordination, and shall be dealt with accordingly."[123] The consequences were shockingly severe. Students could be expelled, and in addition might be sentenced to live in reformatories for juvenile delinquents. Parents could face fines or up to thirty days in jail.[124]

Covington took up the Barnett sisters' case, along with five other children from two different families, all of whom had been expelled. The families sought a court order to stop the state board of education from enforcing the mandatory flag salute resolution.[125]

In the West Virginia federal district court, the Barnetts achieved a surprising victory, despite the fact that *Gobitis* was still good law. "Ordinarily we would feel constrained to follow an unreversed decision of the Supreme Court of the United States, whether we agreed with it or not," Judge John Johnston Parker acknowledged.[126] However, Parker continued, "developments with respect to the Gobitis case . . . are such that we do not feel that it is incumbent upon us to accept it as binding authority. Of the seven justices now members of the Supreme Court who participated in that decision, four have given public expression to the view that it is unsound. . . ."[127] After this pragmatic beginning, Parker concluded that the West Virginia resolution could not be enforced against the children, because "the salute to the flag is an expression of the homage of the soul. To force it upon one who has conscientious scruples against giving it, is petty tyranny unworthy of the spirit of this Republic and forbidden . . . by the fundamental law."[128]

As the West Virginia State Board of Education was appealing the district court's *Barnette* decision to the Supreme Court (the Barnetts, like the Gobitases, had their last name misspelled in the case name of the Supreme Court decision with which they would be forever identified), a major development in the history of the Pledge of Allegiance took place. Although it seems shocking today, when the pledge was created in 1892 by Christian socialist Francis J. Bellamy (who wrote it for a children's magazine's celebration of the four hundredth anniversary of Columbus's arrival), the prescribed accompanying flag salute had a disturbing similarity to what would become the infamous Nazi "Heil Hitler" salute.[129] As Richard J. Ellis describes in his book *To the Flag: The Unlikely History of the Pledge of Allegiance*, both salutes involved having "the arm stiffly extended and raised at about eye level. The only substantial difference was that the Nazis performed the salute with the palm facing down, whereas the Pledge of Allegiance was performed with the palm facing upward."[130] In December 1942, Congress acted to adopt a new recommended gesture—what has been called the "Lincoln hand-over-the-heart salute."[131] This change in the nature of the pledge was a telling example of how fluid Americans' reactions to expressions of patriotism were in the midst of fighting World War II. And although this evolution in the mechanics of the flag salute had no direct impact on the Supreme Court's forthcoming *Barnette* decision, redefining American liberties in stark contrast to fascism would prove a considerable factor in the constitutional shift to come.

* * *

By 1943, the lone dissenter in *Gobitis*, Harlan Stone, had become the chief justice. There were now six votes to overturn *Gobitis* and prohibit compulsory flag salutes for public school students. As chief justice, Stone had the power to decide who would write any decision in which he was in the majority.[132] Yet rather than take the opinion for himself and vindicate his past position, Chief Justice Stone assigned the formidable task to a junior justice who had been on the Supreme Court for less than two years: Robert Jackson. It is not known whether Chief Justice Stone made this selection in an effort to shore up a vote that he felt could waver, or because he knew that as FDR's attorney general when *Gobitis* had been decided Jackson would have been keenly aware of the subsequent violence against Jehovah's Witnesses.[133] What soon would become clear was that the choice was an outstanding one. The decision has been called "the most eloquent and enduring opinion in the Court's history."[134] Justice Jackson's majority opinion was announced on June 14, 1943, which in a poetic coincidence happened to be Flag Day.[135]

Justice Jackson commenced his 6–3 majority opinion with a discussion of the expressive power of symbols. Jackson characterized the flag salute symbolism as "a primitive but effective way of communicating ideas. The use of an emblem or flag to symbolize some system, idea, institution, or personality is a short-cut from mind to mind."[136] He points out that the state "employs a flag as a symbol of adherence to government as presently organized. It requires the individual to communicate by word and sign his acceptance of the political ideas it thus bespeaks."[137] However, Jackson also cautions that "[o]bjection to this form of communication, when coerced, is an old one, well known to the framers of the Bill of Rights."[138]

Having established that symbolic expression can raise constitutional problems, Jackson then presented an entirely new approach to considering whether students could be forced to salute the flag. He radically reframed the constitutional question: the right at issue was not primarily about freedom of religion, but rather freedom of speech. In Jackson's analysis, the *Gobitis* decision

> *assumed* . . . that power exists in the State to impose the flag salute discipline upon school children in general. The Court only examined and rejected a claim based on religious beliefs of immunity from an unquestioned general rule. The question which underlies the flag salute controversy is whether such a ceremony so touching matters of opinion and political attitude may be imposed upon the individual by official authority under powers committed to any political organization under our Constitution.[139]

In this masterstroke, Jackson transforms the question from whether Jehovah's Witnesses should be granted a religious exception to a presumptively valid rule, to whether there is a free speech right for all citizens to be protected from compelled speech.[140] In other words, the issue is not about seeking a religious excuse to skip the Pledge, but rather recognizing that the government has no right to force students to say the Pledge in the first place.

Examining the nature of the speech freedom involved, Jackson embraces the idea that since the First Amendment protects the right to speak, it must also protect the right *not* to speak.[141] "To sustain the compulsory flag salute," he contends, "we are required to say that a Bill of Rights which guards the individual's right to speak his own mind left it open to public authorities to compel him to utter what is not in his mind."[142] The right to remain silent, the Supreme Court recognized for the first time, is an inherent part of free speech.

Jackson also vigorously rejects Frankfurter's arguments in *Gobitis* for judicial restraint and deference to state legislatures. "The very purpose of a Bill of Rights was to withdraw certain subjects from the vicissitudes of political controversy," he proclaims, "to place them beyond the reach of majorities and officials, and to establish them as legal principles to be applied by the courts." In no uncertain terms, Jackson makes clear the vital role judicial review plays as a check on the political process: "One's right to life, liberty, and property, to free speech, a free press, freedom of worship and assembly, and other fundamental rights may not be submitted to vote; they depend on the outcome of no elections."[143]

Dismantling Frankfurter's argument at "the very heart of the *Gobitis* opinion," that the need for "national unity" superseded other First Amendment interests, was Jackson's next step.[144] "National unity, as an end which officials may foster by persuasion and example, is not in question. The problem," Jackson clarifies, "is whether, under our Constitution, compulsion as here employed is a permissible means for its achievement."[145] To answer this question, Jackson sweeps through history and highlights that the "ultimate futility of such attempts to compel coherence is the lesson of every such effort from the Roman drive to stamp out Christianity as a disturber of its pagan unity . . . down to the fast failing efforts of our present totalitarian enemies."[146] He then emphasizes the inherent danger of forced unity with two blunt sentences, the truth of which feels like a punch to the gut: "Those who begin coercive elimination of dissent soon find themselves exterminating dissenters. Compulsory unification of opinion achieves only the unanimity of the graveyard."[147]

In his exquisitely expressed conclusion, Justice Jackson shows that the path to avoiding the deadly results of fascism can be found only by remaining true to our First Amendment values:

> It seems trite but necessary to say that the First Amendment to our Constitution was designed to avoid these ends by avoiding these beginnings. There is no mysticism in the American concept of the State or of the nature or origin of its authority. We set up government by consent of the governed, and the Bill of Rights denies those in power any legal opportunity to coerce that consent. Authority here is to be

controlled by public opinion, not public opinion by authority. The case is made difficult not because the principles of its decision are obscure, but because the flag involved is our own. Nevertheless, we apply the limitations of the Constitution with no fear that freedom to be intellectually and spiritually diverse or even contrary will disintegrate the social organization.[148]

In the final lines of his opinion, Jackson has a closing thought for the ages.[149] He wrote: "If there is any fixed star in our constitutional constellation, it is that no official, high or petty, can prescribe what shall be orthodox in politics, nationalism, religion, or other matters of opinion, or force citizens to confess by word or act their faith therein."[150]

Accordingly, the Court held that the West Virginia flag salute regulation "invades the sphere of intellect and spirit which it is the purpose of the First Amendment to our Constitution to reserve from all official control," affirmed the lower court judgment putting an end to its enforcement, and overruled *Gobitis*.[151]

In a furious dissent, Justice Frankfurter doubled down on his insistence that *Gobitis* was rightly decided. Incredulous, Frankfurter seems to almost spit out the words that he could not "bring my mind to believe that the 'liberty' secured by the Due Process Clause gives this Court authority to deny to the State of West Virginia the attainment of that which we all recognize as a legitimate legislative end, namely, the promotion of good citizenship."[152] He continued (in twenty-five pages) to strenuously argue that "it is not enough to strike down a nondiscriminatory law that it may hurt or offend some dissident view."[153] The restriction of dissenting views was constitutionally OK for Frankfurter, as long as it applied to everyone equally.

Frankfurter reserved his greatest ire for the lack of deference to state lawmakers and the majority's willingness to overturn such a recent precedent. He lectured his fellow justices on the consequences of this aspect of their decision by raising a series of bitter questions:

We are dealing with matters as to which legislators and voters have conflicting views. Are we as judges to impose our strong convictions on where wisdom lies? That which three years ago had seemed ... to lie within permissible areas of legislation is now outlawed by the deciding shift of opinion of two Justices. What reason is there to believe that they or their successors may not have another view a few years hence? Is that which was deemed to be of so fundamental a nature as to be written into the Constitution to endure for all times to be the sport of shifting winds of doctrine?[154]

In short, Frankfurter could not forgive them for rejecting the judicial principle of *stare decisis*.

Stare decisis, which is Latin for "to stand by things decided," lies at the heart of our judicial system.[155] It means simply that to promote legal stability, courts traditionally follow past decisions on previously adjudicated issues. As Justice Brandeis put it, "Stare decisis is usually the wise policy, because in most matters it is more important that the applicable rule of law be settled than that it be settled right."[156] Of course, even Justice Frankfurter acknowledged that stare decisis was not absolute, and that sometimes the Supreme Court should change course and overturn a past decision.[157] Flashing forward in time, the most famous example of the Court choosing to not follow stare decisis was *Brown v. Board of Education*, which in 1954 held that racial segregation in public schools was unconstitutional and finally overturned the noxious "separate but equal" concept approved of by *Plessy v. Ferguson*, decided in 1896.[158] However, unlike the troublingly long road to overturning *Plessy*, what both Frankfurter and Jackson would have agreed on was that the timing of overturning *Gobitis*—in just three years—was indeed highly unusual.[159]

Despite Frankfurter's outrage, the *Barnette* decision was greeted with unbridled enthusiasm from the press.[160] A representative headline in *Time* magazine hailed "Blot Removed," and the article championed the decision for reaffirming the Supreme Court's "faith in the Bill of Rights—which [in *Gobitis*] it had come perilously close to outlawing."[161] The wartime nature of the decision was also crucial in elevating its reception. As Cornell Law School Professor Steven Shiffrin has astutely observed, "*Barnette* was written in the midst of World War II, a time when America's self-understanding was that it was fighting to preserve democracy. It is illuminating that the Court would call forth the idea of protecting dissent as fundamental to what the society stood for."[162]

On a more practical level, as a result of *Barnette*, most schools across the United States quickly abandoned punishments for those who would not pledge allegiance to the flag.[163] And while the Barnett sisters and their cousins had only lost a half a year at school, what about the Gobitas children?[164] It had been eight years since Lillian and William Gobitas had been expelled, and they were now twenty and eighteen years old, respectively. But at least for their four younger siblings, it meant that they finally were allowed to return to public school.[165] Notwithstanding the hardships they endured, years later, Lillian remained steadfast in her beliefs, and her protest. "I would do it again in a second," she said avidly, "without reservations!"[166]

* * *

The complex path to *Barnette* ends with an arrival at a clear free speech principle: the government is restricted from compelling its citizens to express a message they don't support. But what does this mean for Colin Kaepernick?

In his legal action against the NFL, an arbitrator would rule that there was sufficient evidence supporting his claims to justify moving forward to a full hearing.[167] Six months later, in early 2019, Kaepernick and Eric Reid entered into a settlement with the NFL.[168] It had been two and a half years since their Take a Knee protests had sparked nationwide attention to their actions and the issues of racial injustice that they sought to expose. Although the NFL admitted no wrongdoing as part of the confidential agreement, it's still hard to view the deal (which almost certainly involved a substantial financial payout) as anything but at least a partial victory for the former player.[169] Even during the time he was excluded from the NFL, his status as an icon of determination and dissent continued to rise. When Nike made Kaepernick the spokesperson for its thirtieth-anniversary "Just Do It" campaign, and signed him to a lucrative expanded endorsement contract, he proved at the very least that protest can be profitable.[170]

The fact that *Barnette* does not directly prevent the NFL, as a private business, from disciplining its players for their speech on the field does not lessen its impact on the Take a Knee protests in two other significant ways.

First, as the Take a Knee protests swept through professional sports, student athletes were also inspired to engage in their own protests during the national anthem at high school or college games.[171] Unlike private professional sports leagues, public schools at all educational levels from elementary through college are considered the equivalent of governmental actors for constitutional purposes, and therefore the First Amendment applies to the actions of their students, teachers, coaches, and administrators.[172] Protesting public school students are thus squarely protected by *Barnette* from being penalized by school officials for not participating in any forced patriotic rituals.

Second, *Barnette* provides an instructive guide as our country grapples with the compatability of protest and patriotism. Like the Jehovah's Witnesses in the *Gobitis* and *Barnette* cases, Kaepernick faced unrelenting attacks on his patriotism based on three arguments: the protests were unpopular; done in the wrong place and manner; and disrespected the flag. It is worth examining these criticisms in order to debunk them, as they continue to reoccur when protestors dare to defy conventional patriotic rituals.

Looking at the unpopularity critique, at first glance it does seem like the Take a Knee protests were uniquely unpopular. Polls taken throughout the controversy showed that American adults "view the right to nonviolent protest (79%) and protecting the rights of those with unpopular views (74%) as very important components of a strong democracy."[173] Yet at the start of the protests, a Reuters poll found a whopping 72 percent of those surveyed thought Kaepernick's refusal to stand during the anthem was unpatriotic.[174] A series of later polls also found that generally at least half of those surveyed disapproved of the players' protests.[175]

Given the support for free speech in the abstract, it can appear counterintuitive that the Take a Knee protests were apparently unpopular among a majority of Americans. One explanation could be that objection to the protests, as Trump puts it, "has nothing to do with race. It is about respect for our Country, Flag and National anthem."[176] This viewpoint could seem somewhat plausible given that civil rights protests of the past are now looked at with a rosy aura of moral authority and inevitability. However, the widespread antipathy toward current civil rights protests makes much more sense when looked at in the context of how Americans viewed the civil rights movement in the early 1960s. It bears remembering that, at the time, a majority of Americans disapproved of direct action as a method of protesting racial inequality. In the weeks before the March on Washington in 1963, 60 percent of Americans viewed the protest "unfavorably" and only 23 percent looked on it "favorably."[177] Three years later, even the Rev. Dr. Martin Luther King, Jr., was viewed negatively by 63 percent of Americans![178] It seems then that protest speech in the abstract is often highly praised, and yet in practice protesting and protest leaders are often feared and rejected, particularly when the issue is racial justice.

The second critique claims that the Take a Knee protesters could have better shown their patriotism to white NFL audiences by somehow protesting differently.[179] Progressive Christian pastor John Pavlovitz has characterized this approach that protests be done the supposed "right way" as representing "the arrogant heart of privilege: being the beneficiaries of systematic injustice, and then wanting to make the rules for the marginalized in how they should speak into that injustice."[180] Most importantly, as NBA legend Kareem Abdul-Jabbar discussed in an editorial for the *Guardian*, protesting during NFL games wasn't incidental to the players' protest, but rather "the perfect public platform for discussing racial disparity."[181] Abdul-Jabbar points out that

> the NFL's significant ratings means it reaches not just a lot of people (an average of 18m), but a wider cross-section of people, particularly those whose hearts and minds need to be changed if we are to see progress. This target audience may not be aware of the problem or are reluctant to believe there is a problem until they see their favorite players week after week expressing their sadness and frustration at calculated government inaction.[182]

The final critique of the Take a Knee protests is that they are inescapably unpatriotic because they come during a time set aside to honor the flag. In *The Heritage*, Howard Bryant paints a devasting picture of the way in which "Trump positioned dissenting views as unpatriotic at best, traitorous at worst, to both the United States in general and the country's armed forces in particular. . . . The American flag did not represent ideals. It was supposed to be obeyed."[183] On this point, the story of *Barnette* teaches us precisely how respect for the flag does not take precedence over First Amendment rights. If the United States Supreme Court could bring itself to support the free speech of flag dissenters during the dark days of World War II, we can still follow its lead in today's unsettled times.

Of course, Kaepernick was not without defenders of his patriotism.[184] The singer John Legend wrote a piece for Slate in which he said plainly that "protest is patriotic," and celebrated the Take a Knee protests as "their own form of a pledge-of-allegiance—allegiance to the ideals that are our nation's founding principles, which many heroes have given their lives to defend. They are the definition of patriotism."[185] Another stalwart supporter, Eric Reid, the first person to kneel alongside Kaepernick, writing an op-ed in the New York Times, candidly conveyed both their frustration and the nature of their patriotism:

> It baffles me that our protest is still being misconstrued as disrespectful to the country, flag and military personnel. We chose it because it's exactly the opposite. It has always been my understanding that the brave men and women who fought and died for our country did so to ensure that we could live in a fair and free society, which includes the right to speak out in protest. It should go without saying that I love my country and I'm proud to be an American. But, to quote James Baldwin, "exactly for this reason, I insist on the right to criticize her perpetually."[186]

And then, almost four years after Kaepernick first took a knee, George Floyd was killed on camera.[187] Black Lives Matter protests in the wake of the deaths of Floyd, Breonna Taylor, and so many other Black people at the hands of police have finally moved many white people to realize how right and necessary Kaepernick's actions were.[188] Public sentiment regarding protests about police brutality has shifted so dramatically as a result of the resurgence of the Black Lives Matter movement that even NFL commissioner Goodell felt compelled to issue a quasi-apology. Goodell admitted that the NFL was "wrong for not listening to NFL players earlier and [we] encourage all to speak out and peacefully protest."[189] He did not, however, mention Kaepernick's name.

Howard Byant wrote for ESPN.com that this glaring omission matters more than any apology, because the NFL "was the country's primary apparatus to demonize the kneeling gesture, and indirectly condone the very issue of police brutality it now says has no place." Bryant insists that if the league's new statements are to be believed, "the next step toward real truth is opening the door to signing Kaepernick. . . . If it remains closed, this flashpoint will be remembered as the moment the NFL admitted it handed out a life sentence, admitted it was wrong—and still did nothing about it."[190]

No matter what changes may come from the NFL and the shifting tides of popular opinion, the *Barnette* decision stands with Kaepernick as a persuasive ally in the fight to recognize that not standing for the flag does not dishonor the nation or anyone. "To believe that patriotism will not flourish if patriotic ceremonies are voluntary and spontaneous, instead of a compulsory routine," Justice Jackson insisted, "is to make an unflattering estimate of the appeal of our institutions to free minds."[191] The issues raised by Kaepernick and his fellow Take a Knee protestors concerning police brutality, racial discrimination, and criminal justice may make many Americans uncomfortable to even consider, but they matter deeply to the future of our country. And as Jackson wisely reminds us, "freedom to differ is not limited to things that do not matter much. That would be a mere shadow of freedom. The test of its substance is the right to differ as to things that touch the heart of the existing order."[192] In deciding the *Barnette* case in favor of protestors who refused to stand for the flag, the Supreme Court showed how allowing for dissent—be it from Jehovah's Witnesses or Colin Kaepernick—is the greatest and most patriotic of American values.

3 / LIBEL, ACTUAL MALICE, AND THE CIVIL RIGHTS MOVEMENT

One of Donald Trump's more surprising campaign promises was his vow to "open up our libel laws." At a 2016 Texas rally during the Republican primary, he launched into a familiar attack on the media that soon took an unexpected turn:

> I'll tell you what, I think the media is among the most dishonest groups of people I've ever met. . . . And believe me, if I become president, oh, do they have problems. They're going to have such problems . . . and I've never said this before, but one of the things I'm going to do if I win . . . is I'm going to open up our libel laws so when they write purposely negative and horrible and false articles, we can sue them and win lots of money. We're going to open up those libel laws. So that when The New York Times writes a hit piece, which is a total disgrace, or when the Washington Post . . . writes a hit piece, we can sue them and win money instead of having no chance of winning because they're totally protected. . . . So we're going to open up those libel laws folks and we're going to have people sue you like you never got sued before.[1]

Although it is hard to imagine any cross section of the American public that would consider libel law a pressing concern, this is nevertheless a theme that President Trump returned to over and over again. Lashing out against the publication of Michael Wolff's blistering book *Fire and Fury: Inside the Trump White House*, Trump declared during a cabinet meeting, "We are going to take a strong look at our country's libel laws so that when somebody says something that is . . . totally false and knowingly false, that the person who has been abused, defamed, libeled, will have meaningful recourse."[2] He returned to this refrain again in reaction to the release of Bob Woodward's book *Fear: Trump in the White House*, tweeting, "Isn't it a shame that someone can write an article or book, totally make up stories and form a picture of a person that is literally the exact opposite of the fact, and get away with it without retribution or cost. Don't know why Washington politicians don't change libel laws?"[3]

Within the next six months, Justice Clarence Thomas followed Trump's lead and similarly (if more legalistically) called for a reconsideration of the constitutional foundations of modern libel law. He criticized the Supreme Court's past precedents as "policy-driven decisions masquerading as constitutional law." Thomas chided that the Court "did not begin meddling in this area until 1964, nearly 175 years after the First Amendment was ratified."[4] For Thomas, this gap indicates that the Court has strayed too far from what the framers of the Constitution thought about libel at the time of its enactment. Instead, he advocated for the Court to adopt his originalist approach and "carefully examine the original meaning" of the First Amendment.[5] In his view, if the founding fathers did not understand the constitution as requiring "public figures to satisfy an actual-malice standard in state-law defamation suits, then neither should we."

President Trump's modern complaints about libel lawsuits and Justice Thomas's historical critique of libel law both raise a set of valuable questions for Americans today. Do libel laws allow the press to say things that are "totally false" and get away with it? Can politicians change libel law? What does "actual malice" really mean? The answers to all of these questions can be explained by looking back at the foundational case of *New York Times Company v. Sullivan*. *Sullivan* is the source of the widely misunderstood actual malice test, which extended First Amendment protection for the first time to even some false statements criticizing public figures.

Beyond clarifying the meaning of actual malice, taking a strong look at the case also provides an opportunity to recount its extraordinary history. *Sullivan* is ultimately the story of how a Southern libel judgment against a celebrity-backed ad supporting the Rev. Dr. Martin Luther King, Jr., almost bankrupted the *New York Times*, but resulted in a Supreme Court decision that saved the paper and provided a pivotal victory for the civil rights movement.

* * *

In March 1960, student-led sit-in protests of segregated lunch counters had spread across the South.[6] At the same time Dr. King was supporting the student actions, he was preparing to defend himself against trumped up felony perjury charges for allegedly making false statements in connection with his Alabama state tax returns.[7] Meanwhile in New York, the Committee to Defend Martin Luther King and the Struggle for Freedom in the South was formed at the home of singer and civil rights activist Harry Belafonte in part to raise money for King's legal defense.[8] On the 29th of the month, the Committee took out a full-page advertisement in the *New York Times* to support the student demonstrations and condemn the actions taken against the activists and Dr. King.[9] Bannered "Heed their Rising Voices," the ad began by paying tribute to the "thousands of Southern Negro students [that] are engaged in wide-spread non-violent demonstrations in positive affirmation of the right to live in human dignity as guaranteed by the U.S. Constitution and the Bill of Rights."[10] It also highlighted some of the nonviolent actions taken by students, the terrorizing responses they faced in Montgomery, Alabama, and other Southern cities, and how Dr. King had "inspired and guided the students in their widening wave of sit-ins." The ad copy went on to describe Dr. King's plight:

> Again and again the Southern violators have answered Dr. King's peaceful protests with intimidation and violence. They have bombed his home almost killing his wife and child. They have assaulted his person. They have arrested him seven times—for "speeding," "loitering" and similar "offenses." And now they have charged him with "perjury"—a *felony* under which they could imprison him for *ten years.* Obviously, their real purpose is to remove him physically as the leader to whom the students and millions of others—look for guidance and support, and thereby to intimidate *all* leaders who may rise in the South. . . . The defense of Martin Luther King, spiritual leader of the student sit-in movement, clearly, therefore, is an integral part of the total struggle for freedom in the South.

In conclusion, the committee urgently requested donations (via a mail-in coupon) for "this Combined Appeal for all three needs—the defense of Martin Luther King—the support of the embattled students—and the struggle for the right-to-vote."[11] The request was signed by sixty-four civil rights activists and celebrities including Harry Belafonte, Marlon Brando, Diahann Carroll, Nat King Cole, Dorothy Dandridge, Sammy Davis, Jr., Lorraine Hansberry, Langston Hughes, Mahalia Jackson, Eartha Kitt, Rabbi Edward Klein, John Lewis, Sidney Poitier, A. Philip Randolph, Jackie Robinson, and Eleanor Roosevelt. Underneath these individuals were the names of twenty Southerners, nearly all clergymen, "who are struggling daily for dignity and freedom [and] warmly endorse this appeal."

Only 394 copies of the newspaper containing the advertisement were distributed in Alabama (out of a circulation of about 650,000 copies nationally), but the reaction from officials in the state was fast and furious.[12] L. B. Sullivan, a city commissioner of Montgomery, wrote to the *Times* ten days later demanding a full retraction. Although not named in the ad, Sullivan claimed that it accused him of "grave misconduct" and "improper actions" as a city official.[13]

The *Times* responded to Sullivan that it was "somewhat puzzled as to how you think the statements reflect on you" and that the advertisement was "substantially correct."[14] Sullivan in turn promptly brought a libel lawsuit against the *New York Times* and the four Black ministers from Alabama whose names were listed in the ad as endorsing the appeal—the Reverends Ralph Abernathy, Fred Shuttlesworth, S. S. Seay, Sr., and J. E. Lowery.[15] He sought $500,000 in damages.

The governor of Alabama, John Patterson, who was also not named in the ad, soon followed with a copycat retraction demand.[16] This time the *Times* backtracked, apologizing and retracting the paragraphs that referred to Montgomery and the arrests of Dr. King by "Southern violators" for containing factual inaccuracies.[17] Nevertheless, Governor Patterson sued the *Times* and the ministers for libel as well, including Dr. King as an additional defendant. Not to be outdone, the governor asked for $1 million in damages.

The *Times*, along with Abernathy, Shuttlesworth, Seay, and Lowery, would be sued again for libel by the mayor of Montgomery, another city commissioner, and a former city commissioner, demanding $500,000 each. That meant the defendants were facing damage claims of $3 million in total (approximately $25 million in today's dollars) for publishing a single political advertisement.[18] In the wake of this litigation onslaught, the *Times'* counsel, Louis Loeb, later said, "In all the years I have practiced law . . . nothing scared me more than this litigation."[19]

Who were L. B. Sullivan and John Patterson and why were they seemingly so upset by the "Heed Their Rising Voices" advertisement? Sullivan was a member of the Ku Klux Klan and his campaign for city commissioner attacked the incumbent for using "kid gloves to handle social agitators" like Dr. King.[20] As attorney general of Alabama, Patterson had sought and won a court order to effectively ban the NAACP from the entire state. (It would take the NAACP multiple trips to the Supreme Court over eight years to overturn the prohibition.)[21] Just one month prior to the publication of "Heed Their Rising Voices," Patterson, then Alabama governor, would demand the expulsion of thirty-five Black students from Alabama State College for participating in a sit-in protest at the segregated snack bar in the Montgomery County Courthouse.[22] It is therefore hard to believe that Sullivan or Patterson truly felt their reputation was damaged by being criticized by Black civil rights advocates. To the contrary, their political fortunes had been made in large part by taking an aggressively segregationist stance. There could be little doubt that these cases were not about vindicating real reputational injury, but rather a thinly veiled effort to attack civil rights activists.[23]

The minister defendants, in addition to being religious leaders, were at the forefront of the civil rights movement. Abernathy, Shuttlesworth, and Lowery were cofounders, along with Dr. King, of the Southern Christian Leadership Conference.[24] Seay was one of the leading organizers of the Montgomery bus boycott, and all of them were among Dr. King's closest confidants and advisors.[25]

Presiding over Sullivan's libel trial against the *Times* and the ministers was Judge Walter Burgwyn Jones. Judge Jones maintained strictly segregated courtroom seating. He had also spoken of his admiration for "white man's justice, a justice born long centuries ago in England, brought over to this country by the Anglo-Saxon race."[26] Not surprisingly then, among a panel of thirty-six potential jurors, only two were Black, and both were successfully challenged by Sullivan's lawyer, so that an all-white jury was selected.[27]

At every libel trial, the plaintiff has to prove four crucial elements: that the statements at issue were about the plaintiff; were false; injured the plaintiff's reputation; and were made publicly by the defendants.[28]

To establish this, Sullivan claimed that this paragraph in the ad mentioning Montgomery police was referring to him, given his supervisory role over the department:

In Montgomery, Alabama, after students sang "My Country, 'Tis of Thee" on the State Capitol steps, their leaders were expelled from school, and truck-loads of police armed with shotguns and tear-gas ringed the Alabama State College Campus. When the entire student body protested to state authorities by refusing to re-register, their dining hall was pad-locked in an attempt to starve them into submission.

Sullivan also maintained that the reference to "Southern violators" arresting Dr. King implicated him as well. Sullivan's lawyer, M. Roland Nachman, called six witnesses who said they associated these statements with Sullivan and that if they had believed the statements it would have damaged their opinion of him. On cross-examination, five of the witnesses admitted they never saw the ad until Nachman had shown it to them in preparation for trial and none of them believed the statements.[29]

As for the issue of falsity, it was established at the trial that there were a number of minor factual errors in the paragraphs at issue. Arguably the two most significant were that there was no evidence that the Alabama State College dining hall had been padlocked, and that Dr. King had been arrested not seven times, but "only" four.[30]

The final element that remained for Sullivan to prove as to the ministers was whether or not Abernathy, Shuttlesworth, Seay, and Lowery had anything to do with the advertisement, other than having their names included on it. Although the *New York Times* had obviously published the advertisement, all of the ministers testified that they had no knowledge of the ad until after it was published. Moreover, the author of the ad supported their testimony, and acknowledged on the stand that their names had been added at the last minute without seeking their permission because there wasn't time to reach them. Their attorney, famed civil rights litigator Fred Gray, sought to have the ministers removed from the case since "[t]here was not a scintilla of evidence against our clients. They had no knowledge of the advertisement. They had not written it. They had never seen it. They did not know their names would be in it."[31] Judge Jones denied Gray's motion.[32]

The jury took a little over two hours to find in favor of Sullivan. The twelve white men awarded him the entire $500,000 he had asked for in damages. It was the largest libel award in the history of Alabama.[33]

The reaction of the local press was euphoric. The *Alabama Journal* wrote that the verdict and the "half-million dollar judgment ... could have the effect of causing reckless publishers of the North ... to make a re-survey of their habit of permitting anything detrimental to the South and its people to appear in their columns."[34] A headline in the *Montgomery Advertiser* about multiple libel lawsuits against the *Times* frankly cheered, "State Finds Formidable Legal Club to Swing at Out-of-State Press."[35] The decision had effectively become "one more brick white southerners were using to build a wall against desegregation."[36]

Another libel victory, with another award of $500,000 in damages, followed a few months later—this time in the suit brought by the mayor. With the looming threat of three more pending suits over the advertisement, their cumulative impact could have bankrupted the newspaper. The general counsel for the *Times* later reflected that "[w]ithout a reversal of those verdicts there was a reasonable question of whether the *Times* ... could survive."[37]

At the same time, Sullivan also financially attacked the minister defendants by seizing their property, ostensibly to pay for the damages they would owe if and when the court judgment became final. Cars belonging to Revs. Abernathy, Lowery, and Shuttlesworth were sold, along with land belonging to Rev. Seay and to Abernathy's family.[38]

As Fred Gray indignantly put it, "The plaintiff in this case was so determined to punish African Americans who identified with the movement that his attorneys . . . did not have the human decency to wait until the appeal was over before levying on the ministers' property."[39]

The financial impact on Dr. King was equally pronounced. Fundraising for King through advertising had been crippled.[40] In *Parting the Waters*, the first in Taylor Branch's three-volume history of America in the King years, he describes the situation plainly: "The white authorities of Alabama were serving notice that newspapers willing to publish King's paid messages had to fear that Alabama might haul them into court."[41]

Perhaps most seriously, the strategy of censorship by libel threats was working.[42] As civil rights leader Andrew Young pointed out, the press "was essential to the conduct of non-violent demonstrations. . . . It was no accident that our demonstrations were always in the morning; that we completed them by two o'clock in the afternoon so that we could make the evening news; and so that reporters could file their deadlines for the coming day."[43] Without press coverage of civil rights protests, the impact of the movement would be diminished.

By the time the Alabama Supreme Court had affirmed the trial court ruling in 1962 (noting the newspaper's "irresponsibility in printing the advertisement and scattering it to the four winds"), the *Times* had kept its reporters away from Alabama and relied on wire services for over a year.[44] The threats were also spreading. In their book, *The Race Beat: The Press, the Civil Rights Struggle, and the Awakening of a Nation*, veteran journalists Gene Roberts and Hank Klibanoff paint a stark picture of what was at stake in 1964, as the Supreme Court made ready to hear the *Sullivan* case:

Public officials in three southern states had no fewer than seventeen libel lawsuits pending against newspapers, magazines, and a television station, seeking total damages that exceeded $288 million. . . . The court would decide nothing less than how free the press really could be. If the decision went against the *Times*, would reporters be vulnerable to every libel claim filed by a ticked-off sheriff?[45]

In the legal briefs leading up to the Supreme Court oral argument, the defendants took strikingly different approaches.[46] The *New York Times* team, led by Columbia Law School professor Herbert Wechsler, focused almost entirely on the free press and free speech issues involved—criticism of government officials is essential to the First Amendment, and state libel laws should not be allowed to undermine that freedom.[47] In contrast, the ministers' brief called out the racism of the trial and society in no uncertain terms:

> Where Sullivan, a white public official, sued Negro petitioners represented by Negro counsel before an all-white jury, in Montgomery, Alabama, on an advertisement seeking to aid the cause of integration, the impact of courtroom segregation could only denote the inferiority of Negroes and taint and infect all proceedings thereby denying petitioners the fair and impartial trial to which they are constitutionally entitled.[48]

Interestingly, King's counsel "concurred in the suppression of the racial aspects" as a matter of "strategic realism."[49] Recognizing that the Court would be unwilling to take the systemic racism of Alabama government head-on, King's team instead sought to appeal to "anyone who could imagine being victimized by parochial politics or a runaway jury."[50]

The Court was hearing the oral arguments for *Sullivan* at a traumatic and fragile period in the history of American democracy. Only forty-five days after the assassination of President Kennedy and six months before the passage of the Civil Rights Act of 1964, Wechsler began with a dramatic opening that fit the times: the *Sullivan* libel decision posed "hazards to the freedom of the press of a dimension not confronted since the early days of the Republic."[51]

Wechsler's main argument was that "the First Amendment was precisely designed to do away with . . . punishment for criticism of the Government and criticism of officials," and therefore the First Amendment must limit the ability of state libel laws to punish such criticism. If the Court did not impose free speech constraints on state libel law, he warned that massive damage awards like those in *Sullivan* would be "a death penalty for any newspaper if multiplied."[52]

Speaking on behalf of the ministers was Samuel R. Pierce Jr. In a striking juxtaposition, Pierce, a former judge and the first Black partner of a major New York law firm, was arguing before Justice Hugo Black, the most senior member of the Court and a former member of the Ku Klux Klan.[53] Pierce got to the heart of the case that Wechsler and Nachman both strenuously avoided, declaring,

> The sole purpose of this litigation is to suppress and punish expressions of support for the cause of racial equality and to try to keep those who are actively engaged in their fight for civil rights, such as the [ministers] in this case from continuing to participate in that struggle. . . . [T]he injustice of this action which encroaches on freedom of speech under the guise of punishing for libel is magnified by the fact that the petitioners failed to receive a fair trial.[54]

With the confidence that comes from having history on your side, Nachman argued that the only way in which the defendants could succeed was if the Court granted the *Times* "absolute immunity from anything it publishes." Nachman claimed that the result of such blanket protection for newspapers and the media "would have a devastating effect on this nation."[55] He went so far as to say that even if a newspaper had "a reasonable belief" in the truth of what it published,

it would still be subject to punishment under Alabama law if any statement turned out not to be fully accurate.[56]

Despite having acknowledged that the current state of the law would
leave even reasonable journalists subject to devastating liability, Nachman remained self-assured. He told his family after the argument that
"either I will win the case or they will change the law of the land."[57]

* * *

William Brennan, the highly influential liberal justice, labored over
eight drafts of his opinion in order to ultimately get all nine justices
to agree on a decision in favor of the *New York Times*.[58] The unanimous judgment for the defendants meant that Sullivan's libel victory
was going to be taken away from him, but on what grounds?[59] Justice Brennan's first line of his opinion for the Court telegraphed
that sweeping change was to follow: "We are required in this case to
determine for the first time the extent to which the constitutional protections for speech and press limit a State's power to award damages in
a libel action brought by a public official against critics of his official
conduct."[60]

Brennan set the stage for new developments by expounding on
our free speech priorities in powerful terms: "We consider this case
against the background of a profound national commitment to the
principle that debate on public issues should be uninhibited, robust,
and wide-open, and that it may well include vehement, caustic, and
sometimes unpleasantly sharp attacks on government and public
officials."[61]

Next, Brennan explained why the Alabama state law could not be
saved by having truth as the only defense. "Erroneous statement is
inevitable in free debate," he wrote, and therefore sometimes even
false statements "must be protected if the freedoms of expression are
to have the breathing space that they need to survive."[62] Given the

inevitable potential for error, the consequences of allowing the status quo to continue were presented in stark terms of survival:

> Whether or not a newspaper can survive a succession of such judgments, the pall of fear and timidity imposed upon those who would give voice to public criticism is an atmosphere in which the First Amendment freedoms cannot survive.... Under such a rule, would-be critics of official conduct may be deterred from voicing their criticism, even though it is believed to be true and even though it is, in fact, true, because of doubt whether it can be proved in court or fear of the expense of having to do so.[63]

Brennan at this point had built a foundation that laid out the conflict between free speech and libel law, and the reasons that a new standard incorporating both interests was vital. Since libel litigation was to be constrained by the First Amendment, Brennan went on to proclaim what this new limitation would be—an actual malice requirement. "The constitutional guarantees require," he set forth, "a federal rule that prohibits a public official from recovering damages for [libel] unless he proves that the statement was made with 'actual malice'—that is, with knowledge that it was false or with reckless disregard of whether it was false or not."[64]

Making quick work of applying the new standard to the facts of the case, Brennan found that the defendants did not make any statements with reckless disregard of the truth, even if some of the statements in the advertisement were false and could have been checked more thoroughly.[65] The decision went on to hold that the advertisement was also insufficiently "of and concerning" Sullivan, in that an "impersonal attack on governmental operations" cannot in and of itself constitute libel of an unnamed "official responsible for those operations."[66] For both of these reasons, the libel decision of the Alabama

Supreme Court was reversed and all of the defendants had now won a stunning upset.

As bold as this ruling was, three of the justices wanted Brennan to go even further. Justices Hugo Black and Arthur Goldberg each wrote separate concurring opinions (agreeing with the result reached by the majority, but for different reasons) that asserted the First Amendment granted "the press an *absolute immunity* for criticism of the way public officials do their public duty."[67] Brennan's reasons for using "actual malice" instead of a broader immunity approach were likely influenced by fears of McCarthyism still fresh in his mind. In a revealing lecture Brennan gave just a year after the *Sullivan* decision, he warned of the dangers that came from the "use of the known lie" by "those unscrupulous enough and skillful enough to use the deliberate or reckless falsehood as an effective political tool to unseat the public servant or even topple an administration."[68]

These concerns are reflected in the approach Brennan took toward creating this new speech-protective libel standard. In crafting the actual malice test, Brennan sought to strike a balance between blanket protection for all incorrect statements and no protection for any inaccuracies. Contrary to popular belief, the actual malice standard does not have anything to do with "ill will" or bad intent.[69] Instead, what actual malice really means is that journalists need not be infallible, but they can't make stuff up ("knowledge that it was false") and they also can't turn a blind eye to the truth or contradictory information ("reckless disregard").[70]

The decision was greeted with rapturous enthusiasm. One prominent philosopher and free speech advocate hailed it as "an occasion for dancing in the streets."[71] A Black newspaper remarked that the Black press "should be particularly jubilant over the high court's decision because a ruling the other way would have made them especially vulnerable and could have left them with no bulwark against destruction."[72] And an immediate consequence of the Supreme Court's ruling was that the *New York Times* and other news organizations were free to go back to the business of extensively covering civil rights protests in the South.[73]

Thirty years later, when Justice Elena Kagan was a professor of law at the University of Chicago, she wrote that "the decision speaks to the widest possible audience ... [and] as a statement of enduring principle addressed to the American people—it is indeed a marvel."[74] And on the fiftieth anniversary of *Sullivan*, the *Atlantic* magazine published a tribute for the occasion in modern terms:

> Every person who writes online or otherwise about public officials, every hack or poet who criticizes the work of government, every distinguished journalist or pajama-ed blogger who speaks truth to power, ought to bow his or her head today in a silent moment of gratitude for [the *Sullivan* decision]. It means simply that you can make an honest mistake when writing about a public figure and won't likely get sued.[75]

However, on closer examination, it may be all too easy for lawyers and the media to laud to the skies a decision that could just as easily be cast in far less flattering terms. It could be argued that, in reality, the Court handed the all-white *New York Times* additional power from the all-white Supreme Court, in a case that consistently treated the Black civil rights defendants as an afterthought or worse.[76] How can the protection of the press be treated as a victory for speech or justice when, as Professor Catharine MacKinnon frames it, the "civil rights speech at the case's factual foundation [was] ignored, [and] the Court proceeded as if the underlying substantive inequality between assertion of civil rights and official Southern police suppression of their pursuit ... was irrelevant ..."?[77]

There are no easy answers to these critiques. While the debate over the meaning of *Sullivan* should continue, it is undoubtedly time to shake off the unexamined self-satisfaction that frequently accompanies media accounts of this momentous legal drama. One transformative approach, advocated by civil rights attorney Fred Gray, is to continue to celebrate the importance of *Sullivan*, but also to reframe its origins. "The civil rights movement set the stage for *Sullivan* and served as the catalyst for the Supreme Court's historic decision protecting our First Amendment right to freedom of press," Gray reflected. "History should note the role of the civil rights movement in enhancing the rights of every American for generations to come by the legal precepts announced in *New York Times v. Sullivan*."[78]

* * *

Once the *Sullivan* decision is understood, Trump's claims about libel law are easily dispensed with as inaccurate at best. Most importantly, contrary to his repeated assertions, the press is not at all protected from making "totally false and knowingly false" statements. If the media lies, the actual malice standard does not shield them from the repercussions of publishing statements they know to be false, and they would undoubtedly lose a libel suit regarding any such public remarks. In fact, despite this press-favorable standard, modern media organizations still face libel lawsuits from public figures and expend significant resources to minimize the threat of such actions. In addition, what the Court recognized in *Sullivan* is that the First Amendment itself limits the bounds of state libel law. Consequently, the free press protections that Trump objects to are *constitutional* in nature, and can't be changed by the president or even Congress.

It is not clear whether Trump does not actually understand the actual malice test or is intentionally misrepresenting the state of the law to make the news media look like they are running amok without standards. Whatever the reason, it seemed that this president was following in the direct footsteps of another president who also viewed the media as his enemy. On October 16, 1972, President Nixon's outrage over libel and the press was recorded. "There is no libel anymore,"

Nixon told his advisor John Ehrlichman. "The goddam press can do anything."[79] A few months later, Nixon was back to complaining about actual malice, this time with White House counsel John Dean. "Yeah. Well, malice is impossible, virtually . . . ," Nixon complained. "What the hell happened? What's the name of that—I don't remember the case, but it was a horrible decision."

By March 1974, Nixon was giving a radio speech calling for legislation to change libel laws so that "good and decent people" would be willing to enter politics without fear of "slanderous attack on them or on their families."[80] Going a step farther than Trump (as far as we know), Nixon even had a Justice Department lawyer begin drafting a law to meet his wishes.[81] Unfortunately for the embattled Nixon, other legal pressures would soon derail these plans. Within five months, Nixon resigned, and any plans for legislative libel change went with him.

The similarities between the Nixon and Trump statements on libel are telling. When presidents feel particularly threatened by press scrutiny, they lash out at First Amendment protections. Understanding the history of *Sullivan* enables Americans to better understand the motivations of the president, and any public figure, when they attack the free press protections that are now a constitutionally required part of libel law.

Justice Thomas's intellectual efforts to revisit *Sullivan* are much more troubling. Although no other justice joined his dissent, as one prominent First Amendment scholar editorialized, "It is deeply disturbing to have a Supreme Court justice urging overruling one of the most important decisions protecting the press."[82]

Thomas's rejection of *Sullivan* is directly related to his judicial philosophy of originalism, which adheres to a vision of an unchanging constitution. And he is correct in recognizing that the actual malice standard was not known to the framers, much less written about in the Constitution. In this sense, the challenge the Court faced when it agreed to hear the *Sullivan* case presented a classic battle between legal visions of the Constitution being either immutable or evolving. The Court in *Sullivan* adopted the latter approach. Brennan was comfortable with the idea that while the framers may not have thought the First Amendment could restrict libel law, these men did fundamentally believe that unchecked power to punish criticism of public officials was contrary to free speech, a free press, and our democracy. And from that overriding constitutional principle, Brennan had the basis to develop his new test.

Let's give the last word in this ongoing debate on constitutional interpretation to Justice Thurgood Marshall. In a thought-provoking speech he delivered for the bicentennial of the Constitution, Marshall addressed the conflict inherent between celebrating the Constitution for what it was, and what it was to become.[83] As with *Sullivan*, racial justice was at the heart of the issue, when he said,

> I do not believe that the meaning of the Constitution was forever "fixed" at the Philadelphia Convention. Nor do I find the wisdom, foresight, and sense of justice exhibited by the Framers particularly profound. To the contrary, the government they devised was defective from the start, requiring several amendments, a civil war, and momentous social transformation to attain the system of constitutional government, and its respect for the individual freedoms and human rights, we hold as fundamental today. When contemporary Americans cite "The Constitution," they invoke a concept that is vastly different from what the Framers barely began to construct two centuries ago. . . .
>
> What is striking is the role legal principles have played throughout America's history in determining the condition of Negroes. They were enslaved by law, emancipated by law, disenfranchised and segregated by law; and, finally, they have begun to win equality by law. Along the way, new constitutional principles have emerged to meet the chal-

lenges of a changing society. The progress has been dramatic, and it will continue.

The men who gathered in Philadelphia in 1787 could not have envisioned these changes. They could not have imagined, nor would they have accepted, that the document they were drafting would one day be construed by a Supreme Court to which had been appointed a woman and the descendent of an African slave. "We the People" no longer enslave, but the credit does not belong to the Framers. It belongs to those who refused to acquiesce in outdated notions of "liberty," "justice," and "equality," and who strived to better them. . . .

If we seek, instead, a sensitive understanding of the Constitution's inherent defects, and its promising evolution through 200 years of history . . . [w]e will see that the true miracle was not the birth of the Constitution, but its life . . . as a living document.[84]

4 / STUDENT SPEECH FROM THE VIETNAM WAR TO THE NATIONAL SCHOOL WALKOUT

On March 14, 2018, at 10 a.m., almost one million students across the country walked out of their classrooms. They were saying "#Enough" to gun violence, and the inability of adults in this country to make any significant progress on gun safety.[1] Coming just one month after seventeen students and staff members of Marjory Stoneman Douglas High School had been shot to death in Parkland, Florida, many walkouts included seventeen minutes of silence to honor those victims.[2]

Inspired by the activism of the student survivors from Parkland, the National School Walkout marked the beginning of a new student movement to demand action from Congress on gun control legislation.[3] The Parkland students, some of whom formed the March for Our Lives organization, were determined to disrupt the traditionally brief responses to mass shootings and insist that the issue remain a part of the national conversation.[4] The *New York Times* commented on the unique ability of these "student-led" protests to break through and capture the attention of the nation: "Even after a year of near continuous protesting—for women, for the environment, for immigrants and more—the emergence of people not even old enough to drive as a political force has been particularly arresting, unsettling a gun control debate that had seemed impervious to other factors."[5]

Notwithstanding the success of these student demonstrations in capturing national attention, many of those participating were aware that there could be consequences for making their voices heard. A number of school districts had announced in advance of the walkout that they would punish students who left class.[6] "We will discipline no matter if it is one, fifty, or five hundred students involved. All will be suspended for 3 days and parent notes will not alleviate the discipline," one superintendent in Texas posted on Facebook.[7]

These student activists were faced with real uncertainty about the extent of their First Amendment rights in school and what would happen to them afterward. Although they did not have to worry about the violent retribution that faced civil rights student protestors in the 1960s, their concerns were still real and understandable. In this time of renewed student activism, looking to history will not only offer inspiration for how students make social progress, but will also provide answers.[8] This protest story begins during the Vietnam War, in an unlikely place with three young students, whose efforts would end up forging a new path for student speech rights in America.

* * *

On December 16, 1965, Mary Beth Tinker was a thirteen-year-old student in the eighth grade at Warren Harding Junior High School in Des Moines, Iowa.[9] As she walked to school that morning, she was "really nervous" because she was wearing something that she knew was going to get her into trouble.[10] It was a simple black armband over her sweater, made from cloth found in her mother's sewing materials.[11] Mary Beth was wearing it, she later said, to mourn "the dead in Vietnam on both sides of the war" and to support Senator Robert Kennedy's "call for a Christmas truce . . . when there was this tremendous bombing of North Vietnam."[12]

Mary Beth had recently attended a meeting of a Unitarian youth group, Liberal Religious Youth, where some students "decided to wear these black armbands to school."[13] The group may have chosen armbands as their protest symbol, Mary Beth later recalled, because people wore them at a memorial service for the four Black girls killed in the 1963 Birmingham church bombing by the Ku Klux Klan, which she and her family had attended in Des Moines.[14] It was just one of the many ways in which the civil rights movement had influenced her and others to take a stand.[15]

After the meeting, one of the students who attended wrote an article for his high school newspaper announcing their plans. This quickly led to the school district imposing a ban on armbands in their junior high and high schools.[16] The threat of punishment made most of the fifty students who had planned to wear armbands reconsider.[17] Mary Beth, however, did not waver. She knew that what she was about to do was explicitly forbidden, but she planned to go forward and "didn't think it was going to be that big of a deal."[18]

Mary Beth wore her armband in school that morning. Her fellow students talked with her about it, and some even teased her (boys at lunch said, "I want an armband for Christmas"), but there was no hostility or altercation.[19] After lunch, when she arrived at her "favorite teacher Mr. Moberly's" math class, he was waiting for her by the door with "a pink slip in his hand."[20] She "knew she was in trouble then" and her "heart was racing" as she reported to the principal's office.[21] In the office, Mary Beth felt intimidated by the school authorities, and agreed to take off the armband. Nevertheless, she was suspended and sent home.[22]

That same morning at another school in Des Moines, Christopher Eckhardt, a fifteen-year-old sophomore, was "fearful and trembling" as he got out of his car and entered Theodore Roosevelt High.[23] Walking "quietly" to his locker, Eckhardt said he recollected taking off his coat, "and there for all the world to see, was my scarlet letter. Well, really it was just a two-inch-wide piece of black cloth I had safety pinned to my camel jacket."[24] Christopher then went directly to the principal's office on his own accord.[25]

He spoke with Vice Principal Donald Blackman, who repeatedly asked him to remove the armband. Christopher refused, and asserted that wearing it was his constitutional right. A guidance counselor joined them and told Christopher that "colleges didn't accept protestors" and that if he was suspended he should look for another high school to return to afterward.[26] Blackman then cryptically told him that the "senior boys were not going to like" his actions and asked if he "was looking for a busted nose."[27] Christopher remained undeterred, and Blackman suspended him.[28]

Mary Beth's older brother, John, who was fifteen and a high school sophomore, decided to wear an armband to school the next day.[29] By lunchtime he was sent to the principal's office.[30] Principal Donald M. Wetter tried a respectful approach to convince John to take off the armband. Wetter talked about his personal experiences in World War II and the value of patriotism.[31] John remembered the principal also telling him that

> it was important to support our government during times of war. He said that I might have been influenced by Communist propaganda. . . . But I told him that I had already thought about what I was doing, and that I was not going to remove the armband. So then he told me that I would have to leave the school and not come back with the armband on.[32]

Two other students were also disciplined for wearing armbands.[33] However, it was only the Tinker and Eckhardt families that wanted to pursue the issue. They sought out the help of the Iowa Civil Liberties Union (ICLU), which represented the students at two contentious public meetings of the local school board.[34] As the board deliberated, the controversy received extensive local and national press.[35] Ultimately, the board members voted 5–2 to uphold the ban on armbands in their schools.[36]

On the advice of their counsel, Mary Beth, John, and Christopher returned to school after New Year's Day and did not wear any armbands.[37] Instead, they all wore black clothes to class for the rest of the school year, to continue making a statement. "It was our way of fighting back," Mary Beth explained.[38]

The Tinker and Eckhardt families intended to keep fighting. With the financial support of the ICLU, a local lawyer named Dan Johnston was hired to bring a case on their behalf in federal court. Johnston was only twenty-eight years old and just "one year out of law school" when he prepared to file a lawsuit seeking a court order to rescind the ban on armbands.[39]

The public exposure of their protests resulted in the Tinkers and Eckhardts having to withstand some frightening blowback. On Christmas Eve, the Tinkers got a phone call from someone threatening to bomb their house by the morning.[40] The Eckhardts received hate mail, and one anonymous note told them, "Go back to Russia if you like communism so much."[41] A radio show host "offered to lend a weapon to anyone who would shoot" the Tinkers' father.[42] Perhaps most disturbingly, one morning as Mary Beth was heading out to school, she answered the phone, and a woman's voice said, "Is this Mary Tinker? . . . I'm going to *kill* you!"[43]

The anger directed toward the young protestors and their families must be considered (though not justified) in the context of the national attitude toward the Vietnam War at the time. In 1965, most Americans still strongly supported the war, and dissenting views were far from mainstream. One Gallup poll in 1965 found 60 percent of Americans believed that sending US troops to Vietnam was "not a mistake," as opposed to only 24 percent who answered that it was.[44]

Another element likely fueling the rage against these youthful dissenters was that student protest was still considered a radical new cultural development.[45] Although it was four teenaged students who launched the lunch counter sit-ins that became such a successful part of the civil rights movement, many adults remained highly skeptical of student activism.[46] In the book *Troublemakers: Students' Rights and Racial Justice in the Long 1960s*, historian Kathryn Schumaker captures how "the increased involvement of young people in social movements" was met with condemnation and scorn:

> That high school students had the right to be heard was patently absurd to many and deeply disturbing to others who worried that the disruptions of the era jeopardized the ability of schools to carry out their mission to educate all young people. Their claims were frivolous, their methods crude, and their efforts the result of youthful immaturity. Why should anyone care what teenagers think?[47]

On September 1, 1966, Chief Judge Stephenson, in the District Court for the Southern District of Iowa, ruled in favor of the school district.[48] He acknowledged that wearing the armbands constituted a "symbolic act" that was protected speech under First Amendment.[49] However, Stephenson concluded that the armband prohibition was "reasonable" and therefore ruled that it was "the disciplined atmosphere of the classroom, not the plaintiffs' right to wear arm bands on school premises, which is entitled to the protection of the law."[50]

On appeal, the case was argued before all eight judges of the Eighth Circuit.[51] The judges split evenly, 4–4, and issued a one-paragraph order affirming the lower court's decision.[52] It was the latest in a series of losses for the students, and now they had only one last unlikely chance: the United States Supreme Court.

There was one glimmer of hope in their effort to be granted a hearing by the Supreme Court, and it came from other student protestors.

These students were fighting, not against the war, but for civil rights. In September 1965, more than a year before the Tinkers and Eckhardt wore their armbands, Black students at the segregated Booker T. Washington High School in Philadelphia, Mississippi, were wearing a different kind of protest symbol: "Freedom Now" buttons.[53] (This was the same town where, only months earlier, three civil rights activists, James Chaney, Andrew Goodman, and Mickey Schwerner, were murdered by members of the local Ku Klux Klan.)[54] The circular buttons were about "1½ inches in diameter, containing the wording 'One Man One Vote' around the perimeter with 'SNCC,' which stood for Student Non-Violent Coordinating Committee (the civil rights group led by John Lewis) inscribed in the center."[55] As many as forty students wore the buttons, and the majority of them chose to be sent home when their principal told them that a recently announced regulation required them to remove the pins or be suspended.[56] Ultimately, in the case that would be called *Burnside v. Byars*, the Fifth Circuit determined that wearing the buttons would not "inherently distract students." Even more significantly, the circuit judges also held that school officials could not "infringe on their students' right to free and unrestricted expression . . . where the exercise of such rights in the school buildings . . . do not materially and substantially interfere with the requirements of appropriate discipline in the operation of the school."[57]

The *Burnside* decision meant that two circuit courts had considered very similar cases on the rights of students to symbolically express dissent in their schools, and come to seemingly opposite legal conclusions.[58] This circuit split made *Tinker* even more ripe for review by the Supreme Court.[59] Sure enough, the armband students would soon hear their silent protests argued vigorously before the justices of the high court.[60] Chris Eckhardt captured the sheer improbability of their journey when he later remarked that he "knew at the time that the U.S. Supreme Court consisted of nine dudes in black robes who made decisions that affected the rest of the country. But never in my wildest dreams did I ever think we would end up in front of the Supreme Court."[61]

* * *

In the almost three years between the armband protests in Des Moines and the Supreme Court oral argument for the *Tinker* case in DC, much had changed in the country. Martin Luther King and Robert F. Kennedy had been assassinated. Over thirty thousand Americans had died in Vietnam during this period.[62] Public opinion had continued to shift such that Americans had become equally divided on the Vietnam War.[63]

Anti-war protests were sweeping college campuses.[64] At Columbia University in 1968, almost a thousand students, protesting the war and the school's treatment of its Black neighbors in Harlem, took over five buildings on campus. The standoff lasted a week and ended with over seven hundred arrested in violent confrontations with the police.[65] Black armbands were beginning to look more quaint than shocking. Expressions of student dissent could now be seen as part of a youth revolt.[66]

Amid this national turmoil, on a snowy day in November, Dan Johnston was about to argue his first case before the United States Supreme Court.[67] The leading case supporting Johnston's advocacy for the First Amendment was *Barnette*, which established that students couldn't be compelled to speak a message that went against their beliefs. However, as Yale Law School Professor Justin Driver deftly explains, "*Barnette* did not establish that students possessed an affirmative right to advance their own opinions, on topics of their own selection, much less in the face of school officials' objections. The right to sit out, in other words, did not necessarily confer the right to speak out."[68] Johnston was about to face an uphill battle, and armed with only limited legal firepower.

With Christopher and Mary Beth seated in the front row (John had missed his flight), Johnston began his argument feeling surprised about the fact that he was "at eye-level with the Court and pretty close to them."[69] However that intimacy soon turned uncomfortable as Justice Byron White began to grill him with a series of questions about the distraction the armbands could cause. Even though the symbols, "wouldn't make a noise," White pressed, "don't you think it would cause some people to direct their attention to the armband and the Vietnam War and think about that rather than what they were . . . supposed to be thinking about in the classroom?"[70] Johnston had to concede the armbands "might for a few moments" take students' minds off their work, but attempted to counter that it would do so no more than other distractions which were allowed in the classroom.[71]

The justices also seem very concerned about the difficulty of limiting a ruling that would give students new speech rights at school. Justice White wanted to know whether it would have made a difference if the school district's new regulation had simply banned all "armbands or buttons or placards."[72] Justice Abraham Fortas wanted to know if expressive rights would go so far as to include a "child" wearing an "outlandish costume" because they wanted to "express very strong belief . . . in the utmost freedom for the individual you know Kool-Aid and electronic test kit and all the things that have been written about these days?"[73] Even Chief Justice Earl Warren, the white-haired grandfatherly embodiment of liberalism, seemed to worry that such line drawing would get the Supreme Court "pretty deep in trenches of ordinary day to day school district" business.[74] In response, Johnston replied that he "really would not think it would get you any further in that sort of thing than in *Barnette*," and that "whatever are the delicate functions of school boards . . . they still have no function which cannot be exercised within the purview and within the dictates of this Court's decision under the First Amendment."[75]

Arguing next on behalf of the school district was its longtime counsel, Allan Herrick. In contrast to the youthful and inexperienced Johnston, Herrick was in his late sixties, a law firm partner, World War I veteran, and conservative Republican.[76] A classic establishment figure right out of central casting, Herrick had been described as being infuriated by the anti-war protests.[77]

Herrick started off strong, in a gravelly voice.[78] He clearly stated the school board's position that administrators should not "have to wait until violence, disorder and disruption break out," but rather should be able to restrict speech when "in their reasonable discretion and judgment, disorder and disruption of the scholarly atmosphere of the school will result unless they act firmly and promptly." Resorting to an effective cliché, Herrick reminded the court that "sometimes an ounce of prevention is a lot better than a pound of cure."[79]

However, Justice Thurgood Marshall was not going to let Herrick's claims of the purported reasonableness of the regulation go unsupported. "Do we have anything more than your assertion that they used due care and they were reasonable?" Marshall asked skeptically.[80] Herrick claimed the board's actions were indeed reasonable because of "the explosive situation that existed in the Des Moines schools at the time the regulation was adopted." Marshall wanted to know exactly what made the situation so explosive. Herrick struggled to answer the question directly, but offered that a "former student of one of our high schools was killed in Vietnam. Some of his friends are still in the school. It was felt that if any kind of a demonstration existed, it might evolve into something which would be difficult to control."[81]

Marshall would not accept this feeble explanation, and incredulously questioned him further:

JUSTICE MARSHALL: Do we have a city in this country that hasn't had someone killed in Vietnam?

HERRICK: No, I think not Your Honor. But I don't think it would be an explosive situation in most cases but if someone who's going to appear ... with an armband here protesting the thing that it could be explosive ...

JUSTICE MARSHALL: It *could* be, is that your position?

HERRICK: Yes, sir. It could be.

JUSTICE MARSHALL: And there was no evidence that it *would* be? Is that the rule you want us to adopt?

HERRICK: No, not at all, Your Honor.[82]

Herrick was floundering. It was an unusually terrible performance before the highest court in the land. Herrick was simply unable to provide any factual basis to support his inflammatory rhetoric, and he was unable to improve his situation before his time ran out.

On rebuttal, Johnston quickly tried to emphasize that the record showed "that there was in the school no general prohibition against political emblems" and that "other kinds of political insignia including the Iron Cross were worn in the schools."[83] His implied point was that the school district was not really worried about the potential for distraction when it banned armbands. Instead, the school board members' real goal was to restrict political symbols that expressed a message they disagreed with.[84]

As the clock was running out on Johnston, Justice Hugo Black fired off a final accusatory question: "Which do you think has the most right about control in the school ... the pupils or the authorities that are running the school?"[85] "The authorities that are running the schools," Johnston respectfully answered. And he then managed to turn the attack around by insisting that even the administrators' right to run the schools was still subject to "the authority given by them by the Constitution of the United States and within the provisions of that Constitution. And the whole nub of our case is that . . . they've exceeded their powers under that."[86]

Johnston's time was up. Despite his dismay that one of his heroes, Justice Black, "was really vicious" at the end, the novice lawyer felt optimistic about their chances.[87] As they walked out together, Chris Eckhardt remembered Johnston being "high as a kite on the job he did," and that they all felt "exhilarated."[88]

Three months later, the students' hopeful expectations were fulfilled—they had finally won. It was a 7–2 decision in their favor. Justice Fortas wrote for the majority in a rousing style that reads more like a political essay than a typical Supreme Court opinion.

Fortas began by reaffirming that "wearing the armbands for the purpose of expressing certain views is the type of symbolic act" which was essentially "pure speech" and therefore entitled "to comprehensive protection under the First Amendment."[89] He elaborated on the nature of those First Amendment protections in the schools by casting a dramatic expansion of student rights in the guise of an inarguable truth. In a line that would reverberate for decades to come, he announced, "It can hardly be argued that either students or teachers shed their constitutional rights to freedom of speech or expression at the schoolhouse gate."[90] No matter whatever else *Tinker* would mean in the future, it would forever be credited with bringing about this memorable phrasing that for the first time recognized student speech as having constitutional value equal to that of adults.[91]

Fortas then goes on to deconstruct the school district's justification for limiting the students' protected speech. He determines that there was "no indication that the work of the schools or any class was disrupted."[92] And writing with a poetic fervor, Fortas rejects a "fear of a disturbance" standard because

in our system, undifferentiated fear or apprehension of disturbance is not enough to overcome the right to freedom of expression. Any departure from absolute regimentation may cause trouble. Any variation from the majority's opinion may inspire fear. Any word spoken, in class, in the lunchroom, or on the campus, that deviates from the views of another person may start an argument or cause a disturbance. But our Constitution says we must take this risk, and our history says that it is this sort of hazardous freedom—this kind of openness—that is the basis of our national strength and of the independence and vigor of Americans who grow up and live in this relatively permissive, often disputatious, society.[93]

Once again, Fortas creates a stirring vision that directly links public schools with the free speech freedoms that he views as vital in our pluralistic society.

Fortas did, however, acknowledge that schools needed to have the power to limit or even prohibit student speech or expression in certain circumstances. The test Fortas set forth, taken directly from the *Burnside* case, required school authorities to have "reasonably . . . forecast substantial disruption of or material interference with school activities" or interference with "the rights of others" in order to restrict student speech in advance.[94] In other words, this "reasonable forecast of substantial disruption" test means that to restrict student speech, school officials: need not wait until actual disruption occurs; but they must be able to reasonably point to something more than just unsubstantiated fear; and the disruption they predict must be substantial.

Another point Fortas raises in objection to the school district's ban on armbands was that it did not extend to "prohibit the wearing of all symbols of political or controversial significance."[95] He notes that the record showed, just as Johnston pointed out at oral argument, that students had worn political campaign buttons as well as "the Iron Cross, traditionally a symbol of Nazism."[96] By singling out only one type of message, in this case anti–Vietnam War views, the district was engaging in what is often called "viewpoint discrimination."[97] "Clearly," Fortas scolded, "the prohibition of expression of one particular opinion . . . is not constitutionally permissible."[98]

Justice Fortas wrapped up his opinion by delivering another blow to school authorities' efforts to control student expression. Contrasting the limits on schools with the freedoms of students, he engaged in a final burst of searing language:

> In our system, state-operated schools may not be enclaves of totalitarianism. School officials do not possess absolute authority over their students. Students in school, as well as out of school, are "persons" under our Constitution. They are possessed of fundamental rights which the State must respect. . . . In our system, students may not be regarded as closed-circuit recipients of only that which the State chooses to communicate. They may not be confined to the expression of those sentiments that are officially approved. In the absence of a specific showing of constitutionally valid reasons to regulate their speech, students are entitled to freedom of expression of their views.[99]

It was a remarkable outcome for Mary Beth, John, and Chris. The decision remains a tribute to the power of student protest, and these three teenagers' ability to transform two inches of black cloth into a force that would revolutionize student speech rights.[100]

However, Justice Black was having none of it. In fact, the octogenarian was so furious that he read his dissent from the bench, a symbolic gesture that the justices infrequently employ to emphasize their intense disagreement with the majority opinion.[101] To further underline his point, he prefaced his written text by extemporizing, "I want it thoroughly known that I disclaim any sentence, any word, any part of what the court does today."[102]

Black viewed the issues generationally, as reflecting a societal battle between unchecked freedom for the young versus strict controls by older authorities. He decried the majority opinion as "the beginning of a new revolutionary era of permissiveness in this country fostered by the judiciary."[103] Palpably longing for traditional values, Black disdainfully wrote that "it may be that the Nation has outworn the old-fashioned slogan that 'children are to be seen, not heard,' but one may, I hope, be permitted to harbor the thought that taxpayers send children to school on the premise that, at their age, they need to learn, not teach."[104]

With his antipathy toward youthful protestors boiling over, Black concluded by raging against the anarchy he saw approaching:

> school discipline, like parental discipline, is an integral and important part of training our children to be . . . better citizens. Here a very small number of students have crisply and summarily refused to obey a school order designed to give pupils who want to learn the opportunity to do so. One does not need to be a prophet or the son of a prophet to know that, after the Court's holding today, some students in Iowa schools—and, indeed, in all schools—will be ready, able, and willing to defy their teachers on practically all orders. This is the more unfortunate for the schools since groups of students all over the land are already running loose, conducting break-ins, sit-ins, lie-ins, and smash-ins. . . . This case . . . subjects all the public schools in the country to the whims and caprices of their loudest-mouthed, but maybe not their brightest, students. . . . I wish, therefore, wholly to disclaim any purpose on my part to hold that the Federal Constitution compels the teachers, parents, and elected school officials to surrender control of the American public school system to public school students.[105]

This vitriolic dissent was all the more surprising since for most of Hugo Black's time on the Supreme Court he had been a stalwart defender of First Amendment principles.[106] Chief Justice Warren wryly noted his surprise by reportedly remarking, "Old Hugo really got hung up in his jock strap on that one."[107]

Some have speculated that a large degree of Black's anger stemmed from a highly personal reason. A short time after the *Tinker* oral argument, Black's own grandson, Sterling Black Jr., had been suspended from high school for producing an underground newspaper that criticized school officials.[108] Black told his son, an attorney and president of the New Mexico ACLU, that the family should not sue "the school for doing its duty.'"[109] The youth revolution was hitting very close to home.[110]

Regardless of the political or personal factors behind Black's dissent, his law and order concerns were shared by many Americans at the time. One month after the *Tinker* decision, 52 percent of those surveyed said they did not believe that students had a right to protest, as opposed to just 38 percent who supported such rights.[111] The fact that *Tinker* flew in the face of the prevailing societal norms regarding student protest goes to show how stunningly transformative the decision was in its day.[112]

Tinker would prove to be the high-water mark for student speech rights. In three subsequent cases from the 1980s to 2007, the Supreme Court granted school officials greater authority to restrict student expression in specific contexts. Schools can now control student speech that is "vulgar and lewd" (in a case involving a student giving a high school student government nomination speech that was filled with unsophisticated double entendres), "school-sponsored" (prohibiting publication of student newspaper articles on pregnancy and divorce), and "promoting illegal drug use" (punishing a student for displaying a banner that read "BONG HiTS 4 JESUS").[113] Nevertheless, in his authoritative book, *The Schoolhouse Gate: Public Education, the Supreme Court, and the Battle for the American Mind,* Professor Driver persuasively contends that these decisions should not "be viewed as draining student speech of all vitality . . . [and] did not purport to undercut *Tinker*'s core contribution: students, typically speaking, continue to possess the right to express themselves in schools, even if educators do not support their messages."[114]

* * *

What lessons then do *Tinker* and its progeny hold for the participants in the National School Walkout, March for Our Lives, and millions of other students considering protesting *at* their schools about gun violence *in* their schools? At its most fundamental level, *Tinker* means that students can wear armbands, or buttons, to protest gun violence, draw attention to gun safety laws and mourn the dead, as long as it would not reasonably lead to a substantial disruption in school. And thanks to *Tinker*, this should be true no matter how unpopular or controversial the message is in some communities or with school administrators. Of course, students also have an equal right to wear pro–Second Amendment messages as well.[115]

Yet walking out of class during the school day, for any reason—including Greta Thunberg's popular Fridays for Future, where students skip school to strike for climate change action—is a different story.[116] This type of disruptive activity would not be protected by *Tinker*.[117] As the ACLU has advised, "schools can typically discipline students for missing class, even if they're doing so to participate in a protest or otherwise express themselves. But what the school can't do is discipline students more harshly because they are walking out to express a political view or because school administrators don't support the views behind the protest."[118]

Given the savvy and sophistication displayed by the Parkland students so far, it seems likely that they have known about their First Amendment rights for some time. Dalia Lithwick, Slate's insightful legal correspondent, pointed out that "the effectiveness of these poised, articulate, well-informed, and seemingly preternaturally mature student leaders of Stoneman Douglas" was in large part due to their excellent public school, which "painstakingly taught about drama, media, free speech, political activism, and forensics."[119] Another meaningful learning opportunity that Marjory Stoneman Douglas High School provided was to host a forum for Mary Beth Tinker to speak with students in 2013.[120] Having retired as a pediatric nurse that year, she began a "'Tinker Tour' to promote youth voices, a free speech and a free press."[121] Tinker's message then and now, about how student protest can make a difference, should certainly be one that resonates with many of the students today as they seek to make change in their schools and across the country.

Whatever inspiration the future March for Our Lives organizers may have gained from Mary Beth Tinker, she was inspired to join students participating in the National School Walkout. Tinker told the *Des Moines Register*, her former hometown paper, that she "was really excited that they were taking their grief and turning it into something positive."[122] "I do believe we're at a turning point," Tinker added, "for not only gun violence but for young people having more of a say over the policies that affect their lives."[123]

* * *

In 1968, only six months before hearing oral argument in the *Tinker* case, Justice Abe Fortas had a highly unusual book published. Entitled *Concerning Dissent and Civil Disobedience*, it was described as a "'broadside,' a timely political pamphlet in the tradition of the American Revolutionary Press."[124] Fortas strove in the short book to explain, using simple, nonlegal language, "the basic principles governing dissent and civil disobedience in our democracy."[125] He also described with surprising candor how those principles applied "to the revolt of the youth generation—of the sixteen- to twenty-five-year-olds."[126] In one resonant passage from his section on "The Rules" for youthful protest, Justice Fortas wrote:

I do not know how profound in intensity or how lasting the current youth revolt may be. It may presage a new and welcome era of idealism in the nation. It may forecast the development of greater maturity and independence of outlook among our young people, and this may be productive of much good. . . . In any event, it presents a challenge to the older generations as well as to youth to reconsider the goals of our society and its values, and urgently to reappraise the distribution of function and responsibility among the generations.[127]

This sage commentary, from the man who would become the author of the greatest decision for students' rights, manages to simultaneously speak with equal force to the Vietnam War protestors of the past and the March for Our Lives movement of today. America's young people have an essential role to play in fashioning our society's free speech values.

5 / STORMY DANIELS, PRIOR RESTRAINTS, AND THE PENTAGON PAPERS

When a photo of Stormy Daniels posing with Anderson Cooper was tweeted out by her lawyer with a simple reference to "@60Minutes," it triggered the desired effect.[1] The media went into a frenzy of speculation about what the adult-film star would say now that she appeared ready to talk about her alleged affair with Donald Trump. It had been almost two months since the *Wall Street Journal* broke the story that Trump's personal lawyer, Michael Cohen, just days before the presidential election, had arranged a $130,000 payment to Daniels for signing a non-disclosure agreement.[2] It seemed she was ready to break the terms of that agreement. And if you want to speak out and be taken seriously, *60 Minutes* would be the ideal place to tell your story.

However, just a few days after the social media announcement, the conversation about the interview began to turn from *when* the interview would air to questions about *if* it would air at all. Buzzfeed was the first to assert that President Trump's legal team was considering legal action to stop the forthcoming broadcast.[3] A growing chorus of media outlets were soon reporting that Trump's legal team might seek a court order to stop *60 Minutes* from televising the interview.[4] The speculation grew to such a fever pitch that CBS News president David

Rhodes felt compelled to state, "It has been reported there will be an injunction to prevent it from running. I haven't seen such an injunction, and I don't know what the basis of such an injunction would be."[5]

Rhodes was understandably at a loss to think of a sufficient legal argument to support this restriction on the press. His confidence stemmed from what has become known as the Pentagon Papers case, which struck a decisive blow against censorship of the press, even when the reporting was on top secret military intelligence during wartime. Although the official case name was *New York Times Company v. United States*, the real antagonists were President Nixon versus a free press.[6]

Today we take for granted the right of the press to publish material received from leakers and others who provide it in violation of the law. However, in 1971, the outcome of the fight between these two forces was very much in doubt and set the stage for the most thrilling conflict in First Amendment history. The stakes could not have been higher, the Supreme Court review occurred in record time (fifteen days from injunction to decision), and the result likely flipped on a single answer at oral argument.[7]

* * *

Before the court battle, before publication, even before the leak, there was a document entitled "History of U.S. Decision-Making in Vietnam, 1945–68." What would later become known as the Pentagon Papers began as a study, commissioned in 1967 by an increasingly disillusioned Defense Secretary Robert McNamara, of the history of America's involvement in Vietnam. McNamara's instructions were that the report be "encyclopedic and objective."[8] He got his wish. A year and a half later, the completed study was presented to a new defense secretary, all forty-seven volumes and seven thousand pages, comprising three thousand pages of narrative and four thousand pages of supporting documents. It was classified "top secret," the military's highest level of national security information classification, which applies only to secrets that, if revealed, "could result in exceptionally grave damage to the nation."[9] The government continued to consider the report so secret that it was not fully declassified until 2011.[10]

Daniel Ellsberg, the man responsible for releasing the Pentagon Papers, would later describe the documents as revealing "a policy of concealment and quite deliberate deception from the Truman administration onward" about America's role in Vietnam.[11] Of more immediate interest to the country, the report showed the bombing taking place in North Vietnam was not deterring Viet Cong fighters and wasn't working to bring an end to the seemingly endless war.[12] Floyd Abrams, the lawyer who would defend the *New York Times* in the Pentagon Papers case, put it simply: "The documents were devastating, demonstrating an extraordinary level of governmental duplicity based upon an unprecedented source—the very files of the Government itself."[13]

Who was Ellsberg, the man who was both a contributing author and then leaker of the Pentagon Papers? Dubbed "the most dangerous man in America" by Secretary of State Henry Kissinger, he was one of the most unlikely radicals in American history.[14] A Harvard-educated economist and former marine commander, Ellsberg volunteered to serve in Vietnam as a "State Department civilian."[15] After two years in Vietnam convinced him that "continuing the hopeless war [was] intolerable," he still remained a consummate insider who acted as an advisor on the war to presidential candidates and Henry Kissinger in his role as national security advisor.[16]

While working as an analyst at the Rand Corporation in 1969, Ellsberg attended an anti-war conference and heard a speech by an activist who talked about his plans to go to jail to resist the draft.[17] He surprised himself, he later recalled, by breaking down and sobbing for over an hour, thinking "we are eating our young."[18] Two months later, Ellsberg began secretly removing from a safe in his office portions of one of the copies of the Pentagon Papers—only fifteen existed at the time—to photocopy page by page.[19] He brought the papers to anti-war senators such as J. William Fulbright and George McGovern, but even they refused to make the documents public.[20] Feeling increasingly desperate that the papers would never be released, Ellsberg took the riskier step of giving Neil Sheehan, a respected Vietnam reporter with the *New York Times*, access.[21]

A team from the *Times* soon decamped with the papers to a secret hotel suite and began a voracious three-month review. The reporters would later describe their efforts as a race to absorb what information was revealed in the documents, corroborate its accuracy, and determine what could be reported on without potentially compromising national security.[22] Meanwhile, the editors, lawyers, and publisher of the the *Times* began a fierce internal debate as to whether or not to publish or report on the Pentagon Papers at all. The newspaper's outside law firm, Lord, Day & Lord, strongly warned against it. The publisher, Arthur O. Sulzberger, was advised that publication of the top secret documents would violate the Espionage Act, a law aimed at spies dating back to World War I, and that he could be jailed himself.[23]

Undeterred, on Sunday, June 13, 1971, the *New York Times* published its first article on the Pentagon Papers, with the uninvitingly dry headline: "Vietnam Archive: Pentagon Study Traces 3 Decades of Growing U.S. Involvement."[24] In addition, three pages of documents from the study were published verbatim inside the paper.[25] And although this explosive reporting would soon engulf the paper in controversy, an average reader might be drawn to a more prominent front-page article on the White House wedding of President Nixon's daughter Tricia, with a large accompanying photo.[26]

Thanks to Nixon's tape-recorded telephone conversations, we know that on the day the Pentagon Papers were published, the president hadn't even seen the article. Initially, Nixon did not appear very concerned about the publication since he was advised it would mostly reflect badly on the Democrats.[27] Over the phone, Kissinger assured him that the press had "tried to make [Vietnam] 'Nixon's War,' and what this massively proves is that, if it's anybody's war, it's Kennedy's and Johnson's."[28] Yet mid-conversation Nixon changed his tone and indignantly declared, "This is treasonable action on the part of the bastards that put it out!" Kissinger readily agreed and goaded him further, saying, "There's no question it's actionable. I'm absolutely certain that this violates all sorts of security laws."[29] By the end of the call they agreed to have Attorney General John Mitchell examine options on how to respond.[30]

The next day, after the *New York Times* published its second front-page article on the Pentagon Papers, Attorney General Mitchell told Nixon that he thought they would look "a little foolish" not to take action against the newspaper.[31] In a fateful and extremely brief exchange, Nixon asked a pivotal question: "Has this ever been done before?"

"A publication like this, or—" Mitchell responded.

"No, no, no. Have you—has the government ever done this to a paper before?"

"Oh, yes, advising them of their . . ."

"Oh."

"Yes," Mitchell said. "We've done this before."

"Have we? All right."[32]

Mitchell's answer was shockingly misleading. In fact, the federal government had never before in American history brought an action to stop a newspaper from publishing.

Perhaps bolstered by this false precedent, in just another minute Nixon had made up his mind. He proclaimed, "As far as the *Times* is concerned, hell, they're our enemies. I think we just ought to do it."[33] He then authorized the attorney general to warn the *Times* that by publishing these top secret documents they were violating federal law.[34]

Later that day, Mitchell sent a telegram to the publisher of the *New York Times*, stating that continued publication of information from the Pentagon Papers "will cause irreparable injury to the defense interests of the United States."[35] The attorney general concluded with a "request" that the newspaper stop publishing "information of this character" and return the documents to the Defense Department.[36]

The *Times* refused to give in to the government's request, and published an article the next morning with the blaring, all-caps headline, "Mitchell Seeks to Halt Series on Vietnam, but Times Refuses."[37] Underneath this declaration of independence was a third article on the Pentagon Papers and how President Johnson had "secretly opened the way to ground combat."[38] Later that day, the chief of the Civil Division of the United States Attorney's Office in Manhattan went to court seeking an emergency order to prevent the *New York Times* from publishing another word of the Pentagon Papers.[39]

Meanwhile, the *Times* was unceremoniously dumped by the law firm that had represented the newspaper for over sixty years. Shockingly, their counsel at Lord, Day & Lord refused to represent them in what was shaping up to be the most momentous First Amendment challenge in history.[40] This abandonment at the altar was an unmistakable sign of how radically the *Times'* decision to continue publishing was perceived in some legal circles. Fortuitously, the chief in-house lawyer for the *Times* had made a middle of the night call to hire two lawyers who had recently defended the newspaper against having to disclose confidential sources.[41] The new legal team—Yale constitutional law professor Alexander Bickel and up-and-coming First Amendment attorney Floyd Abrams—eagerly took on the case and confidently told the *Times'* leadership that it "would obviously win."[42] However, on heading to court to fight the government's efforts to halt publication, Abrams later recalled that his initial exuberance diminished as he realized that his case was about to be "litigated by an academic with no courtroom experience, accompanied by a lawyer who had never even watched a Supreme Court argument."[43]

The request for an injunction (a court order to stop the *Times* from publishing the articles) was filed in federal district court, and randomly assigned to Judge Murray Gurfein.[44] Judge Gurfein was a Nixon appointee, and has been described as a "roly-poly kind of guy with an abbreviated walrus mustache . . . [and] dazzling intellect."[45] He was also so new to the bench that this would be his very first case.[46] At the outset, the *Times* made the risky but principled decision to refuse the judge's request to "voluntarily" stop publishing during his legal review. As a result, Gurfein granted the government's demand for a temporary restraining order, barring the *New York Times* from publishing anything further on the Pentagon Papers.[47]

The *Times* then had to make another fateful decision: whether or not to obey the judge's order. The paper had already defied the attorney general and, indirectly, the president of the United States. How could the newspaper defend the right to publish as fundamental and then just acquiesce to what their lawyers were preparing to argue was an unjust and unconstitutional decision?

Professor Bickel convinced the *Times'* publisher, Arthur Sulzberger, that they must follow the court's order and not publish for the time being. His prevailing argument was that the newspaper could not violate the rule of law to vindicate the rule of law.[48] In other words, to prove that their controversial act of publishing top secret documents was a lawful endeavor, the *New York Times* must follow and abide by the legal process until the bitter end. The presses stopped.

Bickel and Abrams had two primary First Amendment arguments to convince the judge that a permanent order to halt publication must not be granted.[49] First, they made clear that what the government was seeking was a prior restraint—a government action (by statute or court order) preventing speech before it occurs—and that the Supreme Court had "consistently rejected all manner of prior restraints on publication" for over 150 years.[50] In addition, they took a broader view that publication of government documents exposing presidential misconduct in war was exactly the type of press action that the First Amendment was created to safeguard.[51]

In a surprising turn of events, just three days after Judge Gurfein had granted the temporary injunction, he ruled that he was denying the government's request to stop publication. He found that the government had failed to produce enough facts to demonstrate a "sharp clash . . . between the vital security interests of the Nation and the compelling constitutional doctrine against prior restraint."[52] Gurfein then went on to brilliantly expose the false conflict between security and freedom of expression in American society:

> If there be some embarrassment to the Government . . . that flows from any security breach we must learn to live with it. The security of the Nation is not at the ramparts alone. Security also lies in the value of our free institutions. A cantankerous press, an obstinate press, a ubiquitous press must be suffered by those in authority in order to preserve the even greater values of freedom of expression and the right of the people to know. . . . These are troubled times. There is no greater safety valve for discontent and cynicism about the affairs of Government than freedom of expression in any form. This has been the genius of our institutions throughout our history.[53]

It was a resounding victory from a surprising source. Nonetheless, the judge did maintain the temporary stay on publication while the government appealed his decision.[54]

In the meantime, with any future publication of the Pentagon Papers by the *New York Times* in limbo, Ellsberg gave another copy of the secret documents to the *Washington Post*.[55] The same day the *Post* published their own front-page Pentagon Papers article, Assistant Attorney General (and future Supreme Court chief justice) William Rehnquist called the paper's executive editor, Ben Bradlee, and asked him to cease publication.[56] When Bradlee refused, his "hands and legs were shaking."[57] The attorney general's office hauled them into court the same night, launching a new front in the government's litigation war.[58]

Eventually Ellsberg gave copies of the papers to nineteen newspapers, and as the government tried to stop four of the publications, one exasperated judge vented they were "asking us to ride herd on a swarm of bees."[59]

* * *

The separate district court wins for the *New York Times* and *Washington Post* were both appealed by the government, which obtained partial victories that sent the cases back to the district court for further hearings.[60] The *Times* chose to appeal directly to the United States Supreme Court on June 24, and the high court agreed to hear the case, scheduling oral argument for the 26th.[61]

Oral arguments before the Supreme Court are a high-wire act that is a mix of debate and theater. The attorneys desperately try to highlight their most convincing arguments, but the justices will often interrupt them straight out of the gate with a rapid-fire barrage of questions and hypothetical puzzles.[62] On many occassions the justices aren't seeking answers from the lawyers as much as they are attempting to influence one another. Although legal scholars debate what impact oral argument may or may not have on the decision-making of the Supreme Court justices, in this case, given the breakneck pace of the review process and the sheer volume of the materials at issue, it was indisputably meaningful.[63]

Solicitor General Erwin Griswold, representing the United States,[64] sat in the courtroom at the counsel table, beneath which was the cause of everything that would soon be argued: three boxes holding a rare copy of the complete Pentagon Papers.[65] He began his argument by asserting that the *New York Times* and *Washington Post* had obtained the Pentagon Papers as part of a "breach of trust. They know that this material is not theirs, they do not own it."[66] Griswold then boldly claimed that "the heart of our case is that the publication of the [Pentagon Papers] will . . . materially affect the security of United States. It will affect lives, it will affect the process of determination of the war. It will affect the process of recovering prisoners of war." He went on to argue that the standard for stopping publication of the Pentagon Papers should not be that continued publication would result in *"immediate"* harm to the United States, but rather *"irreparable"* harm. His time having run out, Griswold concluded by adding dramatically that "to say that [publication] can only be enjoined if there will be a war tomorrow morning when there is a war now going on is much too narrow."[67]

Appearing on behalf of the *New York Times*, Alexander Bickel began by arguing that the president does not have any inherent power to impose a prior restraint on speech, and that there was no federal law that authorized such an action.[68] He then went on to emphasize that the "rule against the prior restraint" is a fundamental part of First Amendment history because "prior restraints fall on speech with a special brutality and finality and procedural ease all their own, which distinguishes them from other regulations of speech. If a criminal statute chills speech, a prior restraint freezes it."[69]

Toward the end of Bickel's allotted time, Justice Potter Stewart, one of the two likely swing votes on the Court, sprung a potentially devastating hypothetical on Bickel.[70] What should the Court do if the continued publication of the Pentagon Papers would obviously, directly, and immediately cause the death of one hundred American soldiers?[71] Try as Bickel might to dodge the question by doggedly maintaining there was no evidence to support such definite and direct harm in this case, Stewart insisted on an answer to his specific hypothetical question: "You would say the Constitution requires that it be published and that these men die, is that it?"[72]

"No," Bickel replied, "I'm afraid that my . . . inclinations of humanity overcome the somewhat more abstract devotion to the First Amendment in a case of that sort."[73]

The answer seemed to surprise Justice Stewart, and indeed some of the newspapers' most ardent supporters were also taken aback, viewing it as a misguided concession on the limits of First Amendment protections. The ACLU even took the highly unusual step of filing a post–oral argument brief disavowing Bickel's position.[74] And Justice Black reportedly said in chambers, "Too bad the *New York Times* couldn't find someone who believes in the First Amendment."[75]

In retrospect however, it seems to have been an astute split-second decision to win over a crucial vote. Sometimes to claim a groundbreaking victory you need to set limits on the extent of what you are asking for, if for no other reason than to highlight the reasonableness of your request.

A whirlwind four days later, the Supreme Court held in a 6–3 decision that the government had *not* met the "heavy burden of showing justification for the imposition" of the prior restraint against the press.[76] The divided Court also held that the injunctions against the newspapers were lifted.[77] The next day, the *New York Times* resumed its series—which had been halted for fifteen days—with a banner headline proudly proclaiming the Supreme Court "Upholds Newspapers on Publication of the Pentagon Report."[78]

The triumphant ruling for the press was not, however, as sweeping as it first appears. Three justices (Chief Justice Warren Burger, Justice Marshall Harlan II, and Justice Harry Blackmun) issued stinging dissenting opinions. The dissenters all agreed that further hearings were warranted in order to give the government more time to prove that national security interests in this case necessitated overcoming the heavy presumption against prior restraints. Justice Blackmun's dissent ended on a particularly dire and finger-pointing note:

> I hope that damage has not already been done. If, however, damage has been done, and if, with the Court's action today, these newspapers proceed to publish the critical documents and there results therefrom the death of soldiers, the destruction of alliances, the greatly increased difficulty of negotiation with our enemies, the inability of our diplomats to negotiate, to which list I might add the factors of prolongation of the war and of further delay in the freeing of United States prisoners, then the Nation's people will know where the responsibility for these sad consequences rests.[79]

Even among the majority, "no one opinion by a single justice commanded the support of a majority."[80] This meant that, although six justices voted to allow the newspapers to resume publishing the classified papers, their *reasons* for this decision differed strikingly. Justice Black's opinion, joined by Justice Douglas, took a First Amendment absolutist approach and condemned the prior restraints in the harshest of language, writing that "every moment's continuance of the injunctions against these newspapers amounts to a flagrant, indefensible, and continuing violation of the First Amendment."[81] Switching in tone, he then set forth on a soaring tribute to the role of a free press in general and the *New York Times* and *Washington Post* specifically:

> In the First Amendment, the Founding Fathers gave the free press the protection it must have to fulfill its essential role in our democracy. The press was to serve the governed, not the governors. The Government's power to censor the press was abolished so that the press would remain forever free to censure the Government. The press was protected so that it could bare the secrets of government and inform the

people. Only a free and unrestrained press can effectively expose deception in government. And paramount among the responsibilities of a free press is the duty to prevent any part of the government from deceiving the people and sending them off to distant lands to die of foreign fevers and foreign shot and shell. In my view, far from deserving condemnation for their courageous reporting, *The New York Times*, *The Washington Post*, and other newspapers should be commended for serving the purpose that the Founding Fathers saw so clearly. In revealing the workings of government that led to the Vietnam war, the newspapers nobly did precisely that which the Founders hoped and trusted they would do.[82]

Justices Stewart and White were the swing votes that ultimately turned in favor of the *Times*. Yet Stewart's opinion (joined by White) took a much less celebratory approach than Justice Black's. Stewart stated that he agreed with the government, at least regarding some of the documents, that they should *not* be published in the interest of national security.[83] Nevertheless, sounding almost reluctant, Justice Stewart found that he could not say that publication would "surely result in direct, immediate, and irreparable damage to our Nation or its people."[84] This phrase would later generally be understood as establishing the key legal test to come out of the Pentagon Papers case.[85] It seems Bickel's bold concession that direct loss of life could override the First Amendment not only garnered him the votes needed to win, but contributed to the formation of a test that provided extraordinary—if not absolute—protection of the press.[86]

Along with this ruling in support of the newspapers came a catch. Although there were six votes in favor of the newspapers' right to publish, there was also a majority of justices that indicated that the leakers themselves could still be criminally prosecuted.[87] The First Amendment shield against prior restraints on the press would provide no such protection for the man who gave the top secret documents to the media in the first place. Ellsberg ultimately would be criminally prosecuted under the Espionage Act for revealing classified information.[88]

Nonetheless, the Supreme Court's decision was widely hailed as a decisive victory for the press that would continue to impact the role of the media in significant and unexpected ways. The *Times* went on to publish six more reports on the Pentagon Papers and its reporting won the Pulitzer Prize for Public Service in 1972.[89] Beyond what this award did for the *Times'* reputation, it also marked a crucial turning point for the mainstream media's relationship with the presidency. For the first time, the press had challenged the president head on, and won. The publication of the Pentagon Papers revealed that four presidents had repeatedly and intentionally lied to the media and the American public about the origins, nature, and extent of the Vietnam War. What had always been a fragile and combative relationship between the press and the government had fractured in a way that would not be healed, leading these two entities down a considerably more adversarial path.[90]

On the war front, the continued publication of the Pentagon Papers did not hasten the end of the conflict as much as Ellsberg and other anti-war activists had hoped. America would not withdraw from Vietnam for another four years. Yet despite the fact that these documents never dealt a decisive blow to end the war, they surely lent crucial credibility to "the growing consensus that the Vietnam War was wrong and legitimized the radical critique of the war."[91]

Nixon's ultimately unsuccessful fight to stop publication of the Pentagon Papers lit a raging fire under his building paranoia and desire for revenge against his perceived enemies, particularly leakers. In his fury, Nixon authorized the formation of the White House Special Investigation Unit, soon to become infamously known as the Plumbers. The Plumbers' first task was the burglary of Ellsberg's psychiatrist's office, and their last effort was a botched break-in at the Democratic National Committee headquarters at the Watergate hotel.[92] As a result, the judge in Ellsberg's criminal trial would later drop all charges against him after the evidence of the burglary was put before the court.[93] Ironically, it was Nixon's efforts to stop the Pentagon Papers and leakers at all costs, not anything in the documents or press reports on them, that brought down his presidency and enabled Ellsberg to walk away from any criminal consequences.

For future presidents the impact would be less personal but equally serious. Beyond any specific test in the decision, or the presumption of unconstitutionality now attached to prior restraints, there is a clear takeaway message for the leaders of the free world. That message is simply this: presidents can't stop the publication of information that they don't like, even if they think it will harm the country. As Floyd Abrams succinctly put it, prior restraints are "just not a weapon in the arsenal" of presidents, thanks to the Pentagon Papers.[94]

* * *

Which brings us back to our contemporary conundrum: was President Trump constitutionally prohibited from obtaining a prior restraint to stop *60 Minutes* from broadcasting an interview with Stormy Daniels? To play this scenario out, we can start with what Trump's lawyers actually did. Trump's legal team began their effort to stop Daniels from speaking by attempting to use Daniel's 2016 nondisclosure agreement, or "NDA," against her. Team Trump sought an emergency order to enforce the NDA, and prevent her from disclosing any of the "confidential information" covered in the agreement.[95] They argued that if Daniels was not ordered to abide by the agreement and keep quiet about these claims, then Trump would suffer irreparable harm that the contract was specifically designed to prevent. As a result, a temporary restraining order was issued against Daniels, handing Trump a preliminary win.[96]

Daniels fought back by bringing a separate legal action asking a different judge to declare the NDA unenforceable as a matter of public policy and because Trump never signed the agreement.[97] But before these legal fights were concluded, Daniels sat for the interview with Anderson Cooper.

At this stage, our question becomes hypothetical, since we know the interview proceeded and scored *60 Minutes* its highest ratings in a decade.[98] Yet if Team Trump had gone further and tried to stop the news broadcast, then we can speculate that their thinking would have continued along the following lines. Although *60 Minutes* and CBS News weren't parties to the NDA, their broadcast of the interview would enable Daniels to break her agreement. Trump's lawyers could go on to assert that obtaining a court order to prevent the interview from airing would be the only recourse Trump had to vindicate his paid-for contract rights and protect him from permanent harm by scandalously false claims of an entirely private nature.

But let's not allow Trump's claim about the lack of political significance of Daniels's speech, or what he has called "a simple private transaction," go unchallenged here.[99] Michael Cohen eventually pled guilty to criminal campaign finance violations for his part in a scheme with Trump to hide Daniels's accusations from voters in the final weeks of the presidential campaign.[100] Prosecutors stressed that Cohen's crimes "struck a blow to one of the core goals of the federal campaign finance laws: transparency. While many Americans . . . knocked on doors, toiled at phone banks or found any number of other legal ways to make their voices heard, Cohen sought to influence the election from the shadows."[101] The federal judge at sentencing agreed that Cohen had done "insidious harm to our democratic institutions" and ordered him to serve three years in prison.[102] With Cohen's crimes confirmed, the question of whether Trump broke the law working with Cohen to make "hush payoffs" is an undeniably relevant one.[103]

Nevertheless, Trump's legal team could still argue that even if there was some media interest in Daniel's speech, a balancing test should be used to weigh privacy and contract rights against those of the press.

His lawyers could contend that although there has been an assumption that prior restraints on the media were often unconstitutional, in these circumstances a different outcome is warranted since the potential privacy violation is unusually damaging and the public interest in the material is low. After all, the argument could continue, why should a media company be allowed to help someone break a contractual agreement just because the First Amendment might favor publication over restrictions on the press in some cases?

Thankfully, however, the Pentagon Papers decision and the string of cases reaffirming its principles over the years establish that prior restraints are almost always unconstitutional.[104] It also created a legal test that does more than just *balance* the First Amendment protections against other valid interests. Instead, anyone seeking a prior restraint on the media needs to meet the extremely heavy burden that broadcast or publication would "surely result in direct, immediate, and irreparable damage to our Nation or its people."[105] If publishing top secret government documents during wartime and the resulting potential threats to national security interests were not sufficient to meet this burden, it is clear that very few factual situations will have any chance of doing so.

It must have been the daunting strength of the *New York Times Company v. United States* decision that stopped a hyperaggressive litigator like President Trump from taking any action against CBS.[106] However, in 2020, Trump felt emboldened enough to have the Justice Department try and stop the publication of his former national security adviser John Bolton's political memoir, *The Room Where It Happened*.[107] The effort to block Bolton's disparaging account of his time in the Trump White House was rejected by a federal district court judge just three days before the book's release.[108] Days later, Trump's brother, Robert Trump, attemped to halt publication of another book, this one by the president's niece, Mary Trump. She had written a tell-all entitled *Too Much and Never Enough: How My Family Created the*

World's Most Dangerous Man, and, like the Bolton book, the advance buzz was that it painted a devastating picture of Trump.[109] Once again, the effort to obtain a prior restraint was denied by the courts.[110] In both cases, Trump's surrogates claimed that contractual obligations (a pre-publication review agreement with Bolton and a non-disclosure settlement agreement with Mary Trump) took precedence over free speech.[111] And in both cases the Pentagon Papers precedent was the primary weapon used to fight back.[112]

Legal actions like this serve as a pointed reminder that the Pentagon Papers decision remains an invaluable shield for the media against governmental interference with publication. Moreover, for those that know the Pentagon Papers legal saga, the case also can serve as a sword. Stormy Daniels and her lawyer likely felt emboldened to break her NDA knowing that, if she risked talking, she could wield the Pentagon Papers against a conspiracy to silence her. Daniels knew the power of this vital Supreme Court ruling meant that she could speak out with confidence that her words would be amplified by the full force of a major media outlet that could not be stopped.

Ultimately, what Stormy Daniels had to say about Trump's sex life is not as important as her ability to say it. The Pentagon Papers decision matters because it constrains anyone, all the way up to and including the president of the United States, from stopping the publication of information they do not want to be heard. From Vietnam secrets to claims of sexual and political misconduct, the First Amendment continues to mean that the media's ability to speak truth to power is unabridged. No one can stand in the way of Americans' ability to see, hear, and then judge for ourselves.

6 / FLIPPING OFF THE PRESIDENT AND FUCK THE DRAFT

On a Saturday afternoon in October 2017, a woman was riding her bike down Lowes Island Boulevard near her home in northern Virginia. As about a half-dozen vehicles began to slowly drive past her, she realized it was President Trump's motorcade, leaving the nearby Trump National Golf Course. "My blood started boiling at that point," she recalled. "I lifted my arm and started flipping him off. I started thinking, you're golfing again when there is so much going on right now."[1] After raising her middle finger to the line of SUVs twice, the woman didn't give it much more thought. "I went about my day, my night, my slow Sunday morning," the cyclist remembered, never expecting that this fleeting expression of anger was about to change her life.[2]

Unbeknownst to the woman at the time, observant members of the press corps who were riding along with the motorcade happened to capture the moment of spontaneous protest. A few hours later, the White House bureau chief for Voice of America tweeted a photograph of the "lone cyclist."[3] It shows a woman with a blonde ponytail under a bike helmet, wearing a white T-shirt and black cycling pants. Viewed from behind, so her face is not visible, she has her left arm and middle finger raised defiantly toward three passing black SUVs. The image quickly became a viral sensation, with one commentator calling the defiant gesture "the middle-finger salute seen around the world."[4] On the *Late Show*, host Stephen Colbert quipped, "No one has summed up the mood of the country better. . . . Long may she wave."[5]

The woman being hailed by Trump's critics as a "she-ro" was Juli Briskman, a fifty-year-old marketing analyst and a single mother of two teens.[6] The next day Briskman saw the images on social media, and posted the photograph to her Twitter and Facebook accounts. Even though her employer, a government contractor named Akima, wasn't listed on her personal social accounts, that Monday she decided to tell her company's human resources department that she was the woman in the famous finger photo. One day later, Briskman was fired and escorted out of the building, taking her personal belongings with her in a box.[7]

It was only after Briskman lost her job, allegedly for violating the company's social media policy, that she identified herself to the media. Six months later she sued Akima for wrongful termination.[8] The challenge facing Briskman's lawsuit is that the First Amendment protects only against *government* interference with speech, not the actions of private employers.[9] Nevertheless, Briskman's free speech fight highlights captivating threshold questions about whether the First Amendment protects nonverbal communication, how you communicate a protest message, and the use in public places of "unseemly expletives."[10] Flashing back to a case from the 1960s anti-war movement illuminates the extent to which these speech rights are protected— even when no words are spoken.

* * *

On April 26, 1968, nineteen-year-old Paul Robert Cohen entered the Los Angeles County courthouse.[11] Cohen, who worked at Ohrbach's department store, was there to testify in a misdemeanor trial as a defense witness.[12] As he walked down a "corridor outside of division 20 of the municipal court," past women and children, three police officers took particular note of what Cohen was wearing.[13] It was a dark jacket that had peace symbols painted on it, along with the words "Stop the War."[14] Yet what caught the eye of the police were three more words on the back of the jacket stenciled in red letters: "Fuck the Draft."[15]

Cohen proceeded along without incident, removing his jacket and folding it over his arm before entering a courtroom.[16] One of the policemen, Sergeant Huston Splawn, "sent the presiding judge a note suggesting that Cohen be held in contempt of court."[17] The judge declined to take any action and so the officer waited until Cohen left the courtroom and then promptly arrested him.[18]

At trial, Cohen testified that he knew about the words on the jacket and that they expressed "the depth of his feelings against the Vietnam War and the draft."[19] No one claimed that Cohen, or anyone who saw his jacket, had attempted to commit any violent action during his time in the court building, "nor was there any evidence he uttered any sound prior to his arrest."[20]

Cohen was convicted of a California criminal law that prohibited "maliciously and willfully disturb[ing] the peace or quiet of any neighborhood or person . . . by . . . offensive conduct" and sentenced to thirty days in jail.[21] His conviction was affirmed by the California Court of Appeal, which found that Cohen "carefully chose the forum for his views where his conduct would have an effective shock impact . . . [and] was intent upon attracting the attention of others to his views by the sheer vulgarity of his expression."[22] The court rejected his First Amendment arguments, and firmly asserted that "no one has the right to express his views by means of printing lewd and vulgar language which is likely to cause others to breach the peace to protect women and children from such exposure."[23]

The troublingly harsh sentence, and the almost palpable disdain toward Cohen in the California courts, can seemingly best be explained by a deeply felt hostility to the language *and* content of Cohen's political message.[24] This judicial reaction to Cohen's stenciled slogan also reflected how extremely divided the country was in 1968, both toward the Vietnam War and the student led anti-war movement that was rising up against it.[25]

Events in the three months prior had made a seismic impact on America's perceptions of the war. In January 1968, the Tet Offensive (the series of surprise attacks launched by North Vietnamese and Viet Cong forces against South Vietnamese and American troops in cities across South Vietnam) had badly damaged American morale and the public perception that the war would be won soon.[26] In February, Walter Cronkite, known as the most trusted man in America, concluded a CBS News special report on Vietnam by giving his opinion that "it seems now more certain than ever that the bloody experience of Vietnam is to end in a stalemate. . . . [I]t is increasingly clear to this reporter that the only rational way out then will be to negotiate, not as victors, but as an honorable people who lived up to their pledge to defend democracy, and did the best they could."[27] And in March, Lyndon Johnson shocked the nation by announcing in a live television address that he would not seek or accept another term as president of the United States.[28] Meanwhile, the youth culture of the 1960s was not only increasingly anti-war, but also anti-establishment and "a generation determined to shock with its dress, lifestyle, actions, and language."[29] The impact of all these forces on American society set the stage for Cohen's silent protest, and also amplified its significance.

This boiling national conflict notwithstanding, Cohen would say that his efforts to appeal his case to the US Supreme Court were grounded in a much more practical concern: "I didn't want to serve 30 days in jail."[30]

* * *

On February 22, 1971, oral argument in *Cohen v. California* was about to begin. The war and the draft continued, but Chief Justice Burger had other concerns on his mind. The Supreme Court of the United States was going to hear the "Fuck the Draft" case, but the chief justice did not want the expletive spoken aloud. He tried to telegraph this to Cohen's attorney, Melville Nimmer, by immediately cautioning him: "I might suggest to you that, as in most cases, the Court's thoroughly familiar with the factual setting of this case and it will not be necessary for you I'm sure to dwell on the facts."[31]

Nimmer, a distinguished professor at UCLA School of Law and an expert on copyright, thought he would lose the case if he didn't say "fuck" out loud. Using a euphemism would be tantamount to conceding that the word was indeed unspeakable in courtrooms and society.[32] He decided to take a bold stand. He would politely acknowledge the guidance and then just as politely ignore it. Nimmer began, "[On] the Chief Justice's suggestion I certainly will keep very brief this statement of facts," and then soon added, "may it please the Court what this young man did was to walk through a courthouse corridor . . . wearing a jacket upon which were inscribed the words 'Fuck the draft.'"[33] (Nimmer's sixteen-year-old son was attending the oral argument, and forty years later remembered that his dad had told him on the plane ride home that he half expected the Court marshals "to jump up, yelling 'He said FUCK in the Supreme Court, grab him!'")[34] As Nimmer said the word in question, "the Chief Justice's face turned a bright crimson, almost matching the deep red curtains behind the bench."[35] Despite Burger's displeasure, Nimmer had demonstrated that uttering "fuck" before the justices had neither caused chaos to ensue nor destroyed the sanctity of the Court. None of the justices, however, would follow his lead and utter the word themselves even once during questioning.

Nimmer went on to try and get the justices more comfortable with the youth-driven protest movements of the time that provided the background for Cohen's case, so he cleverly told them they could teach those kids a valuable lesson.[36] "Members of the younger generation tend to . . . equate violent dissent and dissent that may be regarded as objectionable or offensive. It is terribly important," Nimmer encouraged, "that this Court make clear that distinction, that dissent by its very nature involves the right to be offensive. . . . But on the other hand violent dissent is something quite different."[37] If you punish Cohen for an indisputably peaceful protest, he was saying, then that leaves nothing to discourage all those hippies from turning to violence as they continue to express their anti-war messages.

Nimmer then put forth a linguistic argument about why vulgarity was a vital component of Cohen's speech. He contended that the public deserves to know the "depth of the feeling" that sometimes can most effectively be communicated by cursing.[38] He also talked about how "language performs two functions, there is the emotive content of language and there is the intellectual content of language and that these intersperse." Forcing Cohen or any dissenter to express their views without offensive language would rob their speech of its emotive power. Warming to his theme, Nimmer continued,

> Now we get to what the First Amendment is all about. And what it is all about of course is competition in the marketplace of ideas, what ideas are going to prevail. . . . But in order for that system to work, it's important that the state not step in and try to censor . . . the emotive content . . . [because in so doing], the state is thereby enabled to a great degree to determine what group will buy this idea, to what group this idea will appeal. And hence, ultimately we'll be able to determine what ideas prevail in the competition of the market. And so for that reason we submit to the Court respectfully that . . . offensiveness of form no less than offensiveness of substance must be preserved by the First Amendment if the First Amendment is to be meaningful.[39]

Nimmer had ingeniously placed "fuck," not at the periphery, but at the center of First Amendment theory, and rarely has the marketplace metaphor been so persuasively wielded.

Representing the state of California was Michael T. Sauer, a young Los Angeles deputy city attorney.[40] Early on, Justice Potter Stewart pressed Sauer to explain, if the California statute prohibited "tumultuous and offensive conduct" and not speech, then "the conduct was precisely what?"[41] Nailing down a precise answer to that question took quite a bit of back and forth:

MR. SAUER: Displaying the sign on the jacket by the fact he was walking with the sign displayed on his jacket.

JUSTICE STEWART: And the walking wasn't offensive conduct, just the walking was it?

MR. SAUER: Walking with the sign, merely walking, no.

JUSTICE STEWART: And so what was the conduct?

MR. SAUER: Displaying the sign.

JUSTICE STEWART: Displaying?

MR. SAUER: Yes, his conduct of displaying the sign.

JUSTICE STEWART: The words?

MR. SAUER: Yes, where other persons were present.[42]

In the end, it did not bode well for Sauer that his ultimate answers about Cohen's alleged conduct sounded almost entirely like speech.

Justice Thurgood Marshall raised a hypothetical revision of Cohen's words: "Suppose he had on his jacket . . . 'I dislike the draft.'"

Sauer replied, "Then I doubt if we would be here. . . ."

Justice Marshall continued, "So it's the word isn't it? . . . Isn't that all you have?"[43]

"Oh, a word, yes," Sauer responded, without seeming to appreciate that Marshall had gotten him to acknowledge that the state's position boiled down to nothing more than a desire to prohibit the use of a single word.[44]

Sauer did manage to end on a strong note. He framed the state's position as, at most, an inconsequential intrusion on First Amendment values. "Words of this type are no essential part of any exposition of ideas," he insisted, "and are of such slight social value as a step to the truth that any benefit that may be derived from them is clearly outweighed by the social interest in order and morality."[45]

Given two minutes for a rebuttal, Nimmer succinctly urged the Court to reverse the conviction, "and make clear that the language of profanity is not outside the scope of the First Amendment, simply because it's offensive."[46]

* * *

Twice a week when court is in session, the Supreme Court justices gather at a justices' conference to decide the cases they have heard argued in the days prior. Only the justices are allowed in the conference room during the discussion (no law clerks or other assistants) and by tradition they begin their meeting by all shaking hands.[47] The chief justice speaks first to express his views on a case, and then each justice gives their say in descending order of seniority on the court.[48]

At the conference following the Cohen oral argument, Chief Justice Burger discussed what he pointedly called the "screw the draft" case and voted to uphold Cohen's conviction.[49] Justice Black, normally a First Amendment absolutist, surprised everyone by agreeing with the chief justice, telling the group that he viewed Cohen's action as conduct and not speech.[50] Justices Blackmun and White voted with them as well. Justice Stewart and the liberal members of the Court—Justices Douglas, Brennan, and Marshall—all voted to reverse. The justices were evenly divided and the deciding vote belonged to the "ideologically independent" Justice John Harlan. Harlan said he was considering overturning the conviction, but wanted to wait a week to decide.[51]

During the break, Black's clerks tried to sway his vote to be more consistent with his past pro-speech decisions.[52] However, the justice was reportedly "priggish" about language and would not be moved.[53]

"What if Elizabeth [his wife] were in that corridor?" he asked, appalled. "Why should she have to see that word?"[54]

By the next conference, Harlan had made up his mind to reverse the conviction.[55] The vote would be 5–4, and Harlan was assigned to write the decision.[56] Having heard about Black's squeamishness over Cohen's language, Harlan informed his clerks, "'I wouldn't mind telling my wife, or your wife, or anyone's wife, about the slogan.'"[57]

Three months later, Justice Harlan was standing with Chief Justice Burger in the wood-paneled robing room, before announcing the decision.[58] "'John, you're not going to use 'that word' in delivering the opinion, are you?'" Burger inquired. "'It would be the end of the Court if you use it, John.'"[59] Harlan snickered as the justices all walked out, in order of seniority, along the red carpet leading to the courtroom.[60] Although Harlan did not speak the word aloud, "fuck" did appear in his official record of the decision in all of its four-letter glory, for the first time in Supreme Court history.[61]

Justice Harlan's majority opinion begins unusually by sweeping away "what the case is *not* about."[62] He swiftly dismisses the dissenters' idea that California was regulating conduct, writing, "The only 'conduct' which the State sought to punish is the fact of communication. Thus, we deal here with a conviction resting solely upon 'speech.'"[63] He goes on to remind everyone of the core principle that "the State certainly lacks power to punish Cohen for the underlying content of the message the inscription conveyed ... [about] the inutility or immorality of the draft his jacket reflected."[64]

Harlan next discusses why Cohen's speech does not "fall within those relatively few categories of instances where prior decisions have" allowed some limitations on "individual expression."[65] He explains that the use of the word "fuck" is neither "obscenity" (because it is not erotic), nor "fighting words" (because it was not directed at any person), nor a "captive" audience problem (because it took place in public, rather than causing an "intrusion into the privacy of the home").[66]

Having dispensed with these complicated issues, one can almost feel Harlan switch gears and pick up speed as he moves toward boldly reaffirming free speech rights.[67]

Harlan presents the case as really being about the state's efforts to "remove this offensive word from the public vocabulary."[68] He then pulls apart the two theories by which the California courts claimed the right to do so. First, he rejects the idea that the use of the word "is inherently likely to cause violent reaction."[69] Referring to the *Tinker* case, he states that "undifferentiated fear or apprehension of disturbance . . . is not enough to overcome the right to freedom of expression."[70]

Second, he raises the broader notion of whether the government should have a role in "acting as guardians of public morality."[71] Addressing why such legislated propriety is unworkable in our democracy, he launches into an impassioned defense of free speech:

The constitutional right of free expression is powerful medicine in a society as diverse and populous as ours. It is designed and intended to remove governmental restraints from the arena of public discussion, putting the decision as to what views shall be voiced largely into the hands of each of us, in the hope that use of such freedom will ultimately produce a more capable citizenry and more perfect polity and in the belief that no other approach would comport with the premise of individual dignity and choice upon which our political system rests. To many, the immediate consequence of this freedom may often appear to be only verbal tumult, discord, and even offensive utterance. These are, however, within established limits, in truth necessary side effects of the broader enduring values which the process of open debate permits us to achieve. That the air may at times seem filled with verbal cacophony is, in this sense not a sign of weakness but of strength. We cannot lose sight of the fact that, in what otherwise might seem a trifling and annoying instance of individual distasteful abuse of a privilege, these fundamental societal values are truly implicated.[72]

Harlan continues with three more "particularized" reasons why the conviction must be reversed.[73] He calls out the state's limitation on free speech rights as "inherently boundless." "How is one to distinguish this from any other offensive word? . . . Surely the State has no right to cleanse public debate to the point where it is grammatically palatable to the most squeamish among us." And then, in one of the most famous First Amendment lines of all time, he recognizes that although "fuck" may be worse than most curse words, "it is nevertheless often true that one man's vulgarity is another's lyric."[74] This poetic notion encapsulates much of free speech law in a single phrase.[75]

Harlan then endorses Nimmer's formulation that the First Amendment protects both the intellectual and the emotional components of words. "Words are often chosen as much for their emotive as their cognitive force," Harlan observes, and "that emotive function . . . may often be the more important element of the overall message sought to be communicated."[76] As a result, the emotive power of cursing must not be criminalized.

Finally, Harlan points out that it would be a "facile assumption that one can forbid particular words without also running a substantial risk of suppressing ideas in the process."[77] That risk would become even greater, he warned, if there were no check on government power that "might soon seize upon the censorship of particular words as a convenient guise for banning the expression of unpopular views."[78]

In sum, the majority ruled that the First Amendment prohibited the state from making "the simple public display . . . of this single four-letter expletive a criminal offense."[79]

The dissent, written by Justice Blackmun and joined by Chief Justice Burger, Justice Black, and partially by Justice White, was limited in scope and reasoning.[80] Only two paragraphs long, it lashed out at

"Cohen's absurd and immature antic," rejecting it without explanation as "mainly conduct, and little speech."[81] Almost mocking Harlan's grandiose prose, Blackmun wrote that the majority's "agonizing
over First Amendment values seems misplaced and unnecessary."[82]

The sparseness of the dissent may have contributed to the enduring
strength of the majority opinion in *Cohen* over the years.[83] The opinion has been called "a luminous statement on freedom of expression,"
and its First Amendment views continue to influence the Supreme
Court even forty years after it was decided and beyond.[84] More specifically, *Cohen* stands for two crucial free speech principles. Offensive
speech, including but not limited to curse words, is as fully entitled
to First Amendment protection as any other speech.[85] As New York
Law School professor Nadine Strossen eloquently puts it, one of Harlan's "then radical and now-cherished" principles was that "we cannot suppress any word without also suppressing an idea, and that we
may not suppress any ideas."[86] Just as importantly, in public places it
is the speaker's right to choose the language they feel is most effective
to communicate their message.[87] These concepts go hand in hand to
create significant free speech rights for protestors, even when they are
not speaking at all.

Paul Cohen had a more down-to-earth view of the impact of the decision. When he went back to the trial court for the official dismissal
of his charges, "I could tell the judge was upset with the Supreme
Court's ruling in my favor," he remembered. "I probably angered him
even more when I asked for my jacket back." After the years of fighting
over that jacket, Cohen wanted one more thing, for people to know: "I
was and am a patriotic person."[88]

* * *

Juli Briskman's wrongful termination lawsuit was eventually dismissed.[89] *Cohen v. California* makes unconstitutional any *governmental*
punishment for giving the finger.[90] However, the First Amendment

itself offers no protection to private sector employees who express their free speech rights, even if they do so during personal time and outside of the workplace.[91]

Briskman lost her job over a gesture, but received many offers of employment and was soon working again.[92] What would be the next step for this social media symbol of rude resistance to Trump? "It's not like I can run against him," she told the *Washington Post*. "But I can run."[93] So Briskman ran for a seat on her local county board of supervisors in Loudoun, Virginia.[94] Her opponent was an incumbent Republican who campaigned for Trump.[95] "I've gotten some feedback," Briskman said on announcing her campaign, "that folks say you should respect the president. Even if you don't like what they're doing, you shouldn't show this sort of disdain. And I simply disagree, and I think the Constitution grants me that privilege."[96] Many voters must have felt similarly, since Briskman won her race and was elected with over 52 percent of the vote.[97]

7 / SAMANTHA BEE, SEVEN DIRTY WORDS, AND INDECENCY

Samantha Bee, the host and executive producer of TBS's late-night news show, *Full Frontal with Samantha Bee*, has a unique gift for expressing outrage. She focuses her indignant ire on the weekly political scene with ferocious wit and a feminist perspective. A recurring feature on *Full Frontal* is Bee's furious, extended takedowns of mostly conservative politicians.[1] On May 30, 2018, when she set her sights on the Trump administration's immigration and family separation policies—criticizing the president, Chief of Staff John Kelly, and Secretary of Homeland Security Kirstjen Nielsen—it seemed like business as usual.[2]

Bee began to wrap up the segment, saying that "most Americans are finally paying attention" to this issue, with one notable exception. She called out Ivanka Trump for posting an "oblivious" photo with her son on Twitter that week.[3] Starting off in a warm tone that surprisingly shifted gears, Bee said, "You know, Ivanka, that's a beautiful photo of you and your child. Let me just say, one mother to another, do something about your dad's immigration practices, you feckless cunt. He listens to you."[4]

The outrage over this use of the C-word was swift and severe. The day after the show aired, White House press secretary Sarah Huckabee Sanders indignantly asserted that Bee's "disgusting comments and show are not fit for broadcast, and executives at Time Warner and TBS must demonstrate that such explicit profanity about female members of this administration will not be condoned on its network."[5] Bee did apologize later that day to Ivanka Trump and viewers, "for using an expletive on my show to describe her last night. It was inappropriate and inexcusable. I crossed a line, and I deeply regret it."[6] Unsatisfied, or just seeking to stoke the flames of the controversy, a day later President Trump tweeted, "Why aren't they firing no talent Samantha Bee for the horrible language used on her low ratings show?"[7]

Bee would make a further and more nuanced apology in the opening of her next episode of *Full Frontal* the following week, saying in part that she "should've known that a potty-mouthed insult would be inherently more interesting . . . than a juvenile immigration policy."[8] While Bee and others discussed the potential for reclaiming the C-word for women in a positive manner and the "death of civility," one threshold issue went unmentioned in this furious news cycle: are there words that you really can't say on television?[9] Fittingly, the answer to this question comes directly from another comedian whose words shocked and delighted audiences in equal measure.

* * *

In 1972, the countercultural comedian George Carlin recorded his third solo album, *Class Clown*. The last track on the record was called the "Seven Words You Can Never Say on Television," and its most notorious portion began:

> There are four hundred thousand words in the English language and there are seven of them you can't say on television. What a ratio that is! Three hundred ninety-nine thousand nine hundred and ninety-three . . . to seven! They must really be bad. They'd have to be outra-

geous to be separated from a group that large. "All of you over here . . .
You seven, you bad words."

That's what they told us, you remember? "That's a bad word." What?
There are no bad words. Bad thoughts, bad intentions, but no bad words.

You know the seven, don't you, that you can't say on television?
Shit, piss, fuck, cunt, cocksucker, motherfucker and tits. Those are the
Heavy Seven. Those are the ones that'll infect your soul, curve your
spine, and keep the country from winning the war.[10]

The material epitomized Carlin's new approach of challenging societal norms by engaging in hilariously transgressive word play, and it
would help to make him a comic legend. Carlin later observed that
Lenny Bruce "was the first one to make language an issue, and he suffered for it. I was the first one to make language an issue and succeed
with it."[11] Carlin went on to perform the routine in his hometown at
Carnegie Hall and received a standing ovation. However, his rebel-
liousness would not play so well with every audience, and he soon
found that "not only could you not say the Heavy Seven on television,
you couldn't say them in Milwaukee either."[12]

On July 21, 1972, Carlin was headlining the main stage at Summerfest,
a multiday outdoor music festival on the Wisconsin lakefront.[13] Starting his set around sunset before a beer-drinking crowd of thirty-five
thousand, Carlin eventually launched into his "Seven Words."[14] An indignant Milwaukee police officer in the crowd couldn't believe his ears
and orchestrated to have him arrested as he left the stage. A photo of the
long-haired and thickly bearded Carlin being led away by a phalanx of
stout uniformed officers was on the front page of the *Milwaukee Journal*
the next day and subsequently carried all over the country.[15] The charge
of disorderly conduct was ultimately dismissed after a trial in which the
judge reportedly "laughed softly, though self-consciously," while listening
to the cut from a record player set up in the courtroom.[16]

Emboldened by his free speech victory, and building on the words that Carlin gleefully referred to as the "Milwaukee Seven," he soon developed an "equally mind-rotting, spine-curving, peace-without-honor sequel called 'Filthy Words.'"[17] In this new monologue, which appeared on his album that came out the following year, *Occupation: Foole*, he continued to riff on the subject:

> I was thinking one night about the words you couldn't say on the public, ah, airwaves, um, the ones you definitely wouldn't say, ever . . . and it came down to seven but the list is open to amendment . . . a lot of people pointed things out to me, and I noticed some myself. The original seven words were shit, piss, fuck, cunt, cocksucker, motherfucker, and tits. . . . And now the first thing that we noticed was that word fuck was really repeated in there because the word motherfucker is a compound word and it's another form of the word fuck. You want to be a purist it doesn't really, it can't be on the list of basic words.[18]

And it continued on in this way for about another eleven minutes.

On October 30, 1973, at two o'clock in the afternoon, "Filthy Words" was played on radio station WBAI in New York, part of the listener-supported Pacifica Network.[19] The recording was included during a live program called *Lunchpail*, on an episode about "the power of language and how words lose integrity during political debate."[20] Pacifica later maintained that before Carlin's track was played, the host, Paul Gorman, warned "that it included sensitive language which might be regarded as offensive to some; those who might be offended were advised to change the station and return to WBAI in 15 minutes."[21]

Listening to the broadcast was a man named John Douglas, who said he heard it "while driving with his young son."[22] Douglas ended up sending a complaint to the Federal Communications Commission stating that "[a]ny child could have been turning the dial, and tuned in to that garbage."[23] Not a single other complaint was received by the station or the FCC.[24]

It turns out that Douglas was not exactly a typical disinterested listener, as he is often portrayed, but rather an advocate who was on the national planning board of an organization called Morality in Media. He also later admitted that he didn't just happen upon the program, but rather "was listening to Pacifica constantly to see how far they would pull the curtain back."[25] In addition, his "young son" was, in fact, fifteen years old at the time, and the two of them were returning home from a college tour of Yale.[26] Carlin called Douglas "a professional offendee."[27] Douglas's partisan nature notwithstanding, his lone complaint successfully triggered a seismic change in the regulation of radio and television content.

To more fully comprehend the impact of complaints to the Federal Communications Commission, it is helpful to have a brief background on the agency. The FCC is a federal agency, which was created by Congress in the Communications Act of 1934 to regulate broadcasting in the public interest. Both the Communications Act and the First Amendment "prohibits the Commission from censoring broadcast material and from interfering with freedom of expression in broadcasting."[28] However, the agency can place *restrictions* on the material that stations broadcast. The enforcement of these restrictions on objectionable content is driven by complaints from the public. The FCC Enforcement Bureau reviews complaints and then decides whether to launch an investigation if its staff believes a violation may have occurred.[29] If the Commission ultimately finds a violation of its indecency rules, it may issue a warning, impose a fine, or even revoke a station's license to operate.[30]

Within a week of receiving Douglas's complaint, the FCC decided to forward it to the station with a request for comments.[31] Pacifica strongly defended including the recording in their broadcast, which they described as "devoted to an analysis of the use of language in

contemporary society." Pacifica also championed Carlin as "a significant social satirist of American manners and language in the tradition of Mark Twain" and sought to contextualize his choice of words.
"Carlin is not mouthing obscenities," they responded, "he is merely
using words to satirize as harmless and essentially silly our attitudes
towards those words. As with other great satirists . . . Carlin often
grabs our attention by speaking the unspeakable, by shocking in order
to illuminate."[32]

Over a year later, the FCC issued a declaratory order, finding "that
words such as 'fuck,' 'shit,' 'piss,' 'motherfucker,' 'cocksucker,' 'cunt,'
and 'tit' [were] . . . 'indecent' when broadcast on radio or television."[33]
The Commission declared that Carlin's language in the broadcast
was indecent given that it "describes, in terms patently offensive as
measured by contemporary community standards for the broadcast
medium, sexual or excretory activities and organs, at times of the day
when there is a reasonable risk that children may be in the audience."[34]
The FCC asserted that the "obnoxious, gutter language describing
these matters has the effect of debasing and brutalizing human beings
by reducing them to their mere bodily functions," and brushed aside
any consideration of artistic merit or political message.[35] The agency
was also staking a claim that it had the necessary authority to regulate
such language, despite any First Amendment free speech protections.
The FCC implicitly acknowledged that this was breaking new ground,
by imposing no penalty and stating the order was "intended to clarify
the standards which will be utilized in considering the growing number of complaints about indecent speech on the airwaves."[36]

Taking a stand against the FCC's action, Pacifica appealed to the
United States Court of Appeals for the District of Columbia Circuit.
The circuit reversed the FCC's order, by a 2–1 majority, holding that
the order was "censorship, regardless of what the Commission chooses
to call it," and its direct effect was "to inhibit the free and robust exchange of ideas."[37] As for the FCC's professed goal of protecting the

sensitivities of children, the court found that "the Commission has taken a step toward reducing the adult population to hearing or viewing only that which is fit for children. . . . [A] classic case of burning the house to roast the pig."[38] In his concurring opinion, Chief Judge Bazelon also refused to accept the FCC's additional claim that the uniquely intrusive nature of radio and television justified censorship, stating that "the impact of a particular medium constitutes no basis for subjecting that medium to greater suppression."[39]

This time it was the FCC that decided to appeal, despite the fact that some lawyers and commissioners at the FCC thought it was likely the agency would lose at the Supreme Court.[40] The primary question before the justices was whether the First Amendment prohibited the FCC from restricting the broadcast of indecent language that was not obscene.[41] Obscenity, the Supreme Court had ruled in a landmark decision five years earlier, was content so offensive that it was not protected by the First Amendment at all, if "the work, taken as a whole, appeals to the prurient interest" (meaning inappropriate sexual desire), "depicts or describes, in a patently offensive way, sexual conduct" and "lacks serious literary, artistic, political, or scientific value."[42]

At oral argument before the Supreme Court, the most telling moment came right as Chief Justice Warren Burger began, "You may bear in mind that we are familiar with the facts of the case and get directly at your legal argument if you wish. . . ."[43] Court scholars have pointed out that this suggestion was a not so subtle "euphemism for 'Don't repeat any dirty words in *this* court!'"[44] Not a single one of Carlin's filthy words would be uttered by the lawyers or the justices during two days of argument. It was not a good sign for the broadcasters.[45]

On July 3, 1978, a divided Court ruled in favor of the FCC, holding in a 5–4 decision that the agency had the power to regulate even isolated words in otherwise protected speech. Writing for the narrow majority, Justice John Paul Stevens found that the "broadcast of patently offensive words dealing with sex and excretion" had "such slight social value . . . that any benefit that may be derived from them is clearly outweighed by the social interest in order and morality."[46]

Having minimized the importance of the speech based on the words used, rather than the content of the entire work, Stevens set forth two main rationales for allowing speech restrictions in these circumstances. First, he determined that the unique nature of the broadcast medium enabled the government to treat such speech differently in order to shield citizens from its impact. For Stevens, broadcast media's "pervasive presence in the lives of all Americans" meant that "indecent material presented over the airwaves confronts the citizen not only in public, but also in the privacy of the home."[47] In addition, since broadcast audiences were "constantly tuning in and tuning out," Stevens believed that warnings were so ineffective that to say "one may avoid further offense by turning off the radio when he hears indecent language is like saying that the remedy for an assault is to run away after the first blow."[48]

Secondly, Stevens appeared deeply concerned with children being exposed to "offensive expression" on radio and television.[49] He bemoaned that broadcasting was "uniquely accessible to children, even those too young to read."[50] As a result, Stevens maintained that, unlike the prevailing wisdom pertaining to bookstores and movie theaters, protecting America's youth from indecent content necessitated "restricting the expression at its source."[51]

As for First Amendment protections of non-obscene speech, Stevens quickly dismissed such concerns since in his view "supporting parents' claim to authority in their own household justified the regulation of otherwise protected expression."[52] Returning to the strange pork metaphors first raised by the circuit court, Stevens concluded that "when the Commission finds that a pig has entered the parlor, the exercise of its regulatory power does not depend on proof that the pig is obscene."[53]

In dissent, Justice Brennan, joined by Justice Marshall, described himself as "unable to remain silent" in the face of the majority's flagrant "misapplication of fundamental First Amendment principles."[54] Brennan dismissed Stevens's concerns about intrusions in the home as trivial:

> Whatever the minimal discomfort suffered by a listener who inadvertently tunes into a program he finds offensive during the brief interval before he can simply extend his arm and switch stations or flick the "off" button, it is surely worth the candle to preserve the broadcaster's right to send, and the right of those interested to receive, a message entitled to full First Amendment protection.[55]

Brennan found the "children in the audience" rationale equally unpersuasive, insisting that such sweeping treatment impermissibly results in "reduc[ing] the adult population . . . to [hearing] only what is fit for children."[56]

Brennan also took issue with Stevens's seemingly cavalier attitude toward the Court's decision in *Cohen v. California* just seven years earlier. Stevens chose to view *Cohen* as a case demonstrating the importance of context in matters of indecency, and literally turned its most famous pro-expression line on its head, writing "one occasion's lyric is another's vulgarity."[57] Brennan pointed out that even focusing on context, the privacy interests of listeners to the radio are "surely no greater than those of the people present in the corridor of the Los Angeles courthouse in *Cohen* who bore witness to the words 'Fuck the Draft' emblazoned across Cohen's jacket."[58] More crucially, Brennan rebuked Stevens for ignoring the central message of *Cohen*, that "even if an alternative phrasing may communicate a speaker's abstract ideas as effectively as those words he is forbidden to use, it is doubtful that the sterilized message will convey the emotion that is an essential part of so many communications."[59]

In a blistering big picture summary of the Court's ruling, Brennan called out the majority for engaging in "another of the dominant culture's inevitable efforts to force those groups who do not share its mores to conform to its way of thinking, acting, and speaking."[60]

Notwithstanding Brennan's passionate dissent, and the fact that regulating the content of speech seems at odds with the spirit of the First Amendment, *Pacifica* remains the law of radio and television broadcasts to this day.[61] The FCC has the power to restrict when language or images of "sexual or excretory organs or activities" that it finds "patently offensive" can air, and to fine stations for that material.[62] The FCC prohibits indecent speech between the hours of 6 a.m. to 10 p.m., during which time it considers that there is a "reasonable risk that children may be in the audience."[63] The Commission leaves the remaining time period as a "safe harbor" for unregulated (meaning more "adult") content.[64]

* * *

After winning the right to control and punish content it found offensive, the FCC then made no significant effort to exercise its newly recognized powers for nearly a decade.[65] The FCC's post-*Pacifica* restraint lasted until the late 1980s, when Howard Stern became a new favorite target.[66] The agency then began issuing a series of indecency violations against Infinity Broadcasting, which syndicated Stern's radio show, for incidents including ones in which he: taunted the agency by saying, "Hey, FCC, 'penis'"; joking about masturbating to a picture of Aunt Jemima; and discussed another man playing the piano with his penis.[67] Infinity Broadcasting ultimately ended up calling it quits on its seven-year legal war with the FCC over the violations, and paid a then-record $1.71 million fine to settle the matters, but with no admission of wrongdoing.[68]

The next major wave of FCC actions was triggered by a series of celebrities cursing spontaneously on awards shows. At the 2002 Billboard Music Awards, Cher remarked during her acceptance speech, "I've also had my critics for the last 40 years saying that I was on my way out every year. Right. So fuck 'em."[69] Nicole Richie, presenting an award at the Billboard Music Awards the next year, quipped about her reality show *The Simple Life*, "Have you ever tried to get cow shit out of a Prada purse? It's not so fucking simple."[70] Bono hailed his 2003 win for Best Original Song as "really, really, fucking brilliant."[71] The FCC found all of these "fleeting expletives" indecent, holding that the F-word was "one of the most vulgar, graphic and explicit descriptions of sexual activity in the English language," and therefore "any use of that word or a variation, in any context, inherently has a sexual connotation."[72]

At the same time, the FCC became determinedly concerned with "fleeting nudity" as well.[73] A 2003 broadcast of the police drama *NYPD Blue* showing "the nude buttocks of an adult female character for approximately seven seconds and for a moment the side of her breast" was also found to be indecent by the FCC.[74] The FCC was even more scandalized by the infamous "wardrobe malfunction" during the 2004 Super Bowl halftime show, in which Justin Timberlake sang, "Bet I'll have you naked by the end of this song," and then exposed Janet Jackson's breast for nine-sixteenths of a second.[75] After receiving over half a million complaints, the Commission fined CBS the then-maximum penalty of $27,500 per violation against each of the twenty television stations owned by CBS, for a total of $550,000.[76] Yet even that sum was not enough for Congress, which two years later passed the Broadcast Decency Enforcement Act largely in reaction to the Super Bowl debacle.[77] The law raised the top fine to a whopping $325,000 per violation or a maximum of $3 million for the same violation that aired on multiple stations.[78]

The enormously convoluted process of FCC actions and network appeals concerning all of these incidents would not reach the Supreme

Court for a final resolution until 2012.[79] In the "fleeting expletives" and *NYPD Blue* case, known as *FCC v. Fox*, a unanimous Court ruled in favor of the networks and set aside the FCC's orders.[80] The Court held that the agency had failed to provide "fair notice" to broadcasters over the change in policy that "fleeting expletives and momentary nudity could be found actionably indecent."[81] However, the justices punted on the key speech questions, refusing to reach a decision on the "First Amendment implications of the Commission's indecency policy," and the broadcasters' arguments that Pacifica "should be overruled because the rationale of that case has been overtaken by technological change and the wide availability of multiple other choices for listeners and viewers."[82]

A week later, in the *FCC v. CBS* case concerning the Super Bowl scandal (sometimes referred to as "nipplegate"), the Supreme Court denied certiorari, meaning to deny review of the lower court's ruling.[83] Consequently, the Third Circuit's ruling, invalidating the FCC's fine against CBS, was now final.

The Third Circuit had let CBS off the hook on a rationale similar to the Supreme Court's *Fox* decision, that the FCC had failed to give reasonable notice of the Commission's change in policy regarding fleeting nudity.[84] However, in an unusual separate opinion Chief Justice John Roberts wrote to emphasize that going forward all necessary notice had been delivered. One can almost visualize the chief justice wagging a finger, like a parent giving their teenager a final warning, as he admonished, "It is now clear that the brevity of an indecent broadcast—be it word or image—cannot immunize it from FCC censure."[85] In other words, *Pacifica* lives on, and words or images, no matter how brief or arguably nonsexual, can be regulated by the FCC such that broadcasters could face millions of dollars in indecency fines for a single slip of the tongue or clothing.[86]

* * *

Why isn't *Pacifica* a major problem then for Samantha Bee? The C-word must still be indecent by FCC standards. After all, it is a sexual or excretory organ, almost certainly patently offensive, and even one of Carlin's original dirty seven. Although it was only uttered once, such fleeting uses are no longer an exception to FCC indecency regulation. The program airs at 9:30 p.m. in the central time zone, so it does not fall into the late-night safe harbor. How could the show escape FCC censure and huge fines?

The answer is simple and makes little practical sense. The FCC does not regulate indecency on cable at all—neither basic cable nor premium channels.[87] The FCC has explained its lack of authority to regulate indecency on cable and satellite television based on the fact that they are "subscription services" and historical interpretations of statutory language regarding "radio communications" applying only to broadcast channels.[88] Another rationalization for this tradition is that broadcasters disseminate their content via the publicly owned airwaves, while cable and satellite systems deliver programming through privately built systems.[89] Arguably, these are distinctions without a difference, particularly with a generation that has grown up watching everything on their televisions, computers, and phones in equal measure. Does anyone today really distinguish between "cable" and "broadcast" television when thinking about the content of what they are watching? (When I first tried to explain to my young children that I worked for a broadcast television network, their response was "Is that like Netflix or on-demand?") Nevertheless, the FCC's indecency regime still does not extend to cable and satellite TV. This is why HBO could have reoccurring nude dancers at the Bada Bing! strip club on *The Sopranos* and "fuck" was said repeatedly on the FX miniseries *The People v. O.J. Simpson*.[90]

The result of this convoluted indecency system is that Samantha Bee is free to say a word that would almost certainly subject her broadcast colleagues to massive indecency fines.[91] And as for any non-FCC blowback, the comment ended up as little more than a temporary set-back for Bee and her team. A month later, *Full Frontal* was nominated for seven Emmy awards.[92]

As for Carlin, he reflected that he took "perverse pride" in the fact that "*FCC v. Pacifica Foundation* has become a standard case to teach in communications classes and many law schools. . . . I'm actually a footnote to the judicial history of America."[93] Carlin's modest appraisal of his legacy doesn't diminish the fact that his "Seven Dirty Words" continue to resonate beyond the classroom to this day. Carlin's words live on, not only because he dared to swear, but for the way he jubilantly drew attention to the absurdity of our language taboos in the face of an American society racked by cultural upheaval and war.[94] Bee certainly shares Carlin's concerns about the hypocrisy of politeness in the face of devastating political realities. As she put it in her quasi-apology, "Look, if you are worried about the death of civility, don't sweat it. . . . Civility is just nice words. Maybe we should all worry a little bit more about the niceness of our actions."[95]

What both comics appear to be asking for, comedically, is for an openness to all kinds of speech. In cultural historian Melissa Mohr's enlightening book *Holy Shit: A Brief History of Swearing*, she advocates seriously for accepting the use of all kinds of words: "A healthy society needs its 'good' language and its 'bad.' We need irreproachably formal and unassailably decent speech, but we also need the dirty, the vulgar, the wonderful obscenities and oaths that can do for us what no other words can."[96] Carlin and Bee, one can assume, would approve.

8 / SATURDAY NIGHT LIVE, HUSTLER, AND THE POWER OF PARODY

Donald Trump has been obsessed with *Saturday Night Live* for years. He is the only politician to have hosted the show twice—first as a reality television star in 2004, and then as a presidential candidate in 2015.[1] He tweeted about the ratings for his second hosting gig five separate times, and bragged that his appearance had garnered *SNL* its "best ratings in 4 years!"[2]

Yet Trump's love affair with *SNL* was short lived. Just a few weeks before the election, early on a Sunday morning, Trump tweeted that he "Watched 'Saturday Night Live' hit job on me. Time to retire the boring and unfunny show. Alec Baldwin portrayal stinks. Media rigging election!"[3] A month later, despite his election victory, Trump was venting, "I watched parts of @nbcsnl Saturday Night Live last night. It is a totally one-sided, biased show—nothing funny at all. Equal time for us?"[4] He would tweet again that the comedy is "Totally biased, not funny and the Baldwin impersonation just can't get any worse," and again that ".@NBCNews is bad but Saturday Night Live is the worst of NBC . . . always a complete hit job," and again that "It is just a political ad for the Dems."[5]

President Trump's escalating fury toward *SNL* was evident in his increasingly explicit calls to bring federal power to bear on the television program. He wanted legal action taken, declaring, "A REAL scandal is the one-sided coverage, hour by hour, of networks like NBC & Democrat spin machines like Saturday Night Live. It is all nothing less than unfair news coverage and Dem commercials. Should be tested in courts, can't be legal? Only defame & belittle! Collusion?"[6] Trump next raised the specter of reprisals against NBC, questioning "how do the Networks get away with these total Republican hit jobs without retribution?"[7] He even went so far as to threaten a government investigation of the entertainment series, railing in a two-part Twitter offensive:

> It's truly incredible that shows like Saturday Night Live, not funny/no talent, can spend all of their time knocking the same person (me), over & over, without so much of a mention of "the other side." Like an advertisement without consequences. Same with Late Night Shows. . . . Should Federal Election Commission and/or FCC look into this? There must be Collusion with the Democrats and, of course, Russia![8]

Although it's debatable whether *SNL's* mockery of President Trump is any harsher than the show's treatment of past presidents (for example, some have argued that Chevy Chase's portrayal of President Ford as a bumbling fool contributed to his losing the 1976 election), his public attacks on the program are unprecedented for a president.[9] In response, Trump's critics have sounded free speech alarms. Representative Ted Lieu rebuked the president on Twitter: "One thing that makes America great is that the people can laugh at you without retribution. The First Amendment allows Saturday Night Live to make fun of you again, and again, and again."[10] This online debate brings into stark relief a very serious question about comedy. Can satire ever be so offensive that the injured party would be able to successfully sue for hurt feelings? Unfortunately for Trump the television critic, the Supreme Court has seen far more vicious humor before, in the case of the "preacher versus the pornographer."[11]

* * *

The year was 1983. Campari, the Italian aperitif, was running a risqué advertising campaign featuring actors—such as Elizabeth Ashley, Jill St. John, and Tony Roberts—talking about their "first time." The text of each ad consisted of an interview with one of the celebrities talking about their first experience with the liquor; double entendres abounded and it all sounded like they were dishing about sex.[12] The tagline for the ad featuring St. John sums it up: "Campari. You'll Never Forget Your First Time."[13]

On the inside front cover of the November 1983 issue of *Hustler* magazine, published by Larry Flynt, there was a similar-looking faux Campari ad with the headline, "Jerry Falwell Talks about His First Time." A dignified photograph of the famous televangelist was included, along with an image of the Campari bottle next to a cocktail. In a fake interview, Reverend Falwell is portrayed as saying that his "first time" was a drunken tryst with his mother in an outhouse. Shockingly, the more you read the worse it gets. "I never *really* expected to make it with Mom, but then after she showed all the other guys in town such a good time, I figured, 'What the hell!'" The purported interview continues:

> INTERVIEWER: But your mom? Isn't that a bit odd?
> FALWELL: I don't think so. Looks don't mean that much to me in a
> woman.
> INTERVIEWER: Go on.
> FALWELL: Well, we were drunk off our God-fearing asses on Campari, ginger ale and soda—that's called a Fire and Brimstone—at the time. And Mom looked better than a Baptist whore with a $100 donation.
> INTERVIEWER: Campari in the crapper with Mom ... how interesting. Well, how was it?

FALWELL: The Campari was great, but Mom passed out before I could come.

Falwell's last line returns to the subject of trying Campari again: "Oh, yeah. I always get sloshed before I go out to the pulpit. You don't think I could lay down all that bullshit *sober*, do you?"[14]

At the very bottom, underneath the Campari logo, in small print, a final line reads: "AD PARODY—NOT TO BE TAKEN SERI-OUSLY."[15] In addition, in *Hustler's* table of contents for the issue, the page is similarly described as "Fiction: Ad and Personality Parody."[16] It is safe to say that neither disclaimer provided much comfort for Jerry Falwell.

The religious leader lost little time in going on the offensive. Falwell sent out three mailings, some of which contained a copy of the ad parody, to over a million of his supporters, attacking "the billion-dollar sex industry, of which Larry Flynt is a self-declared leader. . . . For those porno peddlers, it appears that lust and greed have replaced decency and morality."[17] Falwell concluded his letters by asking, "Will you help me defend my family and myself against the smears and slan-der of this major pornographic magazine—will you send a gift of $500 so that we may take up this important legal battle?"[18] In a month, Fal-well raised over $1 million for his litigation war chest.[19] He soon sued Flynt, saying it was because the ad "besmirched the memory of [his] dear mother."[20] Relishing the fight, Flynt published the ad parody again in *Hustler's* March 1984 issue, while the case moved forward to trial.[21]

To fully comprehend the almost apocalyptic nature of this free speech war, it is necessary to examine the personal histories of the two men leading their diametrically opposed organizations. In 1956, when Jerry Falwell was twenty-two years old, he founded the Thomas Road Baptist Church in Lynchburg, Virginia.[22] What began in an abandoned Donald Duck Bottling Company building with a congregation of thirty-five people would expand to a thousand members a year later, and to over twenty thousand in the 1980s and beyond.[23] The church also eventually grew to include a school, summer camp, home for alcoholics, international missions, and Liberty University, an "accredited evangelical liberal arts institution."[24]

Six months after founding his church, Falwell began broadcasting the *Old-Time Gospel Hour* on radio and television, developing a nationwide following that would eventually draw in contributions of more than $30 million annually.[25] He liked to say that the program was more widely distributed than the Johnny Carson show.[26]

In 1979 he founded the Moral Majority as a lobbying, educational, and political-action committee, and served as its president.[27] In his autobiography, Falwell wrote that he "was convinced that there was a 'moral majority' out there . . . sufficient in number to turn back the flood tide of moral permissiveness, family breakdown and general capitulation to evil and to foreign policies such as Marxism-Leninism."[28] The Moral Majority was a prominent voice of the Christian Right and campaigned against abortion rights, gay rights, and the Equal Rights Amendment.[29] The organization's political strength grew quickly and, within three years, Falwell proudly claimed that the Moral Majority "had a $10 million budget, 100,000 trained pastors, priests, and rabbis, and several million volunteers. . . . And in the process, we helped elect" President Reagan.[30]

At trial, Falwell would testify that in a *Good Housekeeping* magazine poll he had been named the "second most-admired American behind the President," and that *U.S. News and World Report* had included him "among the twenty-five most influential Americans."[31] However, Falwell's kindly telegenic presence was often in apparent conflict with his fiery and divisive rhetoric. In 1965, he criticized Dr. King and the civil rights movement as having "done more to damage race relations and to engender hate than to help!"[32] He later repudiated the sermon, but in 1985 he called Bishop Desmond M. Tutu, the

Nobel Peace Prize winner, a "phony" and supported the apartheid government.[33] He professed that "AIDS is not just God's punishment for homosexuals, it is God's punishment for the society that tolerates homosexuals."[34] Falwell supported Israel, but said he knew why people "don't like Jews. . . . He can make more money accidentally than you can on purpose."[35] He called feminism "a satanic attack on the home."[36] And one of Falwell's most inflammatory comment came shortly after 9/11, when he cast blame for the attacks on a coalition of liberal groups: "I really believe that the pagans, and the abortionists, and the feminists, and the gays and the lesbians who are actively trying to make that an alternative lifestyle, the ACLU . . . all of them who have tried to secularize America, I point the finger in their face and say 'you helped this happen.'"[37] No matter how his remarks were received by the general public, Falwell continued to willingly embrace his role as a lightning rod for his fundamentalist faith. In everything Falwell said and did, he set himself out as a moral exemplar, preaching what he believed were the old-fashioned values necessary to save America from spiritual ruin.

Meanwhile, Larry Flynt, the pornography publishing titan, did not necessarily see himself as so different from Jerry Falwell. "The truth is, the reverend and I had a lot in common," Flynt reflected years after their litigation had ended. "He was from Virginia, and I was from Kentucky. His father had been a bootlegger, and I had been one too in my 20s before I went into the Navy."[38] In his late twenties, Flynt continued hustling as a small business owner on the fringes of the law, eventually establishing a string of go-go dancing Hustler Clubs across Ohio in the early 1970s.[39] Initially a newsletter to promote his clubs, *Hustler*'s first edition as a glossy magazine was published in July 1974.[40] Flynt saw his vision for the magazine in stark contrast to that of the established *Playboy* and *Penthouse*, saying he "wanted a sex magazine free of pretense and full of fantasy, fiction, satire and biting humor. I wanted to offend everyone on an equal-opportunity basis."[41]

In his first year as publisher, Flynt demonstrated his self-described "hillbilly instincts" for what would sell magazines. He purchased nude photos of Jacqueline Kennedy Onassis sunbathing in Greece from a paparazzo who had been turned down by *Playboy* and *Penthouse.*[42] *Hustler's* August 1975 issue featured four full-page naked pictures of the widowed former first lady and quickly sold a million copies while gaining international publicity in the mainstream media.[43] The *Wall Street Journal* reported that Flynt's unlikely formula of "girlie photos that beg the description 'sexually explicit,' and cartoons and stories of the type that used to circulate only surreptitiously," resulted in "not only the fastest-growing men's magazine around but one of the fastest-growing magazines of any kind, ever."[44]

Hustler was an enormous financial success, but the magazine's exploding public presence also made it a bigger target.[45] Flynt would soon be drawn into a string of trials for obscenity.[46] While fighting obscenity charges in Georgia, on March 6, 1978, Flynt and one of his attorneys were walking toward the "slightly shabby but still dignified" courthouse in the town square, when they were shot multiple times.[47] Flynt survived, but would be left paralyzed from the waist down and suffering from peripheral nerve damage that would cause him years of intense pain.[48]

Years later, a white supremacist convicted of eight murders, who claimed responsibility for killing another twenty African Americans and Jews between 1977 and 1980, also confessed to shooting Flynt.[49] The gunman said he targeted Flynt because he saw photographs in *Hustler's* December 1975 issue of an interracial couple having sex.[50]

The incredibly dramatic twists and turns of Larry Flynt's life would provide the basis for a Golden Globe–winning and Academy Award–nominated film called *The People vs. Larry Flynt* by acclaimed director Miloš Forman in 1996 (the latter portion of the biopic dramatizes Flynt's legal fight with Falwell).[51] The "redemption of Larry Flynt" as a free speech hero on the screen and elsewhere would however be vigorously challenged by a number of feminists and First Amendment scholars.[52] One critic points out that in the movie, "[f]leetingly, we do see the notorious *Hustler* cover of a naked woman being fed into a meat grinder. . . . But we don't see another *Hustler* classic: the picture of a nude woman bagged like a deer and bound to the luggage rack of a car."[53]

"Characterizing Larry Flynt's magazine as sexually explicit, rather than sexually violent, reflects a position," maintained Frederick Schauer, who was the Frank Stanton Professor of the First Amendment at Harvard. He advocated that the public should "resist thinking of Larry Flynt's glorification of violence against women as of a lesser order than the glorification of racial or religious violence."[54]

Gloria Steinem also objected to positioning Flynt in such a sympathetic cinematic light, and sought to draw attention to other disturbing elements of the *Hustler* story. "Filmgoers don't see such *Hustler* features as 'Dirty Pool,' which in January 1983 depicted a woman being gang-raped on a pool table," she wrote in an op-ed for the *New York Times*, "[or] such typical *Hustler* photo stories as a naked woman in handcuffs who is shaved, raped and apparently killed by guards in a concentration-camp-like setting."[55] "So, no, I am not grateful to Mr. Flynt for protecting my freedom, as the film and its enthusiasts suggest I should be," Steinem protested. "No more than I would be to a racist or fascist publisher whose speech is protected by the Constitution."[56]

* * *

Falwell and Flynt, the problematic champions of morality and free expression, would face off at trial in Roanoke, Virginia, only forty-five miles from the headquarters of Falwell's religious empire.[57]

The lawyers for the two sides were an equally pronounced contrast in styles. Norman Grutman, a highly pedigreed New York trial attorney, represented Falwell. Described as having "a melodious basso voice and a rotund Sidney Greenstreet bearing," along with being "a combative man of sweeping self-confidence," Grutman took a pointedly aggressive approach to his dealings with Flynt in the courtroom.[58] Alan Isaacman, a Beverly Hills litigator with a youthful appearance, presented his case with "an informal, unpretentious style . . . and a slight grin on his face."[59] Isaacman and Flynt became good friends over the years. Isaacman has said that one of Flynt's lines in the film—"I'm your dream client. I'm the most fun. I'm rich. And I'm always in trouble"—was based on how the lawyer described their relationship to colleagues when asked how he could represent the notorious pornographer.[60]

Falwell brought two main claims against Flynt: libel and intentional infliction of emotional distress.[61] The essential distinction between the two legal actions is that libel requires a false statement of *fact* and emotional distress does not. In other words, to win a libel action, you need to prove that there was a factual statement that was inaccurate, not an opinion statement. ("Beyoncé has never won a Grammy" is a false statement of fact—she's actually won more than twenty.[62] "Lady Gaga isn't a good singer" is a statement of opinion, in that it's not provably false.) To win on an emotional distress claim, Falwell needed only to convince a jury that Flynt "intended to inflict emotional distress, was outrageous, and did in fact inflict serious emotional" injury.[63] During the trial, Falwell and Flynt's own testimony would be crucial for the jury in determining whether or not Falwell could prevail.

Even before the trial began on December 3, 1984, it had an overheated air.[64] Flynt had flown into town on what he called his "labia-pink jet, a pornographic prerequisite," accompanied by six bodyguards.[65] Two dozen reporters packed the second-floor courtroom as opening statements were given and then Falwell took the stand.[66]

Grutman lead Falwell through questions intended to demonstrate the falsity of the statements in the ad parody. Falwell told the court, "Since I became a Christian in 1952, I have been and am a teetotaler," and that he never endorsed alcoholic beverages or partook of them before services or at any time.[67] He continued to testify that his late mother "was a very godly woman, probably the closest to a saint that I have ever known," and that he "would stake [his] life on her purity."[68] Despite Isaacman's efforts to concede for the record that Falwell's "mother was a person of the finest moral character," and skip over this impassioned line of questioning, Grutman was allowed by the judge to ask, "Mr. Falwell, specifically, did you and your mother ever commit incest?"[69] As the jury watched and listened, the discomfort of even having to answer such a question was successfully brought home, and Falwell answered emphatically, "Absolutely not."[70]

Grutman also led Falwell through a discussion of his work with the Moral Majority and his political views. "Have you attempted to influence public opinion against pornography?" Grutman asked. "With every breath in my body," Falwell dramatically replied.[71] Grutman then wanted to draw the line between political advocacy and personal attacks, asking, "In opposing pornography as a philosophical idea, have either you or the Moral Majority ever personally picked on the intimate personal life of any person who was himself in your judgment a pornographer?" "Never at any time," Falwell responded. "I don't know anything about the personal lives of the people I consider to be the porn kings."[72]

The emotional peak of Falwell's testimony came when Grutman sought to draw out the extent of the emotional distress that the reverend alleged to have suffered. It was an indispensable component of his claim and something of an awkward fit for the personally reserved Falwell. He nevertheless rose to the challenge when Grutman asked him what his "personal reaction was when you read this ad . . . for the first time." Falwell responded,

I think I have never been as angry as I was at that moment. My first impression was that Campari had purchased an ad in the magazine, because I had seen a similar ad in decent magazines earlier, and my first thought was to get on the phone to Campari. Our in-house attorney and I talked it over. My anger became a more rational and deep hurt. I somehow felt that in all of my life I had never believed that human beings could do something like this. I really felt like weeping. I am not a deeply emotional person; I don't show it. I think I felt like weeping.... It is the most hurtful, damaging, despicable, low-type personal attack that I can imagine one human being can inflict upon another.[73]

It would be difficult for Larry Flynt to cut as convincing a figure as the apparently deeply wounded Falwell. However, Flynt rolled into the courtroom in his gold-plated wheelchair ready to be a polished version of his authentic and surprisingly charming self.[74] Isaacman wanted to provide a context for the Falwell parody ad by having Flynt talk about other advertising parodies his magazine had created. Flynt described one *Hustler* parody of Marlboro cigarettes involving "a Marlboro man in the hay with his horse, you know, having a cigarette, you know, after sex, you know, just a sort of a preposterous situation."[75] Isaacman then asked Flynt what was "intended to be conveyed" by this particular Campari ad parody featuring Falwell.

The writer E. B. White once quipped that "humor can be dissected, as a frog can, but the thing dies in the process," and yet Flynt managed to give a detailed and effective explanation of how the ad was intended to be funny.[76] Even more critically, Flynt conveyed why the combination of Campari and Falwell was ripe for parody:

Well, we wanted to poke fun at Campari for their type advertisement because the innuendoes that they had in their ads made you sort of confused as to if the person was talking about their time as far as a sexual encounter or whether they were talking about their first time as far as drinking Campari. Of course, another thing that you had to do is to have a person, you know, that is the complete opposite of what you would expect. If someone such as me might have been in there I don't know how people would have interpreted it. But if somebody like Reverend Falwell is in there it is very obvious that he wouldn't do any of these things; that they are not true; that it's not to be taken seriously. . . . The best example I can say is when somebody asks me why Reverend Falwell, the only thing I can point out is why did Walter Mondale, during the debates in Louisville, [say,] "Do you want Reverend Falwell to be involved in selecting the next Supreme Court?" Now, that was strictly to make a political point, but that means that he, more than any other evangelist is involved in the mainstream of politics. And there is a great deal of people in this country, especially the ones that read *Hustler* Magazine, that feel that there should be a separation between church and state. So, when something like this appears it will give people a chuckle. They know this was not intended to defame the Reverend Falwell, his mother or any members of his family because no one could take it serious.[77]

Isaacman inquired next about the "believability" of what was written in the ad parody, and Flynt seriously replied, "Well, you know, as far as making it with his mother, I mean, that's so outrageous, I mean, that no one can find that believable. . . . I mean, someone may not like it, but that's not what we're here for today is whether somebody likes it or not, but whether it's in violation of the law."[78]

Finally, Isaacman questioned Flynt as to whether his intent with the ad parody was to harm Falwell. "I don't have any, you know, personal animosity towards, towards Reverend Falwell," Flynt explained. "I put him, you know, like all politicians and all evangelists, basically in the same category. *Hustler* satirizes and parodies, and our basic editorial content is built around politics, sex and religion."[79] Guided by Isaacman, Flynt had accomplished all they could hope to with his testimony. Flynt made his position clear: the mockery was not intended to be taken personally, and the extreme nature of the falsehoods was the very reason the parody could not reasonably harm Falwell's reputation or feelings.

At closing argument, the local paper reported that Grutman, in a rising voice, sought to "make a statement about what he saw as the sleaze running wild in America."[80] "Certainly the eyes of the country are on Roanoke," Grutman told the jurors. "And you are going to make a statement. And that statement that you are going to make from this courthouse is going to spread throughout the length and breadth of this land." Grutman's final words could not have painted a starker picture of good versus evil: "The nation is watching. The nation wants to know where the Constitution stands. Which way, America? Are you going to let loose chaos and anarchy? Are you going to turn America into the *Planet of the Apes?*"[81]

Isaacman, in contrast, summed up the matter as a narrow First Amendment question.[82] "It would be ridiculous," he asserted, to award damages "on the basis of something as frivolous as hurt feelings."[83] After the weeklong trial, the all-white, all-Protestant jury of four men and eight women from the Bible Belt deliberated for about six hours before returning their verdict.[84]

The jury answered the questions set forth in the judge's instructions, and specifically found that the ad parody could not "reasonably be understood as describing actual facts about [Falwell] or actual events in which [he] participated," and as a result, found that Flynt did not libel Falwell.[85] The jury then ruled for Falwell on the emotional distress claim, and awarded him $200,000 in damages. The split decision, and the relatively modest damages—a far cry from the $10 million in damages Grutman had asked the jury to award—was surprising and reflected a carefully considered verdict that one juror said was "based on the law and facts rather than emotion." Both sides would claim victory and both sides appealed parts of the decision.[86]

Almost two years later, the Fourth Circuit affirmed the judgment. It rejected Flynt's arguments that the emotional distress claim was limited by the First Amendment in any way.[87] For the first time, a federal court of appeals had held that a public figure could recover damages for emotional distress without a finding of libel or invasion of privacy.[88]

The prospects for Flynt at this stage looked grim. Isaacman later noted that media organizations didn't want to support their last appeal, as the pundits thought they would lose if they got to the Supreme Court.[89] Yet Flynt and Isaacman pressed on, and the case proved to present such a "novel" and significant free speech issue that the high court agreed to hear it.[90]

On the cold December day of the oral argument, there was an additional drama that heightened the tension to an even greater than usual degree. Would Larry Flynt show up? Those who knew about Flynt's last appearance at the Supreme Court four years prior had their doubts.

In *Keeton v. Hustler*, Kathy Keeton, associate publisher of the rival *Penthouse*, had sued Flynt and the magazine for libel.[91] The case reached the Supreme Court on a jurisdictional question and was set to be argued for Keeton by none other than Norman Roy Grutman and for Flynt by a law professor he had hired.[92] Five days before their Supreme Court appearance, Flynt telegrammed the justices that he wanted to argue the case on his own behalf.[93] The request was denied. When the day came for the oral argument and the court-appointed lawyer for Flynt was about to begin, Flynt shouted angrily at the solemn justices, "Fuck this Court. I am being denied the counsel of my choice all because of one token cunt. Goddamm motherfuckers!'"[94] Chief Justice Warren Burger pointed at Flynt and said, "Arrest that man," to the bailiff, and muttered under his breath, "sonofabitch if that isn't contempt."[95]

Ten minutes before the *Falwell* argument began, Flynt entered through a side entrance and was rolled to within twenty feet of where Falwell sat with his wife.[96] Flynt was dressed the part of a respectful participant in a three-piece suit with a red tie and his curly red hair slicked back. Falwell, beaming paternalism, had on a red-and-white-striped tie with his feathery gray hair neatly coiffed.[97] Both stocky men had confident smiles that day—likely projecting Falwell's conviction that he was doing good and Flynt's that he kept getting away with doing bad.

Isaacman began by arguing that the actual malice standard set out in *Sullivan* to protect libel defendants should not be "evaded by a public figure . . . by labeling his cause of action intentional infliction of emotional distress" instead.[98] But Justice Sandra Day O'Connor wanted to approach the issue differently, asking: doesn't the state have "an even greater interest" in protecting its citizens from emotional distress than it does in protecting reputation?[99] Isaacman adroitly replied that reputational injury should be considered more important, since it impacts "what goes on in the minds of other people as well, and not just the minds of one citizen."[100] In saying this, Isaacman was purposefully laying the foundation for his position that the actual malice standard should apply to both emotional distress as well as libel claims.

Justice Byron White probed the limits of what Isaacman was seeking, and queried if he was advocating that "opinion or parody is *never* actionable"?[101] Isaacman qualified that the Court should make clear that parody should always be protected as long as it is concerns public figures and "contains nothing that can be understood as a false statement of fact."[102]

Justice John Paul Stevens then asked a deceptively simple question, "What is the public interest" in parody?[103] Isaacman seemed well prepared for this line of inquiry, answering, "There are two public interests." He described the first interest as arising when "somebody who's out there campaigning against [*Hustler*] saying don't read our magazine and we're poison on the minds of America and don't engage in sex outside of wedlock and don't drink alcohol. *Hustler* has every right to say that man is full of B.S. And that's what this ad parody says."[104]

Isaacman went on to say that there was also a second interest in putting Falwell "in a ridiculous setting." He explained, "Instead of Jerry Falwell speaking from the television with a beatific look on his face and the warmth that comes out of him, and the sincerity in his voice . . . and he's standing on a pulpit, and he may have a bible in his hand, instead of that situation, *Hustler* is saying, let's deflate this stuffed shirt, let's bring him down to our level. . . ." And then Isaacman seemed to catch himself for just a moment, thinking that the justices might never see Falwell as capable of being brought down so low as to be on the same level as Flynt, and added, "or at least to the level where you will listen to what we have to say."[105] The courtroom and the justices exploded in laughter at Isaacman's self-deprecating humor about his own client. Almost apologizing, he remarked, "I was told not to joke in the Supreme Court. I really didn't mean to do that." Afterward, Isaacman vividly remembered "Rehnquist doubled over. . . . I can still picture him bent over at the waist laughing," and thought, "'Boy, this is finally an encouraging sign in the case.'"[106]

Justice Antonin Scalia jumped in with his typically cutting manner. "The rule you give us says that if you stand for public office, or become a public figure in any way, you cannot protect yourself, or indeed, your mother, against a parody of your committing incest with your mother in an outhouse." He continued incredulously, "Do you think George Washington would have stood for public office if that was the consequence?"[107] Isaacman countered that, in a brief submitted by the cartoonist society supporting *Hustler*, there was a political cartoon created in Washington's time showing the founding father "being led on a donkey and underneath there's a caption that, so and so who is leading the donkey is leading this ass. . . ."[108]

Scalia interrupted, "I can handle that. I think George could handle that," receiving uproarious laughter of his own. "But that's a far cry from committing incest with your mother in an outhouse," Scalia pressed. "I mean, there's no line between the two? We can't protect that kind of parody and not protect this?" Isaacman came up with a perfect rejoinder: "What you're talking about, Justice Scalia, is a matter of taste. And as . . . you said [in a previous decision] just as it's useless to argue about taste, it's useless to litigate it."[109]

As the red warning light flashed on his lectern to indicate time was up, Isaacman fielded one last question from Scalia.[110] Apparently seeking to show that an emotional distress claim could be sufficiently limited by an intent to cause harm, he challenged Isaacman one last time: "How often do you think you're going to be able to get a jury to find that [the parody] was done with the intent of creating emotional distress?"[111] "Every time," Isaacman hit back. "Almost every time that something critical is said about somebody, because how can any speaker come in and say I didn't intend to cause any emotional distress, and be believed. If you say something critical about another person, and if it's very critical, it's going to cause emotional distress. . . . That's why that's a meaningless standard."[112] It was an auspicious way to conclude and as Isaacman sat down he winked at Flynt.[113]

Grutman started his argument off with strong words: "Deliberate, malicious character assassination is not protected by the Constitution. Deliberate, malicious character assassination is what was proven in this case."[114] Calling Flynt's conduct "aberrational," Grutman tried to assure the Court that other "responsible" publishers need not worry about any precedent in this case. He emphatically stated that "this is the wanton, reckless, deliberately malicious publisher who sets out for the sheer perverse joy of simply causing injury to abuse the power that he has as a publisher."[115]

But Justice O'Connor was clearly not convinced that a victory for Falwell could be contained. She raised the point that "there are those who think that the conduct of certain newspapers in pursuing Mr. [Gary] Hart [about his alleged extramarital affair, which ended his 1988 campaign for the Democratic nomination for president] was of the same unwarranted character."[116] Rather than distinguishing political reporting as based on truth, Grutman surprisingly would not concede that emotional distress claims could be limited to only those involving *false* statements. O'Connor pushed further: "Well, do you think a vicious cartoon should subject the drawer of that cartoon to potential liability?"[117] Again, Grutman refused to put any limits on emotional distress claims, other than saying a jury would determine if a cartoon "would be regarded by the average member of the community as so intolerable that no civilized person should have to bear it." It was a definite tactical error, which Justice White commented on with some dismay: "Well, Mr. Grutman, you're certainly posing a much broader proposition than is necessary for you to win this case."[118]

Justice Scalia pursued Justice O'Connor's concerns about political cartoons further, commenting that there is "a long tradition of this, not just in this country but back into English history, I mean, politicians depicted as horrible looking beasts, and you talk about portraying someone as committing some immoral act. I would be very surprised if there were not a number of cartoons depicting one or another political figure as at least the piano player in a bordello."[119]

Scalia got another appreciative laugh from the crowd and Grutman tried to play along: "We don't shoot the piano player. I understand that."[120] Scalia, however, would not be deterred, and insisted that Grutman give the court some standard that would allow Falwell to recover, but would not mean that every satirist who offends has to constantly worry about being hauled into court. "Give us something that the cartoonist or the political figure can adhere to," Scalia urged. "I mean, does it depend on how ugly the beast is, or what?" Grutman attempted to jest, "No, it's not the amount of hair the beast has or how long his claws may be," and then, trying to get back on track, added, "I believe that this is a matter of an evolving social sensibility."[121] By saying this, Grutman meant simply: juries could sort it out.

O'Connor was having none of it. "In today's world, people don't want to have to take these things to a jury," she reminded Grutman.

"They want to have some kind of a rule to follow, so that when they utter it or write it or draw it in the first place, they're comfortable in the knowledge that it isn't going to subject them to a suit."[122] Grutman only offered that a "responsible author, artist, or anyone" would somehow know.[123] Even the supremely self-assured Grutman must have realized his argument was not winning over the justices.

* * *

Almost three months later, on February 24, 1988, Larry Flynt answered a phone call at his office. "Larry, I've got some incredible news," Alan Isaacman told him. "We won! It was a unanimous decision."[124] The unexpected victory also had an unexpected author. Chief Justice William Rehnquist, who at that time was viewed as "anti-press," wrote the decision for the Court.[125]

Seeking to frame the opinion in expansive terms, the chief justice began by citing past precedent that "one of the prerogatives of American citizenship is the right to criticize public men and measures. Such criticism, inevitably, will not always be reasoned or moderate; public figures . . . will be subject to vehement, caustic, and sometimes unpleasantly sharp attacks."[126] The First Amendment question before the Court, he set forth, was "whether a public figure may recover damages for emotional harm caused by the publication of an ad parody offensive to him . . . and [that] is intended to inflict emotional injury, even when that speech could not reasonably have been interpreted as stating actual facts about the public figure involved."[127] The answer must be no, Rehnquist wrote, unless a jury finds that "the publication contains a false statement of *fact* which was made with 'actual malice,' i.e., with knowledge that the statement was false or with reckless disregard as to whether or not it was true."[128] Applying *New York Times v. Sullivan* actual malice safeguards was necessary, he added, "to give adequate 'breathing space' to the freedoms protected by the First Amendment."[129]

Rehnquist explained that protecting such parody was absolutely necessary because "were we to hold otherwise, there can be little doubt that political cartoonists and satirists would be subjected to damages awards without any showing that their work falsely defamed its subject."[130] Looking back on Thomas Nast's cartoons of the 1860s and 1870s attacking the corruption of New York City's "Boss" Tweed, he quoted experts who pointed out that such art succeeded in its day through "the emotional impact of its presentation [which] continuously goes beyond the bounds of good taste and conventional manners."[131] "From the viewpoint of history," Rehnquist affirmed, "it is clear that our political discourse would have been considerably poorer without" such artists.[132]

To make sure that no one thought the Court was placing the unseemly Flynt in the elevated company of noble political satirists from the past, Rehnquist indicated that he was holding his nose as he sided with the pornographer.[133] "There is no doubt that the caricature of [Falwell] and his mother published in *Hustler* is at best a distant cousin of the political cartoons described above," he added disdainfully, "and a rather poor relation at that."[134] However, the chief justice concluded, almost reluctantly,

> [i]f it were possible by laying down a principled standard to separate the one from the other, public discourse would probably suffer little or no harm. But we doubt that there is any such standard, and we are quite sure that the pejorative description "outrageous" does not supply one. "Outrageousness" in the area of political and social discourse has an inherent subjectiveness about it which would allow a jury to impose liability on the basis of the jurors' tastes or views, or perhaps on the basis of their dislike of a particular expression.[135]

The Supreme Court's unanimous decision was as impactful as it was surprising. Public figures cannot win money damages for even the most outrageous satiric attacks on them, even when there may be an intent to cause emotional harm. The Court had decisively shut down any future efforts to muzzle such criticism.[136]

The *Hustler* decision also strikingly reaffirmed that the actual malice protections of *Sullivan* were a bedrock principle of the Court's conception of the First Amendment.[137] And in preserving the free speech rights of someone as tawdry as Flynt, the Supreme Court demonstrated that the First Amendment cloaks all of us—not just more civically minded journalists, civil rights activists, and political speakers—in its embrace.[138] As Chief Justice Rehnquist rhapsodized in his decision, "At the heart of the First Amendment is the recognition of the fundamental importance of the free flow of ideas and opinions on matters of public interest and concern. [T]he freedom to speak one's mind is not only an aspect of individual liberty—and thus a good unto itself—but also is essential to the common quest for truth and the vitality of society as a whole."[139]

For Flynt and Falwell, the far-reaching decision would lead to a strange new chapter in their contentious relationship. Immediately after the Supreme Court announced its ruling, the pair traded predictable insults. Falwell called the pornographer a "sleaze merchant" who was using "the First Amendment as an excuse for maliciously and dishonestly" attacking him, and Flynt shot back that the preacher was "just a big windbag."[140]

But almost ten years later, with the opening of *The People vs. Larry Flynt* and the release of Flynt's autobiography, the two men appeared together on CNN's *Larry King Live* and Falwell hugged Flynt![141] Soon after, Falwell came to Flynt's office to propose that the two "go around the country debating . . . moral issues and First Amendment issues."[142]

Over the course of this college tour, and in the years that followed, the two visited with each other and developed a relationship.[143] Flynt said of this time, "Jerry Falwell once made a remark that I didn't save the First Amendment, the First Amendment saved me. And I said 'Jerry, that's the first thing you've ever said that I agree with.'"[144]

A few days after Falwell's death in 2007, Flynt wrote in the *Los Angeles Times* that after spending so much time together "the ultimate result was one I never expected and was just as shocking a turn to me as was winning that famous Supreme Court case: We became friends."[145]

* * *

Whether Trump will ever feel equally friendly toward *Saturday Night Live* is impossible to predict. What we do know, because of *Hustler v. Falwell*, is that there is nothing Trump can legally do to stop the satire. No matter how outrageous, no matter how filled with animus, no matter how hurt the feelings. Mockery, caricature, and ridicule are the price that all public figures pay to keep America's most outlandish ideas freely flowing.

9 / NAZIS IN CHARLOTTESVILLE, FUNERAL PROTESTS, AND SPEAKERS WE HATE

In the darkness of night, punctuated by the fiery glow of tiki torches, the angry chants rang out: "You will not replace us! Jews will not replace us! Blood and soil! White lives matter!" More than three hundred white nationalists were marching in an unannounced processional on the campus of the University of Virginia.[1] They were just some of the self-identified neo-Nazis, Ku Klux Klan members, and other alt-right adherents who had come to Charlottesville for a "Unite the Right" rally scheduled to take place the next day.[2]

The rally had been organized by Jason Kessler, a local resident and University of Virginia graduate, who described himself as a "white advocate."[3] On his permit application, Kessler described the event as a "free speech rally" for an estimated four hundred participants at Emancipation Park.[4] The initially stated purpose for the rally was to oppose the city council's efforts to remove a statue of the Confederate general Robert E. Lee from that park, which, until three months prior, had been named after Lee.[5] However, in a later interview, Kessler said his goal for Unite the Right was to "de-stigmatize white advocacy so that white people can stand up for their interests just like any other identity group."[6]

Five days before the rally was to be held, city officials informed Kessler that they would grant a permit to hold the event only at a different, larger park.[7] The city explained its decision was based on information that "many thousands of individuals are likely to attend the demonstration," and it had determined that "law enforcement, fire, and emergency medical services personnel cannot adequately protect people and property in and around Emancipation Park."[8]

The Virginia ACLU took up Kessler's case and brought a lawsuit in federal court to force the city to allow the demonstration to take place in Emancipation Park. The ACLU argued that the city's denial of the requested permit was "an attempt to undermine the ability of demonstrators to effectively communicate their message" and that the claimed concerns over crowd size were only a "pretext for silencing the 'Unite the Right' demonstration."[9] The judge ruled for Kessler, having determined that since counterprotestors had received their requested permits, it was likely that the "decision to revoke Kessler's permit was based on the content of his speech rather than other neutral factors that would be equally applicable to Kessler and those protesting against him."[10]

On the morning of August 12, 2017, the largest gathering of white nationalists in decades was heading toward Emancipation Park.[11] Violence soon broke out between the alt-right and counterprotestors as police stood by unable or unwilling to do anything to stop it.[12] As the fighting grew more intense, about a half an hour before the rally was officially set to begin at noon, the Charlottesville police chief declared the event an "unlawful assembly."[13] The police ordered the crowd to disperse, and announced that there would be no rally.[14] Alt-right forces began to leave the park, but many continued to spew hate at the counterprotestors, screaming, "Fuck you, n——!"[15] The unintended result of the police action was that the fighting spread beyond the park as "small groups of people wandered through the streets and engaged in frequent skirmishes unimpeded by police."[16]

Almost two hours after the rally was cancelled, a Unite the Right participant drove his gray Dodge Challenger up to a narrow street crowded with counterprotestors and then intentionally accelerated and rammed his car into them.[17] One witness described hearing "this sound of . . . hitting, like traffic cones. This hollow, horrible sound."[18] The driver then reversed quickly, hitting and dragging others.[19] Dozens were injured in the attack and thirty-two-year-old Heather Heyer was killed at the scene.[20] Heyer, a Charlottesville resident, worked as a paralegal at a local law firm. Attending the rally with friends as an anti-racism demonstrator, she had been chanting, "Whose streets? Our streets!" shortly before she was murdered.[21]

President Trump added fuel to the fire when, later that day, he stated in response to the tragic events, "We condemn in the strongest possible terms this egregious display of hatred, bigotry and violence on many sides," adding again for emphasis with a wave of his hand, "On many sides."[22] Equating neo-Nazis, the KKK, and white supremacists with those *protesting* racism triggered a widespread outcry, even from prominent members of his own party.[23] And so, under pressure, Trump reluctantly offered an actual condemnation of racism and hate groups.[24] But another day later, he doubled down on his previous remarks, insisting that "you had some very bad people in that group, but you also had people that were very fine people, on both sides."[25]

Charlottesville mayor Mike Signer responded strongly, "I'm not going to make any bones about it. I place the blame for a lot of what you're seeing in America today right at the doorstep of the White House and the people around the president."[26] Whatever may have caused or exacerbated this hate, the tragedy of Charlottesville and Trump's response had certainly highlighted the festering forces of white nationalism that still exist in this country.

In the aftermath of Charlottesville, the question facing us with renewed urgency is: does the First Amendment protect what is often called "hate speech"? To understand the answer to this question in a modern context we must begin with the Court's most recent and significant examination of hateful speech. The case involved another example of a demonstrations, this time by a fringe church taunting the families of dead soldiers at military funerals.

* * *

The Westboro Baptist Church was founded by Fred Phelps in 1955. During the early years of his church, Phelps made his living as a successful civil rights lawyer in Topeka, Kansas, representing African Americans in discrimination lawsuits, until he was disbarred for unethical behavior in 1979. The church's small congregation was made up primarily of members of his family.[27] He and his wife had thirteen children, fifty-four grandchildren, and seven great-grandchildren, who mostly lived together in a compound of houses they called "the Block."[28]

In the 1990s, Westboro launched an anti-gay crusade and gained attention for protesting against homosexuality at the funerals of people who had died of AIDS.[29] Picketing at the funeral of Matthew Shepard, the twenty-one-year-old gay college student who was beaten to death in Laramie, Wyoming, garnered the church national exposure.[30] The messages on Westboro's signs—"Matt in Hell," "Fags Are Nature Freaks," and "God Hates Fags"—showed the world what would become the church's recognizably signature combination of hate and appalling personal attacks.[31]

In 2001, Phelps attested that 9/11 was God's punishment for America's acceptance of homosexuality. In 2005, Westboro started picketing at the funerals of members of the armed forces who had been killed in Iraq and Afghanistan. Phelps's convoluted rationale for this new outrage was that God wanted those troops dead as a sign to warn Americans of the error of their ways. He believed that the church needed to make this warning clearer and to take it directly to mourners at military funerals. Thereafter, Phelps and his family, including his nineteen-year-old granddaughter, Megan Phelps-Roper, began carrying new signs that continued in their reprehensible tradition: "Thank God for IEDs" and "They Turned the Country Over to the Fags—They're Coming Home in Body Bags!"[32]

The Westboro Baptist Church picketed at hundreds of funerals brandishing such signs, and each demonstration almost certainly added to the trauma experienced by the grieving families at one of the most vulnerable and painful times in their lives.[33] Of all the people impacted, the father of one of the veterans whose funeral was picketed decided to take action. His fight would lead him on a five-year journey as he attempted to change the path of hate speech and First Amendment law.

* * *

Matt Snyder was a senior in high school when he told his father, Albert, that he wanted to join the military. Albert said he would support his son's choice. But he asked Matt to take "a couple of weeks to really think about this," especially since the war in Iraq was ongoing and "not getting any better."[34] Matt decided to join the Marines, and in 2005 during a Christmas visit home, he told his family he was being deployed to Iraq.[35] On March 3, 2006, after serving in Iraq for just a few weeks, Matt was on a mission in Al Anbar Province when he was killed in the line of duty.[36] He was only twenty years old.[37]

A week later, the funeral for Lance Corporal Matthew Snyder was held at the family's Catholic church, St. John's, in Westminster, Maryland. Albert was deeply moved to see thousands of people on the streets paying tribute to Matt, including fire trucks draped in the American flag and elementary school kids holding a sign that said, "We Love You, Matt."[38] As the immediate family was looking out at these expressions of love and sympathy from the windows of their limo, they noticed that their driver took the service entrance to bring them around to St. John's.[39] At the time, Albert didn't know why they had gone that way, but the reason soon became clear: the Westboro Baptist Church.

Fred Phelps, along with two of his daughters and four of his grand-children, had flown in from Kansas to picket Snyder's funeral. Following police instructions, they were standing behind orange snow fencing, on a ten-by-twenty-five plot of public land, about a thousand feet from the church.[40] Some of their despicable signs present that day were "Thank God for Dead Soldiers," "Thank God for IEDs," "Pope in Hell," "God Hates Fags," "Fag Troops," "Semper Fi Fags," and "You're Going to Hell."[41]

Albert Snyder could see only the tops of the signs, but not what they said, from the limo.[42] As he got out of the vehicle to go into the church, he was able to briefly hear the Westboro members singing patriotic songs like "America the Beautiful" and "God Bless the USA," but with new lyrics ("America, America, God showed his wrath to thee" and "Shamed to be an American, where the fags can freely roam" were representative examples of their ham-fisted parodies).[43] After about a half hour of picketing, shortly after the funeral services began in the church and before the burial took place, the Phelps family packed up their signs and left.[44]

Later that day, there was a wake at Matt's grandparents' home. The family turned on the television to see if there was local coverage of the tributes to Matt, and that is when Albert first saw the signs.[45] What the church could not have known is that, although Matt was heterosexual, Albert is gay.[46] Albert's friends and family knew, but his sexual orientation was otherwise a private matter.[47] Many years later, Albert recalled how his loved ones with him at the time "hated to see me and my partner and my friends have to deal with something so vicious at a funeral," adding sorrowfully, "I had one opportunity to bury my son, and it was taken away from me. He should have had a peaceful burial."[48]

Albert Snyder decided to sue Phelps and the Westboro Baptist Church in federal court for intentional infliction of emotional distress and other claims.[49] At the ten-day trial, Snyder testified, "There are nights that, I just, you know, I try to think of my son at times and every time . . . I see those [church protest] signs.'"[50] In his effective closing argument, Snyder's lawyer told the jury:

> Matt Snyder went on a mission for his country. And he wanted to complete that mission and did everything within his power to complete that mission. They disrupted his funeral. Took the dignity and respect that everyone deserves out of that funeral. Matt passed that baton to his father and gave him the mission of holding them accountable for those actions. After that baton was passed to Al Snyder, he had to go through the civil process, and that's why you're here. When I'm done talking, the baton is in your hands. It's your decision. It's your mission to carry out justice.[51]

The jury found in favor of Snyder and awarded him $2.9 million in compensatory damages and $8 million in punitive damages.[52]

Although the loss appeared devastating for the Phelpses' church, Megan Phelps-Roper later described how her family "adopted the sort of position [they] always took: one of exultation."[53] Westboro Baptist Church posted a video in which members jubilantly said that they "thank God for the $10.9 million verdict because it's a small price to pay to get this message—America is doomed—in front of the eyes of the whole word. You can't pay for worldwide publicity that cheap!"[54] Fred Phelps's daughter Margie, who like her father was a lawyer, filed their appeal and was confident God "would turn our apparent defeat into a victory."[55]

On appeal, the Fourth Circuit held the First Amendment fully protected Westboro's speech as involving matters of "public concern" (as opposed to private matters, which are afforded less First Amendment protection).[56] Judge Robert B. King seemed pained to write that, even given "the distasteful and repugnant nature of the words being challenged in these proceedings, we are constrained to conclude" that the church's speech about matters of public concern was protected by the First Amendment.[57] He went on to add, almost apologetically, "it is a fair summary of history to say that the safeguards of liberty have often been forged in controversies involving not very nice people."[58] The judgment in favor of Snyder was reversed, and the multimillion damages were set aside.[59]

Regardless of how distressed Judge King may have been in reaching his decision, the Fourth Circuit's ruling was a nearly fatal blow to Albert Snyder's quest for justice. Snyder had only one remaining chance to try and achieve his goal of holding the Westboro Baptist Church accountable for its actions. To the dismay of some court watchers, the Supreme Court opened the door to that possibility when it agreed to hear the appeal.[60]

As the oral argument drew near, the political impact of the case, beyond just a father's fight, became clearer. Forty-eight states and a bipartisan coalition of forty-three senators filed briefs supporting Snyder.[61] The brief of the attorneys general asserted that this uniquely "intrusive and harassing" speech, which amounted to "emotional terrorism," could and should be restricted without running afoul of the First Amendment.[62] On the opposite side, news and civil liberties organizations lined up to provide briefs that stressed that the media and college campuses would both feel the chill if the Fourth Circuit decision was not upheld.[63] A *New York Times* editorial recommended that it was "in the interest of the nation that strong language about large issues be protected, even when it is hard to do so."[64]

* * *

Outside the Supreme Court on October 6, 2010, the Westboro Baptist Church had once again turned a solemn proceeding into circus. The church had chosen to picket outside the building where one of its own faithful members—Margie Phelps—was about to argue inside.

A nine-year-old grandchild of Fred Phelps held up a "God Hates You" sign as high as he could reach.[65] Over a dozen members of the church held up additional signs, some of which had been brandished at Matthew Snyder's funeral, like "Thank God for Dead Soldiers," along with new ones that read "God Hates Obama."[66]

Counterprotesters responded to the Westboro provocations with humor. One of their signs read, "If You're Going to Heaven, Hell Sounds Nice."[67] A George Washington University student, who identified himself as gay, stripped to his briefs (despite the fifty-degree temperature) and held up his own sign proclaiming, "Fred Phelps Wishes He Were Hot Like Me."[68]

Inside the Supreme Court building, the limits of hateful speech were about to be debated in a much less jocular manner. Albert Snyder was seated next to his partner, Walt Fisher, and Al's daughters and sisters. Near them were members of the church wearing T-shirts with "Jews Killed Christ" emblazoned on them.[69]

Sean Summers, a Maryland attorney who had been representing Snyder pro bono, started off with his strongest point: "We are talking about a funeral. If context is ever going to matter, it has to matter in the context of a funeral. Mr. Snyder simply wanted to bury his son in a private, dignified manner."[70] Westboro Baptist Church's "behavior made that impossible," Summers continued. In these circumstances, he maintained, Snyder should be allowed to bring an intentional infliction of emotional distress claim without it being blocked by the First Amendment.[71] After getting out those few sentences, Summers was on the defensive for the rest of his argument.

He tried to argue that the First Amendment limits on intentional emotional distress claims that prohibited recovery in *Hustler v. Falwell* did not apply in this case. Summers distinguished *Hustler* based on the fact that Reverend Falwell was a *public* figure and here Snyder was a *private* figure. However, Justice Elena Kagan, in just her third day

on the bench, was not persuaded that this distinction made a difference.[72] "Mr. Summers," Kagan interjected,

> *Hustler* seems to me to have one sentence that is key to the whole deci-
> sion, and it goes like this. It says: "Outrageousness in the area of politi-
> cal and social discourse has an inherent subjectiveness about it which
> would allow a jury to impose liability on the basis of the jurors' tastes
> or views or perhaps on the basis of their dislike of a particular expres-
> sion." . . . How is that sentence less implicated in a case about a private
> figure than in a case about a public figure?

Summers replied by saying the parody in *Hustler* was a "traditional
area of public discourse," as opposed to "a private funeral."[73] However,
this seemed to do little to assuage Kagan's concern about the dangers
inherent in giving juries free reign to punish unpopular speech about
matters of public interest.

The questioning by most of the other justices showed they were
also very concerned about how to draw a line that would allow Snyder to obtain monetary damages without leading to a chilling impact
on too much other speech.[74] Summers, responding haltingly and with
a quavering voice, seemed cowed and largely unable to provide any
substantive First Amendment framework that would accommodate
Snyder.

Margie Phelps was in for an equally rough time before the justices,
and got only one sentence out before she was interrupted with a series
of hypotheticals. Justice Samuel Alito posed one that involved an individual who "believes that African Americans are inferior, they are
inherently inferior, and they are really a bad influence on this country.
And so [that] person comes up to an African American and starts be-
rating that person with racial hatred. . . . That's a matter of public concern?" Ms. Phelps replied that she thought "the issue of race is a matter

of public concern," but that "approaching an individual up close and in their grill to berate them gets you out of the zone of protection, and we would never do that."[75]

Justice Anthony Kennedy then challenged her seemingly unlimited definition of public concern, saying Phelps's answer

> simply points out that all of us in a pluralistic society have components to our identity; we are Republicans or Democrats, we are Christians or atheists, we are single or married, we are old or young. Any one of those things you could turn into a public issue and follow a particular person around, making that person the target of your comments; and in your view because this gives you maximum publicity, the more innocent, the more removed the person is, the greater the impact. . . . So, I . . . think your . . . public concern issue . . . may not be a limiting factor in cases where there is an outrageous conduct.

Kennedy's point left Phelps little room to maneuver and showed how difficult it is to define matters of public concern. Attempting to redirect attention to the nature of her church's speech, Phelps fell back to saying that "this Court has given substantial, longstanding protection to speech on public issues, and how could it be gainsaid that the dying soldiers is not on the lips of everyone in this country?"[76]

With much of the discussion centering on *what* could be said, Justice Ruth Bader Ginsburg pointedly zeroed in on the issue of *where* the picketing should be allowed to occur. "This is a case about exploiting a private family's grief," she stated, "and the question is, Why should the First Amendment tolerate exploiting this bereaved family, when you have so many other forums for . . . getting across your message?"[77] Phelps got hung up objecting to the term "exploited" and never answered the question. It was indicative of her performance throughout her oral argument, technically respectful but intransigent in her repeated refusal to directly answer many of the questions.[78] Both counsels appeared to have done little to advance their causes.[79]

After the arguments were finished, Snyder told the press gathered outside that he had no issue with Westboro picketing near him that day with hateful messages similar to the ones at his son's funeral. "Take it to the White House, take it to Congress, take it to the Supreme Court, that's what they're supposed to do," he explained. "But 99% of Americans would agree that you can't protest a funeral," Snyder implored. "Everybody deserves to be buried with dignity and respect."[80]

Not surprisingly, Westboro Church members were acting far less reasonably. Fresh off of her first appearance before the high court, Margie Phelps joined her family as they "burst into song, as one," when asked by a reporter whether they had any concern for the Snyder family's feelings.[81] They sang a parody of Ozzy Osbourne's "Crazy Train": "Cryin' 'bout your feeeeeelings, / For your sin, no shame! / You're goin' straight to Hell on your crazy train!" Megan Phelps-Roper recalled that at the time she was "delighted in the fact that NBC's camera angle had allowed it to capture one extra piece of the picture: me, standing just behind my mom and Margie, lifting my hand for a high five and laughing with a cousin who promptly indulged me." Displaying a passion and ease unheard in her interaction with the court, Margie crowed, "That's our answer about feelings. Stop worshipping your feelings, and start obeying God!"[82]

* * *

Chief Justice John Roberts loves the First Amendment. In a highly unusual declaration, he told a law school audience, "I don't know where you put conservative or liberal in the First Amendment area, but I think I'm probably the most aggressive defender of the First Amendment on the court now."[83] Whether the chief justice is as stalwart a supporter of First Amendment rights as he claimed is debatable, given that he has written major decisions both granting and denying First Amendment claims.[84] But his statement does certainly demonstrate the degree to which he wants to be perceived as a champion of free speech values and how much he relishes leading the Court in this area.

As chief justice, Roberts gets to assign who writes the majority opinion for every case in which he is part of the winning side. Not surprisingly, he gave himself the honor in *Snyder v. Phelps*.[85] Despite the justices' apparent struggle at oral argument with the facts and devising limits for both sides, the vote was nearly unanimous. The Westboro Baptist Church had prevailed, 8–1, with only Justice Alito dissenting. The majority ruled that the First Amendment protected the church from liability for their speech on a matter of public concern in a public place, which did not disrupt or physically interfere with a funeral.[86]

Roberts's opinion articulating *why* the Court reached this decision, more than the victory of Westboro, was the truly impactful part of this very personal and painful speech battle. "Whether the First Amendment prohibits holding Westboro liable for its speech in this case turns largely on whether that speech is of public or private concern," Roberts began, "as determined by all the circumstances of the case."[87] "The First Amendment reflects 'a profound national commitment to the principle that debate on public issues should be uninhibited, robust, and wide-open,'" he continued, quoting *New York Times Co. v. Sullivan*, "because speech concerning public affairs is more than self-expression; it is the essence of self-government. Accordingly, speech on public issues occupies the highest rung of the hierarchy of First Amendment values, and is entitled to special protection."[88]

In something of an understatement, the chief justice acknowledged that "the boundaries of the public concern test are not well defined," but that the Court had provided "guiding principles . . . that accord broad protection to speech to ensure that courts themselves do not become inadvertent censors."[89] The somewhat vague guidance he then offered is that "speech deals with matters of public concern when it can be fairly considered as relating to any matter of political, social, or other concern to the community, or when it is a subject of legitimate news interest," adding that the "inappropriate or controversial character of a statement is irrelevant."[90]

To determine whether Westboro's speech was "of public or private concern," Roberts examined its content and context.[91] As for the content of the church's signs, he found:

> While these messages may fall short of refined social or political commentary, the issues they highlight—the political and moral conduct of the United States and its citizens, the fate of our Nation, homosexuality in the military, and scandals involving the Catholic clergy—are matters of public import. The signs certainly convey Westboro's position on those issues, in a manner designed . . . to reach as broad a public audience as possible.[92]

Roberts went on to briskly dispose of the idea that having personal messages thrown into the speech mix might potentially tip the balance between speech of a public nature to speech concerning private matters. "Even if a few of the signs—such as 'You're Going to Hell' and 'God Hates You'—were viewed as containing messages related to Matthew Snyder or the Snyders specifically, that would not change the fact that the overall thrust and dominant theme of Westboro's demonstration spoke to broader public issues."[93] The key then is whether the "dominant theme" or main point of the speech is about a matter of public concern. In this way, the majority cuts off the problem of courts having to read every sign at a protest to determine if any isolated personal or targeted messages might enable punishment of the speakers.[94]

Reviewing the "context" of Westboro's speech, Chief Justice Roberts arrived squarely at the funeral issue. He rejected Snyder's argument that "Westboro's speech should be afforded less than full First Amendment protection . . . because the church members exploited the funeral 'as a platform to bring their message to a broader audience.'"[95] Roberts wrote that although the funeral picketing may have caused extraordinary pain, being on the public streets afforded the Westboro members extraordinary First Amendment protections:

> Westboro's choice to convey its views in conjunction with Matthew Snyder's funeral made the expression of those views particularly hurtful to many, especially to Matthew's father. The record makes clear that the applicable legal term—"emotional distress"—fails to capture fully the anguish Westboro's choice added to Mr. Snyder's already incalculable grief. But Westboro conducted its picketing peacefully on matters of public concern at a public place adjacent to a public street. Such space occupies a special position in terms of First Amendment protection.[96]

In other words, the fact that Westboro was picketing essentially on a public street meant that despite being near the funeral, it had located itself squarely in a quintessential "public forum," a place where making space for free speech is traditionally most protected by the Court.[97]

Almost as an aside, the chief justice recognized that even in such a public forum, the state can still impose "reasonable time, place, or manner restrictions" on expressive activity, as long as the laws are "content neutral."[98] (In the First Amendment speech context, "content neutral" means a law that applies the same to all speech no matter what the subject matter or content of the speech may be. For example, a law restricting all demonstrations near a funeral would be content neutral, but a law restricting political demonstrations would not. Content-based laws, particularly those that appear to be based on the state's disagreement with a particular message, are constitutionally suspect, and more likely to be overturned for violating First Amendment protections.)[99] In this case, however, content-neutral restrictions were not at issue, since the damages were imposed entirely because of the content of the message expressed. "Rather than any inference with the funeral itself," Roberts pointed out, "it was what Westboro said that exposed it to [intentional infliction of emotional distress] damages."[100]

For the majority, this punishment of Westboro for the content of their messages was the fatal flaw at the heart of the case. The chief justice reminded us that Westboro's "speech cannot be restricted simply because it is upsetting or arouses contempt."[101] To the contrary, Roberts emphasized, "if there is a bedrock principle underlying the First Amendment, it is that the government may not prohibit the expression of an idea simply because society finds the idea itself offensive or disagreeable. Indeed, the point of all speech protection . . . is to shield just those choices of content that in someone's eyes are misguided, or even hurtful."[102]

Roberts then summed up the reasons why it was necessary to protect the hateful speech of the Westboro Baptist Church, and how those protections are tied to America's free speech path:

Westboro believes that America is morally flawed; many Americans might feel the same about Westboro. Westboro's funeral picketing is certainly hurtful and its contribution to public discourse may be negligible. But Westboro addressed matters of public import on public property, in a peaceful manner, in full compliance with the guidance of local officials. The speech was indeed planned to coincide with Matthew Snyder's funeral, but did not itself disrupt that funeral, and Westboro's choice to conduct its picketing at that time and place did not alter the nature of its speech.

Speech is powerful. It can stir people to action, move them to tears of both joy and sorrow, and—as it did here—inflict great pain. On the facts before us, we cannot react to that pain by punishing the speaker.[103]

And then, the chief justice concluded with his most consequential pronouncement: "As a Nation we have chosen a different course—to protect even hurtful speech on public issues to ensure that we do not stifle public debate."[104]

In these lines, Chief Justice Roberts, the self-described First Amendment advocate, strongly reaffirmed a few fundamental tenets of the Supreme Court's established view of free speech and its role in our society. Robust debate on public issues is a central part of the American experience. Protecting hateful speech is necessary to maintain free debate. Therefore, as a necessary trade-off for the greater good, some will suffer great pain from the speech of others.[105]

Justice Alito, in his solitary dissent, responded contemptuously to all of his fellow justices, and put forth a very different interpretation of what the First Amendment requires.[106] He began by framing the case in the starkest of terms:

> Our profound national commitment to free and open debate is not a license for the vicious verbal assault that occurred in this case. . . . Albert Snyder is not a public figure. He is simply a parent . . . [who] wanted what is surely the right of any parent who experiences such an incalculable loss: to bury his son in peace. But . . . members of the Westboro Baptist Church, deprived him of that elementary right.[107]

Alito then challenged the majority on two points underlying their decision.[108] First, he described why in his view the church went "far beyond commentary on matters of public concern," and in fact had "specifically attacked Matthew Snyder because (1) he was a Catholic and (2) he was a member of the United States military."[109] In his opinion, this "attack on Matthew was of central importance" to Westboro's speech.[110] And Alito contended that even if he were to accept the majority's finding that "'the overall thrust and dominant theme of [their] demonstration spoke to' broad public issues," he did not agree that "actionable speech should be immunized simply because it is interspersed with speech that is protected."[111]

Second, Justice Alito criticized the majority for overvaluing the fact that the picketing occurred on a public street. With an almost mocking tone, he asserted that "there is no reason why a public street in close proximity to the scene of a funeral should be regarded as a free-fire zone in which otherwise actionable verbal attacks are shielded from liability."[112] (In an endnote to the majority opinion, the chief justice addressed this line of the dissent, responding that Alito's suggestion was "wrong": "The fact that Westboro conducted its picketing adjacent to a public street does not insulate the speech from liability, but instead heightens concerns that what is at issue is an effort to communicate to the public the church's views on matters of public concern.")[113]

Alito finished by focusing on the brutality of speech and the feelings of the grieving family members. "In order to have a society in which public issues can be openly and vigorously debated," he insisted, "it is not necessary to allow the brutalization of innocent victims. . . ."[114] With this blistering last line, Justice Alito rejected the majority's conception that for free speech to flourish, hateful speech must be allowed to exist.

* * *

In the wake of Charlottesville, it can be hard to accept the free speech principles that *Snyder v. Phelps* prescribes. Hate speech about matters of public concern, in public places, is entitled to full First Amendment protection.[115] Just as with the Jehovah's Witnesses in *Barnette*, civil rights activists in *Sullivan*, Vietnam War protesters in *Tinker* and *Cohen*, and pornographer in *Hustler*, the Supreme Court has resolved that controversial and objectionable speech should be safeguarded despite how much people may object to the content of that speech. Although today most people would acknowledge that the controversial speech of years past feels either correct or at least acceptable—with Nazis and Westboro both at the irredeemably abhorrent end of the hated-speakers continuum—the Court is committed to a First Amendment theory of government neutrality in order to protect all speech at the time it is threatened.

Even so, it is also important to recognize that the protection of hate speech as a matter of free speech law in no way obligates us as a society to accept the messages of hate or to turn a blind eye to the harm that such words can cause. Responding to the racist and anti-Semitic speech in Charlottesville, civil liberties lawyer Burt Neuborne observed, "I don't quarrel with the president's recognition that people had a right to march." However, he added, "this is a time to distinguish legal rights from moral condemnation."[116]

In addition, the *Snyder* case also reminds us that the government can impose time, place, and manner restrictions on demonstrations for a wide range of content-neutral reasons. For example, a city may constitutionally require protestors on two sides of an issue be separated for public safety (as long as neither side is privileged or disadvantaged because of their viewpoints), require the submission of pre-march plans, and set boundaries on the use of public property.[117] And of course, violence of any kind, including the terrorist car attack that took the life of Heather Heyer, can be prosecuted without any First Amendment restrictions. Case in point, the "avowed neo-Nazi" who killed Heyer was sentenced to life in prison for murder and federal hate crimes.[118]

This is the state of the law on hate speech today, and given the Supreme Court's relatively recent recommitment to these principles, by a broad coalition of liberal and conservative justices, it seems unlikely it will change any time soon. Nevertheless, given the seeming resurgence of neo-Nazism in this country, this approach can be disturbing enough to shake the confidence of even the most stalwart First Amendment adherent. Whether free speech law should evolve to be more concerned about the harm caused by hateful messages, and less protective of free speech for all, is a burning First Amendment question that has no simple answers.[119] The only certainty is that understanding the current shape of the law in this area is essential for either defending or challenging the development of free speech in the next decade and beyond.

* * *

Returning to the combatants in the *Snyder* case, we can see one justification for free speech including hate speech—the ability of raucous debate to change people's minds—play out in very unexpected ways. Megan Phelps-Roper, granddaughter of Westboro founder Fred Phelps, responded to the news of their Supreme Court victory in her typical fashion: she used social media to triumphantly proclaim their church's joy in the face of others' misery. "WE'RE DANCIN IN THE STREET! @ Westboro Baptist," she tweeted, and on Instagram she posted a photo of two women jumping in the air, one holding a sign that said "Destruction Is Imminent," the other with the words "Supreme Court" over an upside-down American flag that had stick figures engaging in symbolic anal sex.[120] Since 2009, Phelps-Roper had become her church's social media spokesperson, saying, "The Lord has given us a new platform."[121] After the Supreme Court decision, Megan ramped up her social media activity even further, as she later described, using "Twitter to bait celebrities with anti-gay messages, to publicly celebrate Japan's Fukushima nuclear disaster, and to debate the merits of the *Snyder* case with anyone who would listen."[122]

And then, "heated but friendly" discussions she had with people on Twitter actually led her to begin to question her faith.[123] One turning point came in an exchange with @Jewlicious, an Israeli Jewish blogger with whom she communicated frequently, when he used New Testament quotations to dispute Westboro's belief in the death penalty for gay people. Megan began to consider, "if the church was wrong" about these issues brought up by her Twitter community, "what else were we wrong about?"[124] It may seem remarkable that there were, as Megan put it, "these individuals who found ways of kindly and effectively challenging [her] beliefs at Westboro," but they did.[125] Her hate speech had brought her in touch with counterspeech. Most of this speech Megan ignored or further fueled her convictions, but "in the midst of that digital brawl," some of it changed her.[126] This change and doubt felt to Megan "like an iron key sliding into the lock of a long-sealed door."[127] In 2012, at the age of twenty-six, she walked out that door and departed the Westboro Baptist Church. She had left most of her family, and their hateful beliefs, behind for good.[128]

Now Megan uses her story to show that it is possible to break through the walls of our increasingly polarized society in which we frequently demonize the other side. "What gives me hope is that we can do something about this," she says in a TED Talk that has been viewed over nine million times. "The good news is that it's simple, and the bad news is that it's hard. We have to talk and listen to people we disagree with."[129]

Free speech, in Megan's view, is at the heart of making this simple and hard approach possible.[130] From her personal experience, she sees the growing popularity of the idea that "refusing to grant mainstream platforms to hated ideas will halt their spread . . . [as] a fundamentally flawed strategy, one that ignores the practicalities of human nature."[131] Instead, she now believes that "the principles enshrined in the First Amendment are no less relevant to social media than they are in public spaces: that open discourse and dialectic is the most effective enabler of the evolution of individuals and societies."[132]

Megan's remarkable transformation mirrors an equally remarkable change of heart experienced by Albert Snyder. After the Supreme

Court ruling, which came the day before the fifth anniversary of Matthew's death, Snyder spoke out at a press conference: "We found out today that we can no longer bury our dead with dignity."[133] To Snyder, the decision meant "anything goes," and as a result there is "nothing stopping Westboro from going to your daughter's wedding."[134] With sadness as well as anger, he said he was "just very disappointed in America today."[135]

When Fred Phelps died in 2014, at the age of eighty-four, Albert still felt angry. "I hate the man," Snyder stated flatly, but he did not wish on Phelps what his family had suffered from Westboro's funeral protest.[136] "I still feel everybody has the right to be buried in peace," he said, "people should just say good riddance."[137] (Perhaps fearing protests, Margie Phelps told a local radio station there would be no funeral for her father.)[138]

Over time, Albert's viewpoint evolved. By 2019, in an interview on the legal podcast *Unprecedented*, Albert expressed different feelings about the Supreme Court and free speech: "My son fought and died for freedom of speech, and I do understand what they did, and I may not have when the decision came down. I remember being very upset, but the reality set in, and I started to reflect on everything. And I realized that the Supreme Court made the right decision, as painful as it was."[139] With that simple statement of acceptance, Albert and Megan—two First Amendment foes—had come to a profound agreement about the meaning of free speech in America. Sometimes the theoretical power of free speech can be realized even in the most trying real-world circumstances.

10 / SOCIAL MEDIA AND THE "VAST DEMOCRATIC FORUMS OF THE INTERNET"

Sacha Baron Cohen, the comedian and actor famous for pranking people on camera as Borat and other fictional characters, walked into the Anti-Defamation League's 2019 summit, and it was no joke. In a scathing speech, he blamed surging hate crimes around the globe on "a handful of internet companies that amount to the greatest propaganda machine in history."[1] Cohen warned that "our pluralistic democracies are on a precipice . . . and the role of social media could be determinant."[2] Pointing the finger at the group he dubbed the "Silicon Six"—the billionaire leaders of Facebook, Google, YouTube, and Twitter—he said,

> it's time for a fundamental rethink of social media and how it spreads hate, conspiracies and lies. Last month, however, Mark Zuckerberg of Facebook delivered a major speech that, not surprisingly, warned against new laws and regulations on companies like his. . . . Zuckerberg tried to portray this whole issue as "choices . . . around free expression." That is ludicrous. This is not about limiting anyone's free speech. This is about giving people, including some of the most reprehensible people on earth, the biggest platform in history to reach a third of the planet. Freedom of speech is not freedom of reach.[3]

Cohen's keynote speech was just one of many high-profile statements decrying the proliferation of hate speech online, and demanding that social media companies remove hate speech more aggressively from their platforms.[4] In Lindy West's feminist memoir, *Shrill*, she describes being "on the receiving end of a viral internet hate mob," including threats to rape and kill her, for having the temerity to suggest "that comedy might have a misogyny problem."[5]

"It's hard to convey the confluence of galloping adrenaline and roaring dread," she wrote of the experience. "It is drowning and falling all at once."[6]

After the release of the female-led remake of the *Ghostbusters* movie, costar and comedian Leslie Jones was subject to hundreds of racist and sexist tweets.[7] Jones took the unusual step of challenging and retweeting the horrid comments that she received, and the abuse that she had been suffering received national news coverage.[8] Twitter CEO Jack Dorsey reached out to Jones, and the company released a statement: "We know many people believe we have not done enough to curb this type of behavior on Twitter. We agree."[9] The admission was a start, but if it takes a savvy movie star and a CEO to deal with such a conspicuous onslaught of hate, what relief could Twitter's regular 300 million users hope for?[10]

Hate speech and personal attacks by online trolls are of course just part of the problems plaguing social media. As David Kaye, the United Nations' special rapporteur on the promotion and protection of the right to freedom of opinion and expression, has observed, "Hatred is spreading through [online platforms] with the help of manufactured amplification; incitement to violence and discrimination seem to flow through their veins; and they have become highly successful and profitable zones for disinformation, election interference, and propaganda."[11] Given that seven in ten adults use social media, the scale and importance of these internet speech issues are undeniable.[12]

In our online lives today, burning questions about social media speech appear before us even faster than we can scroll through our feeds. Can hate speech on social media be restricted? What about the spread of "fake news" posts?[13] Are government officials free to block users from their social media accounts?[14] Although social media hardly seems like cutting-edge technology anymore, the Supreme Court has only very recently even started to address "the relationship between the First Amendment and the modern Internet."[15] To comprehend how we can begin to approach free speech questions involving social media, we need to first ask how the First Amendment applies to restrictions on internet speech. For the Supreme Court, the answer would turn on how much cyberspace is like a public park IRL.[16]

* * *

On April 27, 2010, Lester Gerard Packingham was thrilled to have beaten a traffic ticket, and so he did what many of us do to share our good fortune: he went on Facebook. Packingham posted, "Man God is Good! How about I got so much favor they dismissed the ticket before court even started? No fine, no court cost, no nothing spent... Praise be to GOD, WOW! Thanks JESUS!"[17] Unfortunately for Packingham, around the same time, Officer Brian Schnee of the Durham Police Department was investigating registered sex offenders who were violating a North Carolina law that prohibited them from accessing social media.[18] Officer Schnee saw the traffic ticket statement on Facebook, posted by someone named "J. R. Gerrard." Looking at the profile photo, Schnee thought he recognized the man as a sex offender. So he tracked down the court records of traffic tickets dismissed around the time of the post and came up with Packingham's name. Schnee followed up by obtaining a search warrant for Packingham's home, which turned up the evidence needed to confirm that Packingham had been using Facebook under the alias J. R. Gerrard.[19]

A year later, Packingham was tried for violating North Carolina law, Section 14–202.5, which made it a crime for a registered sex offender "to access a commercial social networking Web site where the sex offender knows that the site permits minor children to become members or to create or maintain personal Web pages."[20] This broadly worded statute meant simply that sex offenders were prohibited from using social media. The purpose of the law was to prevent sex offenders from gathering information about children, in order "to target an unwitting victim . . . under the guise of familiarity or shared interests."[21] Since 2008, the law had applied to about twenty thousand North Carolinians and more than a thousand people had been prosecuted for violating it.[22]

At trial, the basis for Packingham being on the sex offenders' registry was presented to the jury. Nine years before, when Packingham was twenty-one years old, "he had sex with a 13-year-old girl," and pleaded guilty to "taking indecent liberties with a child."[23] Packingham was on supervised probation for two years, and had not had any problems with the law since his conviction.[24] Prosecutors did not claim that he had ever contacted a minor or committed any other illegal acts on the internet.[25] Packingham was found guilty of breaking the law banning sex offenders from accessing social media and sentenced to up to eight months of imprisonment. He did not serve any jail time and was placed on supervised probation.[26]

On appeal, the law was struck down for violating the First Amendment.[27] The Court of Appeals for North Carolina held the law unnecessarily prevented "a wide range of communication and expressive activity unrelated to achieving" the state's legitimate interest in protecting children from sex offenders.[28] The North Carolina Supreme Court disagreed and ruled, 4–2, that law was "constitutional in all respects" and "carefully tailored."[29] North Carolina's highest court also found that the law provided access to websites that served as sufficient alternatives to social media, giving the Paula Deen Network and a local NBC station as (particularly unconvincing) examples.[30]

When the Supreme Court granted review in *Packingham*, it was not clear how eager the justices would be to directly engage with the social media aspects of the case.[31] At oral argument in 2017, however, their questioning quickly made clear that the nature of social media was central to their views about the constitutionality of the speech limits at issue.

At the outset, Chief Justice John Roberts expressed dissatisfaction with the lack of precedent regarding the First Amendment and social media. "We don't have a lot of history here concerning access to websites and all the sort of things we're dealing with here," he said, referring in part to the "broad access to minors" that the internet provides. Packingham's lawyer, David Goldberg, agreed that "as with any manner of new technologies the Court has confronted, there isn't . . . a framing . . . or reconstruction-era analogue." However, he pointed out that "when you talk about all the things that the State historically has restricted, they never said you lose your right to publish a newspaper because you've been convicted" of a crime.[32] Regardless of the technology, Goldberg contended, the wide-ranging amount of speech restricted by the North Carolina law as a post-prison punishment was still historically unprecedented.

Expressing concern about "the safety of children," Justice Ruth Bader Ginsburg wanted to know: "Suppose the law simply said that someone who was a sex offender could not communicate with a minor on social media. Would you agree that that would be constitutional?" Goldberg initially hedged, and only answered that such a law would be "much less restrictive" of First Amendment rights. But Justice Ginsburg insisted on a direct answer from her former law clerk, and Goldberg agreed that "it probably would be."[33] Goldberg's reluctance seemed misplaced, as if he didn't recognize that accepting the limitation presented by Ginsburg would support his case. If there was a less speech-restrictive alternative available to North Carolina that still served the state's goal of protecting children, then the Court would likely find the current law to be overbroad and too restrictive.

After Goldberg reserved the remaining time for his rebuttal argument, Robert C. Montgomery, senior deputy attorney general of North Carolina, stood up before the Court. He spoke for less than a minute before he was interrupted by Justice Elena Kagan. Making the point that being excluded from social media had serious political implications, she asked:

> so a person in this situation, for example, cannot go onto the President's Twitter account to find out what the President is saying today? . . . Not only the President. I mean, we're sort of aware of it because the President now uses Twitter. But in fact, everybody uses Twitter. All 50 governors, all 100 senators, every member of the House has a Twitter account. So this has become a . . . crucially important channel of political communication. And a person couldn't go onto those sites and find out what these members of our government are thinking or saying or doing; is that right?[34]

Montgomery had no choice but to answer, "That's right. However, there are alternatives. Usually those congressmen also have their own web page."[35]

The unsatisfying quality of that alternative lingered only for a moment as Justice Anthony Kennedy built on Kagan's comments. "Well, it seems to me," he began, "assuming we had a public square a hundred years ago, could you say that this person couldn't go into the public square? . . . [T]he sites that Justice Kagan has described and their utility . . . are greater than the communication you could ever had, even in the paradigm of public square."[36] Justice Kennedy's focus here on public squares is referring to the idea that in public spaces (sometimes called "public forums" by the Court), where people can freely gather and talk, freedom of speech should receive the highest level of First Amendment protection.[37]

In response, Montgomery accepted the metaphor, but argued that "in essence, States have said that sex offenders can't go into the public square; that they can't go into parks or they . . . can't go near playgrounds."[38]

Kagan soon spoke up again to touch on the centrality of social media in American life. "50 million Americans use [social media] for religious community purposes," she emphasized. "So whether it's political community, whether it's religious community, I mean, these sites have become embedded in our culture as ways to communicate and ways to exercise our constitutional rights, haven't they?"

Montgomery tried hard to maintain that "there are other alternatives, still. This is a part of the Internet, but it's not the entire Internet that is being taken away from these offenders. They can still have their own blog. They can read blogs. They can do podcasts. They can go to nytimes.com. They can do other things to communicate with people."[39]

Justice Ginsburg had a last issue she wanted to raise that had not been mentioned. "These people are being cut off from a very large part of the marketplace of ideas. And the First Amendment includes not only the right to speak, but the right to receive information," she reminded counsel and her fellow justices. Montgomery could do little other than acknowledge that Packingham and other sex offenders were in fact "being cut off" from this significant right.[40]

After Montgomery sat down, Goldberg said he wished to make a number of points in his remaining four minutes, but Justice Samuel Alito cut him off to challenge the idea of social media as vital to contemporary life. "Now, I know there are people who think that life is not possible without Twitter and Facebook and these things and that 2003 was the dark ages," he remarked sarcastically. But if people got along perfectly well without social media such a relatively short time ago, and some people still do, then Alito wanted to know how taking away these new "channels of communication" could really be such a dramatic limitation on speech. As his time expired, Goldberg responded with a well-defended conclusion:

> So it is an extraordinary argument to say not everybody does it. I don't think that's the test. The test is how much of your core First Amendment activity is foreclosed. And the ability to speak with this networked group of people all over the world is as strong—this is, as Justice Kennedy said, well beyond the traditional town square.

* * *

The vote in favor of Packingham was unanimous. Justice Kennedy, who was known for most of his thirty years on the Supreme Court as both a swing vote and a frequent, if not entirely consistent, defender of First Amendment values, wrote the opinion.[41] It would be one of his last free speech decisions before he retired the next year, and the only Roberts Court case directly engaging with free speech issues related to the internet.[42]

Justice Kennedy began with an expansive look at how social media fits within the core of First Amendment protections. Drawing on the public forum theme raised at oral argument, he wrote:

> A fundamental principle of the First Amendment is that all persons have access to places where they can speak and listen, and then, after reflection, speak and listen once more. The Court has sought to protect the right to speak in this spatial context. A basic rule, for example, is that a street or a park is a quintessential forum for the exercise of First Amendment rights. Even in the modern era, these places are still essential venues for public gatherings to celebrate some views, to protest others, or simply to learn and inquire. While in the past there

may have been difficulty in identifying the most important places (in a spatial sense) for the exchange of views, today the answer is clear. It is cyberspace—the vast democratic forums of the Internet in general, and social media in particular.[43]

Justice Kennedy went on to discuss the prevalence and possibilities of social media. "Social media offers relatively unlimited, low-cost capacity for communication of all kinds," he noted admiringly.[44] Kennedy went on to extoll how "social media users employ these websites to engage in a wide array of protected First Amendment activity on topics as diverse as human thought."[45]

He then urged that the Court tread lightly in this relatively new area of speech and cyberspace. Setting the stage for the decision to come, Kennedy heralded:

> While we now may be coming to the realization that the Cyber Age is a revolution of historic proportions, we cannot appreciate yet its full dimensions and vast potential to alter how we think, express ourselves, and define who we want to be. The forces and directions of the Internet are so new, so protean, and so far reaching that courts must be conscious that what they say today might be obsolete tomorrow. This case is one of the first this Court has taken to address the relationship between the First Amendment and the modern Internet. As a result, the Court must exercise extreme caution before suggesting that the First Amendment provides scant protection for access to vast networks in that medium.[46]

Turning to evaluate the North Carolina statute, Kennedy recognized the serious state interest of protecting "children and other victims of sexual assault from abuse."[47] At the same time, however, he admonished that "the law must not burden substantially more speech than is necessary to further the government's legitimate interests."[48]

Kennedy took pains to note that states could constitutionally "enact specific, narrowly tailored laws that prohibit a sex offender from engaging in conduct that often presages a sexual crime, like contacting a minor or using a website to gather information about a minor."[49] Yet that was not what had occurred here. To the contrary, the Court found the statute at issue was "unprecedented in the scope of First Amendment speech it burdens."[50]

In conclusion, Kennedy described how social media's newly indispensable role in society, when matched with the sweep of the prohibition, was a constitutionally unsustainable combination. He declared:

> By prohibiting sex offenders from using those websites, North Carolina with one broad stroke bars access to what for many are the principal sources for knowing current events, checking ads for employment, speaking and listening in the modern public square, and otherwise exploring the vast realms of human thought and knowledge. These websites can provide perhaps the most powerful mechanisms available to a private citizen to make his or her voice heard. They allow a person with an Internet connection to become a town crier with a voice that resonates farther than it could from any soapbox. In sum, to foreclose access to social media altogether is to prevent the user from engaging in the legitimate exercise of First Amendment rights.[51]

Therefore, the Court agreed that there was no choice but that the "law must be held invalid."[52]

Although there was unanimity as to the judgement that the law violated the First Amendment, there was still disagreement as to the scope of the opinion. Justice Alito wrote a concurring opinion, joined by Chief Justice Roberts and Justice Thomas, that took Kennedy to task for going too far.[53] Troubled by what he called "the implications of the Court's unnecessary rhetoric," Alito scolded the other justices for being "unable to resist musings that seem to equate the entirety of the internet with public streets and parks."[54] He feared that States would consequently be "largely powerless to restrict even the most dangerous sexual predators from visiting any internet sites, including, for example, teenage dating sites and sites designed to permit minors to discuss personal problems with their peers."[55]

The concurring justices also wanted to raise a flag to signal that they were disturbed by Kennedy's overarching approach to internet speech.[56] "The Court is correct that we should be cautious in applying our free speech precedents to the internet. Cyberspace is different from the physical world," and accordingly, Alito warned, "we should proceed circumspectly, taking one step at a time. It is regrettable that the Court has not heeded its own admonition of caution."[57]

* * *

Unlike the other contemporary speech controversies that we have explored, in this area of social media the Supreme Court has not yet provided answers to the questions many Americans have at the beginning of the 2020s. Unfortunately, *Packingham* doesn't tell us what can be done to mitigate the problems created by social media trolls and hate mobs. Sacha Baron Cohen will continue to tear into Mark Zuckerberg, but the Court has remained silent on how to combat Nazi propaganda on Facebook.[58] However, while *Packingham* doesn't contain easy answers, it does provide us with constructive guidance on how to approach these issues within a First Amendment framework.

Before reflecting on the impact of *Packingham*, we need to remember that all social media platforms are private entities and so do not have to abide by the First Amendment. Accordingly, since Facebook, Twitter, and YouTube are not government actors, they can abridge the freedom of speech all they want.[59] They can kick people off their platforms or restrict speech based on its message or refuse to accept ads from whomever they choose.[60] These choices, in fact, represent editorial decisions that reflect the free speech rights of the social media companies themselves.[61] And while this raises its own host of political and social issues (for example, what if Twitter kicks off only right-wing commentors, or Facebook restricts any post supporting Black Lives Matter?), they are not going to be found by courts to be unconstitutional violations of the First Amendment.[62]

It is also imperative to note the fact that social media platforms (along with other internet providers) are immune by federal statute from liability for anything their users post. This blanket protection from liability comes from Section 230 of the Communications Decency Act, enacted in 1996.[63] The Electronic Frontier Foundation, a leading digital rights advocacy organization, has described Section 230 as "the most important law protecting internet speech," arguing that this relatively obscure provision has enabled "the kind of innovation that has allowed the Internet to thrive."[64] As a result, without any foreseeable legal pressure from either lawsuits or constitutional challenges, any major social media reforms will most likely come from somewhere other than the courts.

While furious debates continue about what actions social media companies should take to make their platforms better for their users and society, *Packingham* does provide insights into how the Supreme Court looks on government regulation of social media at this time.[65] *Packingham* at its core shows all of the participating justices unwilling to allow the government to place blanket restrictions on social media. And the majority in *Packingham* views the internet as a vast public forum, like an endless cyber park or town square, and social media like a supercharged combination of a megaphone, printing press, and broadcast channel all in one.[66] Taking this view, longstanding decisions providing heightened protections for free speech in such spaces can apparently be transplanted, without any loss of strength, to the internet era. That means that the Court is likely to look on the constitutionality of any government regulation of social media with extreme skepticism.[67]

Just as notably, *Packingham* highlights both sides of the threshold question of how to consider questions about free speech on the internet. Should these online platforms be conceptualized in what cyberlaw theorists have described as "exceptionalist" or "unexceptionalist" positions?[68] In other words, should social media be treated as unexceptional, and receive the same stringent protections accorded to speech in general? Or is social media somehow so different that it should be treated as exceptional, a type of speech that can be more directly regulated in ways that the press is not.[69] Kennedy's opinion, with its embrace of past metaphors, sees social media as unexceptional. Whereas Alito's concurrence maintains that the internet *is* exceptional in ways that pose greater dangers, and therefore may require more intrusive speech regulations.[70] Terminology aside, this debate demonstrates that how we frame future social media free speech controversies can determine how such questions are decided.

Floyd Abrams, who made his name as the country's preeminent First Amendment litigator before the invention of the internet, has spoken persuasively from an unexceptionalist perspective. He says that while the internet has created powerful new town criers (as Kennedy refers to them in *Packingham*) we cannot deny that "those town criers now include Nazis and child pornographers."[71] And yet he does not believe that such loathsome cyber speakers

> should change our view of the First Amendment. None of the new technological innovations embedded in the Net make anything Justice Holmes said any less true than when he said it. . . . [And] as the threats to Internet freedom mount—as they will—we should keep recalling that the only circumstances in which Holmes' (at least in his later *Abrams*-like) articulations would countenance limitations on speech is when an immediate check is required to save the country, whenever crowded-theater speech would itself cause immediate panic, or the like. So as we go to sleep each night, we could do worse

than to remind ourselves that the ultimate good is better reached by the free trade in ideas than any other way.[72]

Although this view would likely be embraced by a majority of the Supreme Court, it may not suffice to make those of us worrying over the state of social media rest easy.[73] Nevertheless, whether we accept past speech protections as appropriate for the internet or seek to break new ground, it remains essential to understand the free speech rights that the Supreme Court has already established. The future of free speech is certainly online. How we as Americans seek to chart that future can only begin by taking in and learning from our First Amendment stories of the past.

AFTERWORD

When new free speech questions arise in the future, taking stock of what First Amendment rights have already been established will always be a worthwhile starting point. In the preceding chapters, I recounted how ten of these rights have developed and continue to define American society today. My approach to telling these stories has been to focus on brevity and clarity as much as possible. To that end, and going even further, here is a list of the ten cases presented in this book distilled to their essence. As The Clash sing, "Know your rights, these are your rights. . . ."[1]

- Right to Advocate for Illegal Action (Unless It Likely Causes Imminent Harm)
- Right Not to Speak
- Right to Criticize Public Figures and Make Mistakes
- Right to Non-disruptive Protest in School
- Right to Offend
- Right to Publish Without Being Stopped
- No Right to Curse on Broadcast Television and Radio
- Right to Parody
- Right to Espouse Thought We Hate
- Right to Use Social Media as a Public Forum

I hope these bullet points serve as helpful memory triggers for readers' later reference when confronted with free speech challenges of all kinds.

And while knowing your rights is the best first step, applying those rights to uncharted contexts is a greater leap forward. Until now this book has been more descriptive than proscriptive. But as advice for how to consider future free speech controversies, here are my recommended maxims, drawing on the principles behind these rights we have come to know well:

Protect Dissent

Defend the Press

Resist Government Speech Restrictions

Expand the Marketplace of Ideas

Allow Speakers to Express Messages How They Choose

Print them on a T-shirt, tape them up over your bed. Take them to heart, but not for granted. These lines don't encapsulate all of the ideas behind our free speech rights today, but I believe they are uniquely beneficial for guiding us in the years to come.[2]

We also may well need to put these precepts into practice sooner rather than later. Shortly after the end of World War II, George Orwell wrote a cautionary essay, observing that

the relative freedom which we enjoy depends on public opinion. The law is no protection. Governments make laws, but whether they are carried out, and how the police behave, depends on the general temper in the country. If large numbers of people are interested in freedom of speech, there will be freedom of speech, even if the law forbids it; if public opinion is sluggish, inconvenient minorities will be persecuted, even if laws exist to protect them.[3]

Orwell's insights still feel essential and relevant today, as free speech values seem to be on the cusp of change, no matter how steadfast our First Amendment legal protections appear to be.

Having read this book, you can make a difference in shaping public opinion on free speech. You have the knowledge to speak freely with confidence. But even more importantly, you also have the power to engage in debate about legislation and policies that curtail speech or champion it. Although ultimately the Supreme Court will be the final word in determining First Amendment law, the process of getting review by the highest court is long and unlikely. Meanwhile, speech happens on the ground every day—at schools, community boards, houses of worship, city council meetings—and these local places are where an informed citizenry can have the greatest impact. Promoting and protecting free speech is not out of reach, it is an everyday grass roots activity. Because the fight for free speech continues on, and now you can be a part of it too.

ACKNOWLEDGMENTS

The first person, outside of my family, who told me that I should definitely write this book was Nicola Wheir. Her enthusiastic encouragement, wise counsel, and pragmatic guidance enabled me to make this dream a reality. My advice to would-be writers everywhere is to talk to Nicola and follow her advice to the letter—you won't regret it.

To be able to say that I am represented by Carrie Hannigan and Jesseca Salky still strikes me as an incredible stroke of luck. I could not ask for better advocates, and their expert abilities to navigate the publishing world and its mysterious ways are second to none. As an added bonus, they managed to make even the most stressful elements of the process pretty fun.

My editor Clara Platter championed this work from the very beginning. To be included among the authors published by NYU Press is an extraordinary honor, and it would not have been possible without Clara's vision. I am so grateful for her efforts and those of everyone at NYU Press, including Mary Beth Jarrad, Laura Ewan, Megan Madden, Betsy Steve, Martin Coleman, and Dan Geist.

Thanks to the Fair Harbor gang—Tom Jesulaitis, Megan McQuillan, and Adam Riggs—for taking the time and effort to read and thoughtfully comment on my draft.

Thanks also to Townsend Davis, a valued colleague and friend, for listening to me talk about this book over countless lunches and occasional subway rides and always boosting my spirits.

More thanks to: Larry Bercow, Ronald Collins, Mary Karen Dahl, James DeFrancisco, Kevin Fogarty, Katherine Fry, Jason Hill, OVO, Katya Rogers, Steven Shiffrin, Karen Sorensen, Rabbi Joshua Stanton, Angela Tucker, and my Brooklyn College Media and Communication History and Regulation students.

This would not be a legal book without a legal disclaimer. So please note that for all of the help these good people have given me, of course any faults in this book are mine, and all opinions expressed are my own and are not the views of my employer.

Speaking of the law, I want to thank and recognize my legal mentors: Donald Downs, John Siliciano, Marc Fajer, Floyd Abrams, and John Zucker. I have learned so much from you about the law and I would not have been able to have had such a fulfilling career were it not for you.

Thank you to my parents, Richard and Susan Rosenberg. I owe you so much and could write a book of thanks for all the love you have given me and all you have done for me, but here are just a few. Thank you, Dad, for suggesting I write a book about free speech. Thank you, Mom, for teaching me how to read and write. Thank you both for instilling in me a love of books and teaching me that being patriotic and being critical are not mutually exclusive.

I am unbelievably fortunate to have such remarkable children. Thank you, Alice and Leo, for being interested in talking with me about free speech at the dinner table and everywhere else. More importantly, thank you for being yourselves, you inspire me every day.

Lastly, thank you to my wife, Caroline Laskow. At every stage, her suggestions and support made the crucial difference. This book, as with all the best things in my life, would not have been possible without her.

NOTES

Introduction

1   *See* Chauncey Devega, "Historian Timothy Snyder: 'It's Pretty Much Inevitable'
That Trump Will Try to Stage a Coup and Overthrow Democracy," Salon, May 1,
2017, www.salon.com (Snyder says, referring to his brilliant and inspiring short book
On Tyranny: Twenty Lessons from the Twentieth Century, "we have a century of
wisdom and very smart people who confronted situations like our own . . . and that
wisdom can be condensed").

2   This book is limited to exploring the free speech and press clauses of the First
Amendment: "*Congress shall make no law* respecting an establishment of religion, or
prohibiting the free exercise thereof; or *abridging the freedom of speech, or of the press*;
or the right of the people peaceably to assemble, and to petition the government for a
redress of grievances." *See* U.S. Const. amend. I (emphasis added).

3   *See* Frederic William Maitland, "A Prologue to a History of English Law," 14 *Law
Quarterly Review* 13 (1898).

4   *PBS NewsHour*, "Former Supreme Court Justice Souter on the Danger of America's
'Pervasive Civic Ignorance,'" YouTube, September 17, 2012, www.youtube.com.

Chapter 1. The Women's March and the Marketplace of Ideas

1   *See* Anemona Hartocollis and Yamiche Alcindor, "Women's March Highlights as
Huge Crowds Protest Rump: 'We're Not Going Away,'" *New York Times*, January 21,
2017 ("In a sly allusion to the crude remarks Mr. Trump made in the [2005 *Access
Hollywood*] recording, many marchers, men and women alike, wore pink 'pussyhats,'
complete with cat ears"); Colin Dwyer, "Women's March Floods Washington,
Sparking Rallies Worldwide," NPR, January 21, 2017, www.npr.org.

2   *See* Poster House, "20/20 Insight: Posters from the 2017 Women's March," 2019,
www.posterhouse.org.

3 *See* Susan Chira and Yamiche Alcindor, "Defiant Voices Flood U.S. Cities as Women Rally for Rights," *New York Times,* January 21, 2017.

4 *See* Lyndsey Matthews, "Here's the Full Transcript of Angela Davis's Women's March Speech," *Elle,* January 21, 2017.

5 *See* CBS News, "America Ferrera Speaks at Women's March on Washington," YouTube, January 21, 2017, www.youtube.com.

6 *See* CBS News, "Watch: Scarlett Johansson Speaks at Women's March on Washington," YouTube, January 21, 2017, www.youtube.com.

7 *See* Spencer Kornhaber, "How Madonna Gave Trump Ammo with a Cry for Peace," *Atlantic,* January 23, 2017; Associated Press, "Madonna: 'Thought about Blowing Up White House,'" YouTube, January 22, 2017, www.youtube.com.

8 *Id. See also* Lisa Respers France, "Madonna: 'Blowing Up White House' Taken Out of Context," CNN.com, January 23, 2017, www.cnn.com (containing Madonna's Instagram clarification, which includes: "I am not a violent person, I do not promote violence . . . I spoke in metaphor and I shared two ways of looking at things—one was to be hopeful, and one was to feel anger and outrage, which I have personally felt").

9 *See* Chira and Alcindor, "Defiant Voices Flood U.S. Cities."

10 *See* "Newt Gingrich: Madonna Should Be Arrested for Women's March Remarks," *Hollywood Reporter,* January 23, 2017.

11 *See* Richard Polenberg, *Fighting Faiths: The Abrams Case, the Supreme Court, and Free Speech* (Ithaca, NY: Cornell University Press, 1987), 4, 18.

12 *See* Geoffrey R. Stone, *Perilous Times: Free Speech in Wartime* (New York: W. W. Norton & Company, 2004), 203–4; Anthony Lewis, *Make No Law: The Sullivan Case and the First Amendment* (New York: Vintage Books, 1991), 69; Paul Avrich, *Anarchist Portraits* (Princeton, NJ: Princeton University Press, 1988), 214; Polenberg, *Fighting Faiths,* 4, 126.

13 *See* Polenberg, *Fighting Faiths,* 126.

14 Emma Goldman, *Living My Life, Vol. II* (New York: Dover, 1970), 701–2.

15 *See* Polenberg, *Fighting Faiths,* 11, 18; Avrich, *Anarchist Portraits,* 214.

16 *See* Polenberg, *Fighting Faiths,* 18.

17 *Id.*

18 *Id.* at 18–22. For a captivating look at anarchists in fiction, *see* Joan Silver's *Fools* (New York: W. W. Norton & Company, 2013), a collection of linked stories about anarchists and their loved ones, which begins, "A lot of people thought anarchists were fools."

19 *See* Thomas Healy, *The Great Dissent: How Oliver Wendell Holmes Changed His Mind—and Changed the History of Free Speech in America* (New York: Henry Holt, 2013), 169; Polenberg, *Fighting Faiths,* 22–23.

20 *See* Polenberg, *Fighting Faiths,* 23; Abe Bluestein, ed., *Fighters for Anarchism: Mollie Steimer & Senya Fleshin, a Memorial Volume* (Minneapolis: Libertarian Publications Group, 1983), 80 (quoting "With Jack Abrams: Imprisonment and Deportation, a Memoir by Mollie Steimer").

21 *See* Polenberg, *Fighting Faiths*, 22–23.

22 *See* Healy, *The Great Dissent*, 171; Polenberg, *Fighting Faiths*, 42.

23 *See* Polenberg, *Fighting Faiths*, 40–41.

24 *See* Erick Trickey, "The Forgotten Story of the American Troops Who Got Caught Up in the Russian Civil War," *Smithsonian*, February 12, 2019; Healy, *The Great Dissent*, 171; Peter Irons, *A People's History of the Supreme Court* (New York: Penguin, 1999), 277.

25 Polenberg, *Fighting Faiths*, 42 (quoting Steimer leaflet).

26 *See id.* at 49–51.

27 *See id.* at 23.

28 *See* Polenberg, *Fighting Faiths*, 49–50.

29 *Abrams v. United States*, 250 U.S. 616, 621–22 (1919) (quoting passages from the government translation of the Yiddish leaflet).

30 *See* Avrich, *Anarchist Portraits*, 216; Polenberg, *Fighting Faiths*, 66 (Steimer later admitted to police that she had distributed "the leaflets at various locations on the Lower East Side—on Rivington Street, Clinton Street, and East Broadway").

31 *See* "Wilson Attacked in Circulars from Roofs of East Side," *New York Tribune*, August 23, 1918 (accessible at https://chroniclingamerica.loc.gov).

32 *See* Polenberg, *Fighting Faiths*, 43.

33 *See* Avrich, *Anarchist Portraits*, 216.

34 *See* Polenberg, *Fighting Faiths*, 43–46.

35 *Id.* 45–46 (quoting Steimer's letters).

36 *See id.* at 47–48. A friend of Abrams's named Gabriel Prober was also arrested. With unfortunate timing, Prober had stopped by the 104th Street apartment while the police were searching it. He would be charged and tried along with the rest of the group, but acquitted by the jury. *Id.* at 138.

37 *See id.* 61–66.

38 "Seven Taken as Anarchists in N.Y.," *Washington Times*, August 26, 1918 (accessible at https://chroniclingamerica.loc.gov).

39 *Id.*

40 *See* Polenberg, *Fighting Faiths*, 48–49.

41 *See* Healy, *The Great Dissent*, 176; Stone, *Perilous Times*, 191.

42 *See* Stone, *Perilous Times*, 151–53; Polenberg, *Fighting Faiths*, 34.

43 *Abrams*, 250 U.S. at 617. The charges also included an additional count "that the defendants conspired, 'when the United States was at war with the Imperial German Government, unlawfully and willfully, by utterance, writing, printing and publication, to urge, incite and advocate curtailment of production of things and products, to-wit, ordnance and ammunition, necessary and essential to the prosecution of the war.'" *Id.*

44 *See* William H. Rehnquist, *All the Laws but One: Civil Liberties in Wartime* (New York: Alfred A. Knopf, 1998), 183. The Sedition Act was ultimately repealed in 1920. A decade later, FDR would grant amnesty to all those convicted under the acts. *See* Stone, *Perilous Times*, 230–32.

45 *See* Polenberg, *Fighting Faiths*, 88.

46 "Girl Anarchist Defies the Court to Air Her Philosophy," *New York Tribune*, October 23, 1918 (accessible at https://chroniclingamerica.loc.gov).

47 *See* Polenberg, *Fighting Faiths*, 89.

48 *See* Healy, *The Great Dissent*, 177; Stone, *Perilous Times*, 205; Polenberg, *Fighting Faiths*, 96–101. *See also* "Free Speech Does Not Protect Disloyalty," *New York Times*, September 13, 1918 ("Judge Clayton added that when in Congress he had voted to restrict immigration and that he was now satisfied that he voted right on that question").

49 Polenberg, *Fighting Faiths*, 76 (quoting Weinberger).

50 *Id.* at 107 (quoting Clayton). Blatant anti-Semitism was also present on the United States Supreme Court at the time. Justice James McReynolds would leave the room when Justice Brandeis, the Court's first Jewish justice, would speak in conferences. He also once wrote to Justice Holmes, on a draft dissent joined by Holmes and Brandeis, "Did you ever think that for four thousand years the Lord tried to make something out of Hebrews, then gave it up as impossible and turned them out to prey on mankind in general—like fleas on the dog for example." *See* Stephen Budiansky, *Oliver Wendell Holmes: A Life in War, Law, and Ideas* (New York: W. W. Norton & Company, 2019), 360–61.

51 Polenberg, *Fighting Faiths*, 121 (quoting Clayton).

52 *Id.* at 118.

53 *See id.* at 127.

54 Avrich, *Anarchist Portraits*, 218 (quoting Steimer).

55 *See* Polenberg, *Fighting Faiths*, 132.

56 *See id.* at 133.

57 *Id.* (quoting Weinberger). Judge Clayton made clear at the defendants' arrangement that he had no interest in Steimer's free speech claims: "'What you term free speech does not protect disloyalty. I am sorry for the people of New York that have to deal with individuals who have no more conception of what free government means than a billy goat has of the gospel.'" *See* "Free Speech Does Not Protect Disloyalty," *New York Times*, September 13, 1918.

58 *See* Polenberg, *Fighting Faiths*, 138.

59 Heywood Broun, "Act Three—The Courtroom," *New York Tribune*, October 27, 1918 (accessible at https://chroniclingamerica.loc.gov).

60 *See* Polenberg, *Fighting Faiths*, 145.

61 *Id.*

62 Broun, "Act Three—The Courtroom" (quoting Clayton).

63 *Id.* (quoting Steimer).

64 Polenberg, *Fighting Faiths*, 228 (quoting Weinberger).

65 *Id.* at 229.

66 *See Abrams*, 250 U.S. at 619–21.

67 *See* Healy, *The Great Dissent*, 188.

68 Polenberg, *Fighting Faiths*, 229 (quoting Weinberger).

69 *See* United States Department of Justice, "Robert P. Stewart," April 12, 2016, www. justice.gov.

70 *See* Healy, *The Great Dissent*, 190; Polenberg, *Fighting Faiths*, 233.

71 Healy, *The Great Dissent*, 190 (quoting Stewart's brief).

72 Stone, *Perilous Times*, 192.

73 *See Schenck v. United States*, 249 U.S. 47, 48–49 (1919).

74 *Id.* at 49–51.

75 *Id.* at 50.

76 *Id.* at 51–53. *See* Ronald K. L. Collins and Sam Chaltain, *We Must Not Be Afraid to Be Free: Stories of Free Expression in America* (New York: Oxford University Press, 2011), 109 (noting Charles Schenck's ten-year sentence). Some legal terms used throughout this book will be defined in these notes. Legal definition of "affirm": when an appellate court affirms a case, it agrees with the results reached by the court below and upholds the decision.

77 *See* Healy, *The Great Dissent*, 1; Stone, *Perilous Times*, 199–200; Andy Bowers, "What's a Boston Brahmin?," Slate, March 1, 2004, www.slate.com; G. Edward White, "Oliver Wendell Holmes, Jr.," in *The Supreme Court Justices: Biographical Dictionary*, edited by Melvin I. Urofsky (New York: Garland Publishing, 1994), 225; Polenberg, *Fighting Faiths*, 208.

78 Healy, *The Great Dissent*, 12 (quoting Holmes in connection with his support of America's involvement in World War I).

79 *Schenck*, 249 U.S. at 52 (internal citation omitted). Holmes said in 1912 that his goal as a justice was "to put as many new ideas into the law as I can, to show how particular solutions involve general theory, and to do it with style." *See* White, *The Supreme Court Justices*, 234.

80 Trevor Timm, "It's Time to Stop Using the 'Fire in a Crowded Theater' Quote," *Atlantic*, November 2, 2012.

81 For the continuing popularity, and misunderstanding, of the metaphor, *see* Eugene Volokh, "Shouting Fire in a Crowded Theater," *Washington Post*, May 11, 2015; Timm, "It's Time to Stop."

82 In *Schenck*, Holmes also introduced his "clear and present danger" test. *See Schenck*, 249 U.S. at 52 ("The question in every case is whether the words used are used in such circumstances and are of such a nature as to create a clear and present danger that they will bring about the substantive evils that Congress has a right to prevent. It is a question of proximity and degree"). Holmes's refinement of this test in *Abrams* will be discussed in note 93 below.

83 *See Frohwerk v. United States*, 249 U.S. 204, 205 (1919) (affirming conviction of German-language newspaper publisher for anti-draft articles attempting "to cause disloyalty" in the armed forces; *Debs v. United States*, 249 U.S. 211 (1919). In *Debs*, the Supreme Court affirmed the conviction of Eugene Debs, the leader of the Socialist Party and a presidential candidate, for a speech before a crowd of over one thousand

people, supporting the rights of others to protest the war and the draft. Debs was sentenced to ten years in prison, from which, in 1920, he ran for president, receiving over nine hundred thousand votes! In 1921, his sentence was commuted by the man who beat him, President Harding. *See* Terence McArdle, "The Socialist Who Ran for President From Prison—and Won Nearly a Million Votes," *Washington Post*, September 22, 2019; Stone, *Perilous Times*, 196–98, 232.

84　For more on the unlikely intellectual and personal friendship of Holmes and Brandeis, *see* Budiansky, *Oliver Wendell Holmes*, 357; Healy, *The Great Dissent*, 69–70; David M. Rabban, *Free Speech in Its Forgotten Years* (Cambridge, UK: Cambridge University Press, 1997), 356–57 ("As one of Holmes's law clerks summed up the difference between the two Justices, 'Brandeis felt sympathy for the oppressed, Holmes contempt for the oppressor'").

85　Healy, *The Great Dissent*, 198.

86　*Id.* at 203, 211 (quoting Holmes's November 1, 1919, letter to Frankfurter). Legal definitions of "majority," "concurring," and "dissenting" opinions: a majority opinion is the decision of an appellate court joined by more than half the members of the court reviewing that case. A concurring opinion is written by one of the members of the court who agrees with the majority on the result of the decision, but wants to express a different reason for reaching that decision. A dissenting opinion is written by a member of the court that explicitly disagrees with both the result and the reasons of the majority opinion. A dissenting opinion is not binding precedent, but can be influential in future cases and draw public attention to the issues discussed.

87　*See* Healy, *The Great Dissent*, 1.

88　*Id.* at 5. The men that called on Holmes were Justice Willis Van Devanter, Justice Mahlon Pitney, and a third, unknown justice. *See also id.* at 213–14.

89　*See Abrams*, 250 U.S. at 631. Brandeis would later advance the spirit of Holmes's dissent in *Abrams* with his own landmark concurrence in *Whitney v. California*. Brandeis wrote, in a perpetually repeated line: "If there be time to expose through discussion the falsehood and fallacies, to avert the evil by the processes of education, the remedy to be applied is more speech, not enforced silence." 274 U.S. 357, 377 (1927).

90　*Abrams*, 250 U.S. at 618–19.

91　*Id.* at 621.

92　*See* Healy, *The Great Dissent*, 217. It is unusual for Supreme Court justices to read their dissents from the bench, and doing so is intended to demonstrate that, as Justice Ginsburg has said, "in the dissenters' view, the Court's opinion is not just wrong, but grievously misguided." Ruth Bader Ginsburg, "The Role of Dissenting Opinions," 95 *Minnesota Law Review* 1, 2 (2010).

93　*Abrams*, 250 U.S. at 628 (emphasis added). Much academic writing about *Abrams* focuses on the changing nature of the "clear and present" danger test. *See, e.g.*, Collins and Chaltain, *We Must Not Be Afraid to Be Free*, 107–33; Stone, *Perilous Times*, 192–211. In contrast to the formulation in *Schenck*, the test in *Abrams* added a requirement that the danger not just be clear and present, but also "immediate" or "imminent," thereby making it more speech protective. *See Abrams*, 250 U.S. at 627. For the ultimate development of a version of this test in *Brandenburg v. Ohio*, 395 U.S. 444 (1969), *see* note 115 below.

94 *Abrams*, 250 U.S. at 628.

95 *Id*. at 629.

96 *Id*.

97 *Id*. at 630–31.

98 Vincent A. Blasi, "Rights Skepticism and Majority Rule at the Birth of the Modern First Amendment," in *The Free Speech Century*, edited by Lee C. Bollinger and Geoffrey R. Stone (New York: Oxford University Press, 2019), 21; *see also* Melvin I. Urofsky, *Dissent and the Supreme Court: Its Role in the Court's History and the Nation's Constitutional Dialogue* (New York: Vintage Books, 2015), 169–71 (cataloging forty-one Supreme Court opinions citing Holmes's dissent in *Abrams*, between 1941 to 2011).

99 *See, e.g.*, Collins and Chaltain, *We Must Not Be Afraid to Be Free*, 111 ("A signpost in the history of the First Amendment had been erected—the two greatest jurists then sitting on the court had broken ranks and urged a far more liberal approach to resolving free-speech claims in time of war"); Lewis, *Make No Law*, 80 ("The Supreme Court's recognition of freedom of expression as a paramount constitutional value began with Justice Holmes's dissent in *Abrams v. United States*").

100 *See* Bollinger and Stone, eds., *The Free Speech Century*, 5 (Stone in "Dialogue," preface: "One thing the Court came to understand is that the First Amendment forbids government officials from suppressing particular ideas because they don't want citizens to accept those ideas in the political process. This principle, which was first clearly stated in the Supreme Court in Justice Holmes' dissenting opinion in *Abrams*, is central to contemporary First Amendment doctrine").

101 *But see* Steven H. Shiffrin, *The First Amendment, Democracy, and Romance* (Princeton, NJ: Princeton University Press, 1990), 95 ("If the marketplace metaphor counsels us that the market's version of truth is more worthy of trust than any that the government might dictate, a commitment to sponsoring dissent counsels us to be suspicious of both").

102 Ginsburg, "The Role of Dissenting Opinions," 4 (quoting Chief Justice Charles Hughes).

103 Urofsky, *Dissent and the Supreme Court*, 426 (quoting Tushnet).

104 *See* Healy, *The Great Dissent*, 207 (Holmes "was not claiming that . . . free speech magically produces an objective and verifiable truth via the mechanism of the invisible hand. . . . He was drawing a picture to help us see the way in which free and open debate promotes the ultimate good even if there are short-term costs").

105 *See* Collins and Chaltain, *We Must Not Be Afraid to Be Free*, 43–44 ("This market-place of ideas theory of the First Amendment sees the Madisonian guaranty as a mechanism not so much for necessarily securing truth as for testing the truthfulness of various positions").

106 This astute and convincing idea was suggested to me by Jamaal Orr, one of my outstanding Brooklyn College graduate students, during a discussion in my Media and Communication History and Regulation class in spring 2018.

107 Charles R. Lawrence III, "If He Hollers Let Him Go: Regulating Racist Speech on Campus," 1990 *Duke Law Journal* 431, 481 (1990).

108 Catherine A. MacKinnon, *Feminism Unmodified: Discourses on Life and Law* (Cambridge, MA: Harvard University Press, 1987), 209–10. *See also* MacKinnon, "The First Amendment: An Equality Reading," in *The Free Speech Century*, ed. Bollinger and Stone, 160–61 ("the tired canard that truth will triumph in the marketplace, so nothing that can be considered expression should be restricted, was well addressed by John Stuart Mill in a less commonly quoted passage in *On Liberty*: 'It is a piece of idle sentimentality that truth, merely as truth, has any inherent power denied to error of prevailing against the dungeon and the stake'").

109 *See* Laurence H. Tribe, *American Constitutional Law* (2d ed.) (Mineola, NY: Foundation Press, 1988), 786 ("Especially when the wealthy have more access to the most potent media of communication than the poor, how sure can we be that 'free trade in ideas' is likely to generate truth?").

110 Megan McArdle, "We Finally Know for Sure That Lies Spread Faster than the Truth. This Might Be Why," *Washington Post*, March 14, 2018 (quoting Twain and citing MIT researchers who found, "It took the truth about six times as long as falsehood to reach 1,500 people").

111 *See* Sacha Baron Cohen, "The 'Silicon Six' Spread Propaganda. It's Time to Regulate Social Media Sites," *Washington Post*, November 25, 2019.

112 *See, e.g.*, Budiansky, *Oliver Wendell Holmes* ("Lawyers, scholars, and judges have devoted hundreds of thousands of pages of arguments to disputing the technicalities and legal doctrines of Holmes's free speech jurisprudence, but as the legal scholar Ronald K. L. Collins noted, this is 'lawyers' stuff' that misses the monumental consequentiality of what Holmes did. . . . 'Free speech in America,' Collins concluded, 'was never the same after 1919'"); Jason Stanley, *How Fascism Works: The Politics of Us and Them* (New York: Random House, 2018), 68–69 ("The argument for the 'marketplace of ideas' model for free speech works only if the underlying disposition of the society is to accept the force of reason over the power of irrational resentments and prejudice. If society is divided, however, then a demagogic politician can exploit the division by using language to sow fear, accentuate prejudice, and call for revenge against members of hated groups. Attempting to counter such rhetoric with reason is akin to using a pamphlet against a pistol").

113 *See Stromberg v. California*, 283 U.S. 359 (1931) (California statute prohibiting the flying of a red flag "as a sign, symbol or emblem of opposition to organized government" is held to be an unconstitutional limit on free speech).

114 *Brandenburg v. Ohio*, 395 U.S. 444, 447 (1969). In *Brandenburg*, a Ku Klux Klan leader was convicted under an Ohio criminal syndicalism statute for giving a racist and anti-Semitic speech at a rally. The Supreme Court held that since the statute

punishes "mere advocacy" (and not "incitement to imminent lawless action") it violated the First Amendment. *Id.* at 444–49.

115 *See* Stone, *Perilous Times*, 522 (in *Brandenburg*, "not only did the Court invalidate the Ohio law, but exactly fifty years after *Schenck*, the Supreme Court finally and unambiguously embraced the Holmes-Brandeis" approach); Irons, *A People's History*, 280 ("The Court adopted this [*Abrams* dissent] test exactly fifty years later in 1969, ruling in *Brandenburg v. Ohio* that only speech 'directed to inciting or producing imminent lawless action' could be punished"). The Supreme Court's decision in *Holder v. Humanitarian Law Project*, 561 U.S. 1 (2010), which upheld the federal statutory prohibition of nonviolent, lawful speech that provided "material support" to designated "foreign terrorist organizations," led the counsel for the defendants to write that the decision "calls into question the continuing validity of the *Brandenburg* incitement test." David Cole, "The First Amendment's Borders: The Place of *Holder v. Humanitarian Law* Project in First Amendment Doctrine," 6 *Harvard Law & Policy Review* 147, 148–49 (2012).

116 Healy, *The Great Dissent*, 79–81 (quoting Oliver Wendell Holmes, Jr., *The Common Law* [Boston: Little, Brown, and Company, 1881], 1).

117 *See* Polenberg, *Fighting Faiths*, 285. Abrams and Lipman tried to jump bail, but were captured in New Orleans, while attempting to flee to Russia. *Id.* at 242–48.

118 *Id.* at 339 (quoting Harding's attorney general, Harry Daugherty).

119 *See* Bluestein, *Fighters for Anarchism*, 28 (quoting a statement by Steimer in the documentary film *Anarchism in America*).

120 *Id.; see* "Girl Won't Accept Deportation Offer: Mollie Steimer, Russian Anarchist, May Have Prison Term Cut if She Will Agree," *New York Times*, July 15, 1921.

121 *See* Polenberg, *Fighting Faiths*, 341.

122 *See id.* at 341–42; "Freed Radicals Off to Russian Exile: Mollie Steimer and Her Three Associates Sail Hoping for Government's Overthrow," *New York Times*, November 24, 1921 (quoting Steimer).

123 *See* Polenberg, *Fighting Faiths*, 352–56.

124 *See id.* at 358–59, 362.

125 *See id.* at 353, 363.

126 *See id.* at 357–62.

127 *See* Avrich, *Anarchist Portraits*, 214, 225–26.

128 Irons, *A People's History*, 281 (quoting Steimer's writing from 1960).

Chapter 2. Take a Knee and the Pledge of Allegiance

1 *See* Mark Sandritter, "A Timeline of Colin Kaepernick's National Anthem Protest and the Athletes Who Joined Him," SB Nation, September 25, 2017, www.sbnation.com; John Branch, "The Awakening of Colin Kaepernick," *New York Times*, September 7, 2017.

2 *See id.;* Jennifer Lee Chan, "Colin Kaepernick Did Not Stand during the National Anthem," Niners Nation, August 27, 2016, www.ninersnation.com.

3   Steve Wyche, "Colin Kaepernick Explains Why He Sat during National Anthem," NFL.com, August 27, 2016, www.nfl.com.
4   *Id.*
5   *Id.*
6   Chris Biderman, "Transcript: Colin Kaepernick Addresses Sitting during National Anthem," Niners Wire, August 28, 2016, www.ninerswire.usatoday.com.
7   *See* Branch, "The Awakening."
8   *See* "Two Police Shootings, Two Videos, Two Black Men Dead," CNN.com, July 7, 2016, www.cnn.com; Leah Donnella, "Two Days, Two Deaths: The Police Shootings of Alton Sterling and Philando Castile," NPR Code Switch, July 7, 2016, www.npr. org; *see also* Colin Kaepernick (@Kaepernick7), Instagram, July 6, 2016 and July 7, 2016, www.instagram.com (posting video of Sterling's death—"This is what lynchings look like in 2016! Another murder in the streets because the color of a man's skin, at the hands of the people who they say will protect us"—and of Castile's death: "We are under attack! It's clear as day! Less than 24 hrs later another body in the street!").
9   Biderman, "Transcript: Colin Kaepernick."
10 *Id.*
11 Nate Boyer, "An Open Letter to Colin Kaepernick, from a Green Beret-Turned-Long Snapper," *Army Times*, August 30, 2016.
12 *Id.*
13 *See* Nick Wagoner, "From a Seat to a Knee: How Colin Kaepernick and Nate Boyer Are Trying to Effect Change," ESPN.com, September 6, 2016, www.espn.com.
14 *See id.*
15 *See* Eric Reid, "Why Colin Kaepernick and I Decided to Take a Knee" (op-ed), *New York Times*, September 25, 2017.
16 Wagoner, "From a Seat to a Knee."
17 *See* Sandritter, "A Timeline."
18 The history of the national anthem is intimately entwined with the dual themes of racism and sports. *See* Brent Staples, "Strains of the National Anthem," *New York Times*, June 9, 2018 (discussing the complicated relationship between African Americans and the anthem, as well as its creation by a "slave-owning Washington lawyer," and its "long suppressed third stanza ('No refuge could save the hireling and slave/From the terror of flight or the gloom of the grave') that can be read as reflecting the composer's embrace of slavery and the anger felt toward the British officers who used the promise of emancipation to recruit enslaved African-Americans"); Luke Cyphers and Ethan Trex, "The Song Remains the Same," ESPN.com, September 8, 2011, www.espn.com ("Congress didn't officially adopt 'The Star-Spangled Banner' until 1931—and by that time it was already a baseball tradition steeped in wartime patriotism").
19 Tony Drovetto, "Seahawks Cornerback Jeremy Lane Sits Down during National Anthem," Seahawks.com, September 1, 2016, www.seahawks.com.

20 Euan McKirdy, "USWNT Star Megan Rapinoe Takes Knee in Solidarity with Kaepernick," CNN.com, September 5, 2016, www.cnn.com.

21 *See* John Breech, "Second Sponsor Dumps Broncos' Marshall following Anthem Protest," CBS Sports, September 12, 2016, www.cbssports.com.

22 *See* James Dator, "Chiefs' Marcus Peters Raises Fist during National Anthem," SB Nation, September 11, 2016, www.sbnation.com; Adam Stites, "Seahawks Players Link Arms during National Anthem instead of Kneeling," SB Nation, September 11, 2016, www.sbnation.com.

23 *See* Jonah Engel Bromwich, "Entire Indian Fever Team Kneels during Anthem before Playoff Game," *New York Times*, September 21, 2016.

24 *See* Associated Press, "Colin Kaepernick Opts Out of Contract, Becomes Free Agent," ESPN.com, March 3, 2017, www.espn.com. To this day, no team in the NFL has been willing to hire him, despite his proven abilities as a football player. *See* Colin Kaepernick (@Kaepernick7), "5am. 5 days a week. For 3 years. Still Ready," Instagram, August 7, 2019, www.instagram.com (video ends with a graphic that shows "DENIED WORK FOR 889 DAYS"); Reid, "Why Colin Kaepernick" ("Anybody who has a basic knowledge of football knows that his unemployment has nothing to do with his performance on the field"); Kyle Wagner, "Colin Kaepernick Is Not Supposed to Be Unemployed," FiveThirtyEight, August 9, 2017, www. fivethirtyeight.com (using statistics to show that "it's practically unheard of" for a quarterback of his caliber to remained unsigned so long into his free agency).

25 Jill Martin, "Michael Bennett: 'I Can't Stand for the National Anthem,'" CNN.com, August 17, 2017, www.cnn.com.

26 Michael Bennett and Dave Zirin, *Things That Make White People Uncomfortable* (Chicago: Haymarket Books, 2019), xviii.

27 Although some described Trump's remarks as "stream of consciousness" (*e.g.*, Ben Jacobs, "Kim Jong-un, the NFL and 'Screaming at Senators': Trump's Strange Night in Alabama," *Guardian*, September 23, 2017), many commentators found them intentionally calculated. *See* Howard Bryant, *The Heritage: Black Athletes, a Divided America, and the Politics of Patriotism* (Boston: Beacon Press, 2018), xi ("With the opportunistic demagoguery that won him the presidency, Donald Trump engaged in a twenty-first-century version of McCarthyism"); "The N.F.L. Kneels to Trump" (editorial), *New York Times*, May 23, 2018 ("The president, smelling an issue sure to fire up his base, pounced").

28 *See* Ian Schwartz, "Trump: NFL Owners Should Fire the 'Son of a Bitch' Player Who 'Disrespects Our Flag' by Kneeling," RealClearPolitics, September 23, 2017, www. realclearpolitics.com.

29 *Id.*

30 Associated Press, "First-Time NFL Protesters Explain How They Became Woke," *U.S. News & World Report*, September 26, 2017.

31 See Associated Press, "More than 200 NFL Players Sit or Kneel during Anthem," *USA Today*, September 24, 2017 (including summary breakdown at each game).

32 *See* "The Latest: More than 200 NFL Players Don't Stand for Anthem," Associated Press, September 24, 2017, www.apnews.com.

33 Arnie Stapleton, "More than 200 NFL Players Sit or Kneel during National Anthem," *Chicago Tribune*, September 24, 2017; *see also* Emma Baccellieri, "Seth DeValve Is the First White Player to Kneel for the National Anthem," Deadspin, August 21, 2017, www.deadspin.com (including video interview with DeValve, who said, "We wanted to draw attention to the fact that there's things in this country that still need to change, and I myself will be raising children that don't look like me [DeValve's wife is Black] and I want to do my part as well to do everything I can to raise them in a better environment than we have right now"); Erica Harris DeValve, "I'm Proud of My Husband for Kneeling during the Anthem, but Don't Make Him a White Savior," The Root, August 24, 2017, www.verysmartbrothas.theroot.com ("To center the focus of Monday's demonstration solely on Seth is to distract from what our real focus should be: listening to the experiences and the voices of the black people who are using their platforms to continue to bring the issue of racism in the U.S. to the forefront").

34 Bryant, *The Heritage*, 13. *See also* Shaun R. Harper, "There Would Be No NFL without Black Players. They Can Resist the Anthem Policy," *Washington Post* (Perspective), May 24, 2018 ("According to data from the Institute for Diversity and Ethics in Sport, 94 percent of NFL franchise owners and 75 percent of head coaches are white. NFL Commissioner Roger Goodell and most of the league's top executives are white. . . . Yet 70 percent of NFL players are black").

35 *See* ESPN.com News Services, "QB Colin Kaepernick Files Grievance for Collusion against NFL Owners," October 16, 2017, www.espn.com. Legal definition of "grievance": a grievance is an employee's formal complaint regarding an alleged violation of a union agreement, which provides a procedure for reviewing and resolving that complaint.

36 *Id.*

37 Geragos & Geragos, "Claimant Colin Kaepernick's Demand for Arbitration," ESPN. com, October 15, 2017, page 2, www.espn.com.

38 Associated Press, "Colin Kaepernick Files Grievance against NFL, Alleging Collusion," *Los Angeles Times*, October 16, 2017.

39 *Id.*

40 *See* Tom Lutz, "Anthem Protester Eric Reid Files Grievance Alleging He Is Being Kept Out of NFL," *Guardian*, May 2, 2018; A. J. Perez, "Free-Agent Safety Eric Reid Files Grievance against NFL, Claiming Collusion," *USA Today*, May 2, 2018.

41 Ken Belson, "Colin Kaepernick's Collusion Case against the N.F.L. Will Advance," *New York Times*, August 30, 2018; *see* Chris Chavez, "Roger Goodell Deposed in Colin Kaepernick Collusion Case, QB Sat through the Hearing," *Sports Illustrated*, April 17, 2018.

42 *See* Tom E. Curran, "NFL Teams Being on the Field for Anthem Is a Relatively New Practice," NBC Sports, August 29, 2016, www.nbcsports.com.

43 Daniel Roberts, "There's No 'NFL Rule' That Players Must Stand for the Anthem—
but There's a 'Policy,'" Yahoo Finance, September 29, 2017 www.finance.yahoo.com
(quoting NFL game operations manual, emphasis added). *See also* Alex Fitzpatrick,
"Does the NFL Require Players to Stand for the National Anthem," *Time*, September
25, 2017.

44 National Football League, "Roger Goodell's Statement on National Anthem Policy,"
May 23, 2018, www.NFL.com.

45 *See* John Fritze and Gregory Korte, "Trump Praises NFL's Anthem Policy, Says
Protesters Maybe 'Shouldn't Be in the Country,'" *USA Today*, May 24, 2018.

46 *See* Jeff Darlington, "NFL, NFLPA Announce 'Standstill' on Anthem Rules after
Dolphins Report," ESPN.com, July 20, 2018, www.espn.com; Austin Knoblauch,
"NFL Anthem Policy On Hold under Standstill Agreement," NFL.com, July 19, 2018,
www.NFL.com. *See also* Scott Chiusano, "Dolphins Policy on Anthem Punishment
Includes Team-Issued Suspensions Up to Four Games," *Daily News*, July 19, 2018
(comparing four-game suspension to lesser punishments issued for two NFL players
accused of sexual assault and repeated domestic violence).

47 *See* Jacob Bogage, "A Trump Fundraiser Could Be the Latest Flashpoint between
NFL Players and Owners," *Washington Post*, August 7, 2019 (noting indefinite
suspension); Sarah Friedmann, "The Super Bowl 2019 Kneeling Policy Leaves That
Decision Up to Players," Bustle, February 2, 2019, www.bustle.com ("Presently, the
anthem policy remains suspended and therefore not intact for the 2019 Super Bowl").

48 Malcolm Jenkins (@MalcolmJenkins), "#TheFightContinues," Twitter, May 23,
2018, www.twitter.com.

49 Eli Rosenberg, "What the NFL's New Rules for Anthem Protests Really Mean for the
First Amendment, According to Experts," *Washington Post*, May 24, 2018. *But see*
Marc Edelman, "Standing to Kneel: Analyzing NFL Players' Freedom to Protest
during the Playing of the U.S. National Anthem," 86 *Fordham Law Review Online* 1,
9–10 (2017) (arguing theoretically that "President Trump's threat to strip 'massive
tax breaks' from team owners who allow players to protest the anthem serves as a
form of" state action sufficient to constitute a violation of players' First Amendment
rights).

50 *See* Vincent Blasi and Seana V. Shiffrin, "The Story of *West Virginia State Board of
Education v. Barnette*: The Pledge of Allegiance and the Freedom of Thought," in
First Amendment Stories, edited by Richard W. Garnett and Andrew Koppelman
(New York: Foundation Press, 2012), 104–5.

51 *See* Peter Irons, *The Courage of Their Convictions* (New York: Free Press, 1988), 25
(interview with Lillian Gobitas).

52 *See* Winston Bowman, "The Flag Salute Cases," Federal Judicial Center, 2017,
www.fjc.gov, 5; Irons, *The Courage of Their Convictions*, 15.

53 Shawn Francis Peters, *Judging Jehovah's Witnesses: Religious Persecution and the Dawn
of the Rights Revolution* (Lawrence: University Press of Kansas, 2000), 27 (quoting
Rutherford's radio speech).

54 *Id.*

55 Irons, *The Courage of Their Convictions,* 26.

56 Peters, *Judging Jehovah's Witnesses,* 27.

57 Irons, *The Courage of Their Convictions,* 26–27.

58 Peters, *Judging Jehovah's Witnesses,* 38.

59 *Id.*

60 Billy Gobitas to Minersville, Pennsylvania, School Directors, November 5 1935, Manuscript Division, Library of Congress, www.loc.gov.

61 Peters, *Judging Jehovah's Witnesses,* 37–38.

62 Leonard A. Stevens, *Salute! The Case of the Bible vs. the Flag* (New York: Coward, McCann & Geoghegan, 1973), 34.

63 *See* Richard J. Ellis, *To the Flag: The Unlikely History of the Pledge of Allegiance* (Lawrence: University Press of Kansas, 2005), 99; Peters, *Judging Jehovah's Witnesses,* 42–43.

64 *See* Ellis, *To the Flag,* 93 (citing ACLU's count of expulsions). *See also* Blasi and Shiffrin, "The Story of *West Virginia State Board of Education,*" 103 (noting prior flag salute protests, such as a 1916 incident involving "an eleven-year-old African-American student named Hubert Eaves [who] refused to salute the flag because of its association with racial discrimination and lynching").

65 Peters, *Judging Jehovah's Witnesses,* 38; *see* Blasi and Shiffrin, "The Story of *West Virginia State Board of Education,*" 105.

66 *See* Bowman, "The Flag Salute Cases," 5, 67–68; Blasi and Shiffrin, "The Story of *West Virginia State Board of Education,*" 105; Peters, *Judging Jehovah's Witnesses,* 42–44; Irons, *The Courage of Their Convictions,* 28.

67 Bowman, "The Flag Salute Cases," 54 (quoting Roudabush's testimony in excerpt from the original trial record); *see* Ellis, *To the Flag,* 101 (Roudabush as the only witness for the defense). Legal definition of "bench trial": a bench trial is one without a jury, in which the judge is the final decision maker.

68 Bowman, "The Flag Salute Cases," 55, 57.

69 *Id.* at 60.

70 *Gobitis v. Minersville School Dist.,* 24 F. Supp. 271, 274 (E.D. Pa. 1938). For the "Gobitis" spelling error, *see* Peters, *Judging Jehovah's Witnesses,* 38.

71 *Gobitis,* 24 F. Supp. at 274.

72 *See* Peters, *Judging Jehovah's Witnesses,* 42.

73 *See Minersville School Dist. v. Gobitis,* 108 F.2d 683 (3d Cir. 1940).

74 *Id.* at 691. (The decision also has an unusually modern take on the overuse of patriotism as a theme in film and daily life: "The noble sentiment of patriotism is worn threadbare not only in our movie houses but also in many schools." *Id.* at 692.)

75 *See* Blasi and Shiffrin, "The Story of *West Virginia State Board of Education,*" 105.

76 *See* Peter Irons, *A People's History of the Supreme Court* (New York: Viking Penguin., 1999), 338; Richard Danzig, "How Questions Begot Answers in Felix Frankfurter's First Flag Salute Opinion," in *The Constitution and the Flag: The Flag Salute Cases,*

edited by Michael Kent Curtis (New York; Garland Publishing, 1993), 86–87 ("*Gobitis* was written against the backdrop of [Frankfurter's] perceptions of the need to mobilize America for war").

77 *See* Bowman, "The Flag Salute Cases," 12; Irons, *A People's History*, 338.

78 Peters, *Judging Jehovah's Witnesses*, 49–50 ("electrifying"); Irons, *A People's History*, 338–39.

79 *See* Bowman, "The Flag Salute Cases," 13; Irons, *A People's History*, 338.

80 *See* Peters, *Judging Jehovah's Witnesses*, 50–51.

81 *See, e.g.*, Legal Information Institute, "Incorporation Doctrine," www.law.cornell.edu; Freedom Forum Institute, "Does the First Amendment Apply to Public Schools," www.freedomforuminsittute.org (discussing the application of the First Amendment to the states); First Amendment Encyclopedia, "*Gitlow v. New York* (1925)," https://mtsu.edu (discussing how the *Gitlow* case started the era of the incorporation doctrine, and found freedom of speech and press protections applied to the states). *See also* Anne Proffitt Dupre, *Speaking Up: The Unintended Costs of Free Speech in Public Schools* (Cambridge, MA: Harvard University Press, 2009), 139 ("The degree to which this doctrine of selective incorporation changed the balance of power between state and federal courts and state and federal government is incalculable").

82 *See* Peters, *Judging Jehovah's Witnesses*, 50–51.

83 *See* Jeffrey Owen Jones and Peter Meyer, *The Pledge: A History of the Pledge of Allegiance* (New York: St. Martin's Press, 2010), 127.

84 *See id.*; Noah Feldman, *Scorpions: The Battles and Triumphs of FDR's Great Supreme Court Justices* (New York and Boston: Twelve, 2010), 11, 36–39; Peters, *Judging Jehovah's Witnesses*, 53–54.

85 *See* David L. Hudson Jr., *Let the Students Speak: A History of the Fight for Free Expression in American Schools* (Boston: Beacon Press, 2011), 33.

86 *See* Bowman, "The Flag Salute Cases," 14.

87 *Minersville School District v. Gobitis*, 310 U.S. 586, 591, (1940).

88 *Id.* at 594.

89 *Id.* at 595.

90 *Id.*

91 *Id.* at 596–97. *See* Blasi and Shiffrin, "The Story of *West Virginia State Board of Education*," 107 ("For Justice Frankfurter . . . the case was all about national identity and patriotic assimilation, matters so fundamental as to dwarf all other considerations").

92 *Id.* at 596.

93 *See* Feldman, *Scorpions*, 233–34 ("Frankfurter's judicial restraint was driven by a deeply romantic conception of the nature and tendencies of the American people living under conditions of democracy. . . . His deep loyalty to the country that had taken him as an immigrant led him to downplay the racism, prejudice, and other types of illiberalism that could be found in America").

94 *Gobitis*, 310 U.S. at 598.

95 *Id.*

96 *Id.* at 604.

97 *Id.*

98 *Id.* at 606.

99 *Id.*

100 *Id.*

101 Irons, *The Courage of Their Convictions*, 30–31 (quoting Lillian Gobitas).

102 *See* Peters, *Judging Jehovah's Witnesses*, 70–71.

103 *See* Curtis, *The Constitution and the Flag*, xxx–xxxi.

104 *See* Peters, *Judging Jehovah's Witnesses*, 77–81.

105 *See* Ellis, *To the Flag*, 106.

106 *See* Steven Waldman, *Sacred Liberty: America's Long, Bloody, and Ongoing Struggle for Religious Freedom* (New York: HarperCollins, 2019), 168.

107 Bowman, "The Flag Salute Cases," 62–63 (quoting from, and including the full text of, Beulah Amidon, "Can We Afford Martyrs?," *Survey Graphic*, September 1940, 457–60).

108 *See* Peters, *Judging Jehovah's Witnesses*, 100.

109 Gregory L. Peterson, E. Barrett Prettyman, Jr., Shawn Francis Peters, Bennett Boskey, Gathie Barnett Edmonds, Marie Barnett Snodgrass, and John Q. Barrett, "Recollections of West Virginia State Board of Education v. Barnette," 81 *St. John's Law Review* 755, 762–63 (2007) (quoting Gregory L. Peterson).

110 *See* Peters, *Judging Jehovah's Witnesses*, 67. Eleanor Roosevelt also wrote with dismay about anti–Jehovah's Witness violence in Wyoming, just a few weeks after *Gobitis* was decided. *See* Eleanor Roosevelt, *My Day: The Best of Eleanor Roosevelt's Acclaimed Newspaper Columns, 1936–1962*, edited by David Emblidge (Cambridge, MA: Da Capo Press, 2001), 46 ("Must we drag people out of their homes to force them to do something which is in opposition to their religion?").

111 *Id.* at 69.

112 *See* Curtis, *The Constitution and the Flag*, xxxi.

113 *See* Justin Driver, *The Schoolhouse Gate: Public Education, the Supreme Court, and the Battle for the American Mind* (New York: Pantheon, 2018), 6.

114 *Id.* at 6–7.

115 *Jones v. Opelika*, 316 U.S. 584, 623–24 (1942).

116 *See* Ronald K. Collins, "Thoughts on Hayden C. Covington and the Paucity of Litigation Scholarship," 13 *FIU Law Review* 599, 625 (2019) ("In the period between 1939 and 1955, [Covington] brought forty-five First Amendment cases involving free speech, press, and religion before the Supreme Court. Like Thurgood Marshall and the plan developed by the NAACP . . . [Covington] formulated a First Amendment litigation strategy by which to foster, try, appeal, and then prevail in a variety of free expression cases. To do that, one needed the right plaintiffs and the right facts, something that the Witnesses, thanks to their legal counsel, did not leave to chance").

117 *See* Jeffrey S. Sutton, *"Barnette,* Frankfurter, and Judicial Review," *Marquette Lawyer,* Fall 2012, 16; Peterson, "Recollections," 767–68; Richard Panchyk, John Kerry, and James Baker III, *Our Supreme Court: A History with 14 Activities* (Chicago: Chicago Review Press, 2006), 79.

118 Stevens, *Salute!* (quoting interview with Marie Barnette Snodgrass).

119 Panchyk, *Our Supreme Court,* 79 (quoting interview with Gathie Barnette Edmonds). *See also* Peterson, "Recollections," 770.

120 Panchyk, *Our Supreme Court,* 80.

121 *See, e.g.,* Dupre, *Speaking Up,* 150.

122 *See* Driver, *The Schoolhouse Gate,* 62; Ronald K. L. Collins and Sam Chaltain, *We Must Not Be Afraid to Be Free: Stories of Free Expression in America* (New York: Oxford University Press, 2011), 245–46.

123 West Virginia Archives & History, *"Barnette v. Board of Education,* State Board of Education Resolution on Salute to the Flag," www.wvculture.org.

124 *See* Driver, *The Schoolhouse Gate,* 62; Dupre, *Speaking Up,* 149.

125 *See* Peters, *Judging Jehovah's Witnesses,* 245; Stevens, *Salute!,* 126. Walter Barnett, Gathie and Marie's father, was the lead plaintiff in the case filed on August 17, 1942, in the US District Court for the Southern District of West Virginia (the other named plaintiffs were Paul Stull and Lucy McClure). As with the Gobitases, the Barnett family's name was misspelled at some point in the litigation. *See* Bowman, "The Flag Salute Cases," 19. The case would be captioned as *Barnette v. West Virginia State Board of Ed.,* 47 F. Supp. 251 (S.D.W. Va. 1942).

126 *Barnette v. West Virginia State Board of Ed.,* 47 F. Supp. 251, 252–53 (S.D.W. Va. 1942). Judge Parker was writing the decision for a three-judge panel of the district court. In a clever and unusual strategic maneuver, Covington brought the lawsuit as one that sought "to enjoin a state statue as [constitutionally] invalid on its face," since such cases "were heard by a three-judge panel . . . [whose] decision was then directly appealable to the Supreme Court, bypassing the intermediate court of appeals." Bowman, "The Flag Salute Cases," 18.

127 *Id.* at 253.

128 *Id.* at 255.

129 *See* Ellis, *To the Flag,* 5–10, 17–21, 113; *see also* Erin Blakemore, "The Rules about How to Address the U.S. Flag Came about Because No One Wanted to Look Like a Nazi," *Smithsonian,* August 12, 2016; Glenn Kessler, "Mitt Romney's Misfire on the National Anthem," *Washington Post,* February 6, 2012 (discussing history of the hand going "over the heart during both the pledge and the anthem").

130 Ellis, *To the Flag,* 113.

131 *Id.* at 118–20. The original Pledge of Allegiance was: "I pledge allegiance to my Flag and to the Republic for which it stands—one Nation indivisible—with Liberty and Justice for all." *Id.* at 19. In 1942, "my Flag" was changed to "the Flag of the United States of America." The words "under God" were not added until 1954. *See* Blasi and Shiffrin, "The Story of *West Virginia State Board of Education,*" 102 n.14, 138–39.

132 *See* United States Courts, "Supreme Court Procedures," www.uscourts.gov ("After the votes have been tallied [during the Justice's post-oral argument Conference], the Chief Justice, or the most senior Justice in the majority if the Chief Justice is in the dissent, assigns a Justice in the majority to write the opinion of the Court").

133 *See* Peterson, "Recollections," 784 (discussing assignment of *Barnette* opinion, by Chief Justice Stone's law clerk at the time, and that the chief justice "decided the best thing to do for the Court to get an opinion which would be subscribed to by the maximum number of Justices . . . would be to assign the opinion to Jackson, whatever chances that might involve taking"); Ellis, *To the Flag*, 111.

134 David Geary, "First Amendment Trial Lawyer addresses Free Expression at the Jackson Center," Robert H. Jackson Center, October 16, 2017, www.roberthjackson.org (quoting Floyd Abrams, "arguably the nation's foremost champion of the First Amendment"). *See also* Driver, *The Schoolhouse Gate*, 65 ("whatever Supreme Court majority opinion might claim the runner-up spot in eloquence lags so far behind Barnette as to render the event no contest at all"); Jeffrey Toobin, "Colin Kaepernick and a Landmark Supreme Court Case," *New Yorker*, September 15, 2016 ("Jackson's opinion in . . . *Barnette* stands as perhaps the greatest defense of freedom of expression ever formulated by a Supreme Court Justice").

135 *See* Ellis, *To the Flag*, 111.

136 *West Virginia State Board of Education v. Barnette*, 319 U.S 624, 632 (1943). *See* Mark Tushnet, Alan K. Chen, and Joseph Blocher, *Free Speech Beyond Words: The Surprising Reach of the First Amendment* (New York: New York University Press, 2017), 138 (in Barnette, "the Court indicated that expressive conduct (in that case, saluting a flag) is 'speech' for constitutional purposes because it conveys 'ideas'").

137 *Barnette*, 319 U.S. at 633.

138 *Id.*

139 *Id.* at 635–36 (emphasis added).

140 *See* Driver, *The Schoolhouse Gate*, 65; Blasi and Shiffrin, "The Story of *West Virginia State Board of Education*," 115; Dupre, *Speaking Up*, 153–54; Curtis, *The Constitution and the Flag*, xxxiii.

141 *See* Driver, *The Schoolhouse Gate*, 65.

142 *Barnette*, 319 U.S. at 634.

143 *Id.* at 638.

144 *Id.* at 640.

145 *Id.*

146 *Id.* at 641.

147 *Id.*

148 *Id. See* Christopher L. Eisgruber, "Is the Supreme Court an Educative Institution?," 67 *NYU Law Review* 961, 979 (1992) ("Throughout [*Barnette*] . . . Jackson identifies America's flag with America's Constitutional principles. The closing passage is a form of flag-waving").

149 *See, e.g.,* Cass R. Sunstein, "The Supreme Court's Five Greatest Moments," Bloomberg, June 1, 2015, www.bloomberg.com (calling Jackson's *Barnette* opinion "the greatest of all time").
150 *Barnette,* 319 U.S. at 642.
151 *See id.*
152 *Id.* at 647.
153 *Id.* at 654.
154 *Id.* at 665.
155 Legal Information Institute, "Stare decisis," www.law.cornell.edu.
156 *Burnet v. Coronado Oil & Gas Co.,* 285 U.S. 393, 406 (1932).
157 *See Barnette,* 319 U.S. at 665 ("Of course, judicial opinions, even as to questions of constitutionality, are not immutable. As has been true in the past, the Court will from time to time reverse its position").
158 *See Plessy v. Ferguson,* 163 U.S. 537 (1896); *Brown v. Board of Education,* 347 U.S. 483 (1954) (Frankfurter was a member of the unanimous court in *Brown*). *See also* A. J. Willingham, "The Supreme Court Has Overturned More than 200 of Its Own Decisions. Here's What It Could Mean for Roe v. Wade," CNN.com, May 29, 2019, www.cnn.com (contemporary overview of representative overturned cases).
159 *See* Sutton, "*Barnette,* Frankfurter, and Judicial Review," 18 ("What is most striking about *Barnette,* and to my knowledge without any counterpart in American constitutional history, is the shift in the number of votes over just three years"); Peterson, "Recollections," 765 ("I am not aware of any other decision that has been overturned so quickly").
160 *See* Driver, *The Schoolhouse Gate,* 69.
161 "Judiciary: Blot Removed," *Time,* June 21, 1943.
162 Steven H. Shiffrin, *The First Amendment, Democracy, and Romance* (Princeton, NJ: Princeton University Press, 1990), 160.
163 *See* Driver, *The Schoolhouse Gate,* 71.
164 *See* Peterson, "Recollections," 772–73. The Barnett sisters and cousins had been allowed to return to school after the district court decision in their favor. *See id.*
165 *See* Panchyk, *Our Supreme Court,* 78.
166 Irons, *The Courage of Their Convictions,* 35.
167 *See* Ken Belson, "Colin Kaepernick's Collusion Case against the N.F.L. Will Advance," *New York Times,* August 30, 2018.
168 *See* "Colin Kaepernick, Eric Reid Settle Grievances against NFL," ESPN.com, February 16, 2019, www.ESPN.com; Kevin Draper and Ken Belson, "Colin Kaepernick and the N.F.L. Settle Collusion Case," *New York Times,* February 15, 2019. Before the settlement, Reid had accepted a $22 million, three-year deal with the Carolina Panthers, while Kaepernick remained unsigned. *See* David Newton, "Safety Eric Reid Signs 3-Year Deal to Return to Panthers," ESPN.com, February 11, 2019, www.espn.com.

169 *See* Ken Belson and Kevin Draper, "In Colin Kaepernick Case, N.F.L. Makes a Familiar, Safe Call," *New York Times*, February 16, 2019; Michael Powell, "Colin Kaepernick Is Silenced by a Settlement, but His Knee Spoke Volumes," *New York Times*, February 15, 2019.

170 *See* Charisse Jones, "Nike Goes All In: Colin Kaepernick Voices 'Just Do It' Ad to Air during NFL's Kick-off Game," *USA Today*, September 5, 2018; Tim Daniels, "Colin Kaepernick Named Face of Nike's 30th Anniversary of 'Just Do It' Campaign," Bleacher Report, September 3, 2018, www.bleacherreport.com; *see also* Soo Youn, "Nike Sales Booming after Colin Kaepernick Ad, Invalidating Critics," ABC News, December 21, 2018, www.abcnews.go.com.

171 *See* Chris Yuscavage, "HS and College Football Players Are Being Unfairly Penalized for National Anthem Protests," Complex, October 11, 2017, www.complex.com; Ariana Figueroa, "How Schools Are Dealing with Students' Right to Protest," NPR, September 29, 2017, www.npr.org; Joyce Tsai, "School Honor Band Kneels While Playing Anthem before Oakland A's Game," *East Bay Times*, September 21, 2016; Joe Davidson, "Echoing Kaepernick, Laguna Creek High Football Players Kneel before Game," *Sacramento Bee*, September 20, 2106; Jayda Evans, "Garfield Football Team Takes Knee during National Anthem prior to Game Friday Night," *Seattle Times*, September 16, 2016 (entire high school team knelt during anthem).

172 *See* Knowles Adkisson, "In Louisiana, High School Players Link Arms but Do Not Kneel during Anthem," *Washington Post*, September 29, 2017 (in response to public school principal's order students to stand for anthem during sporting events, the ACLU of Louisiana cited Barnette: "As long as they're peaceful, students cannot be forced to engage in expressions of opinions that they do not share. And you cannot make that conditional of taking part in a school activity . . . It's counterproductive in addition to being illegal to tell students they can't express their dissent"); Christine Hauser, "High Schools Threaten to Punish Students Who Kneel during Anthem," *New York Times*, September 29, 2017; *see also Brentwood Academy v. Tennessee Secondary School Athletic Assn.*, 531 U.S. 288, 290–91 (2001) (holding even "a statewide association incorporated to regulate interscholastic athletic competition among public and private secondary schools" was engaging in state action).

173 Pew Research Center, "Large Majorities See Checks and Balances, Right to Protest as Essential for Democracy," March 2, 2017, www.people-press.org.

174 Ann Tennery, "Most Americans Disagree with Kaepernick, but Respect His Right to Protest," Reuters, September 14, 2016, www.reuters.com.

175 *See* Carrie Dann, "NBC/WSJ poll: Majority Say Kneeling during Anthem 'Not Appropriate,'" NBC News, August 31, 2018, www.nbcnews.com ("54% of voters called kneeling during the anthem inappropriate"); Scott Clement and Emily Guskin, "Poll: 53 Percent of Americans Say It's 'Never Appropriate' to Kneel during the National Anthem," *Washington Post*, May 23, 2018; Kathryn Casteel, "How Do Americans Feel about the NFL Protests? It Depends on How You Ask,"

FiveThirtyEight, October 9, 2017, www.fivethirtyeight.com (citing four separate polls that found "more people disapprove of the protests than approved"); Daniel Roberts, "Poll: 84% Support NFL Players' Right to Protest," Yahoo Finance, September 28, 2017, www.finance.yahoo.com ("84% of people believe in the players' right to protest, but only 35% support the specific protest of kneeling during the anthem"); *but cf.* Max Greenwood, "Poll: Majority Says NFL Players Taking a Knee Isn't Unpatriotic," *The Hill*, June 7, 2018 ("58 percent said players who kneel during the anthem are not unpatriotic, compared to 35 percent who said they are," but 70 percent of Republicans said that "players who protested during the anthem are unpatriotic").

176 Donald J. Trump (@realDonaldTrump), Twitter, September 25, 2017, www.twitter.com.

177 *See* Elahe Izad, "Black Lives Matter and America's Long History of Resisting Civil Rights Protesters," *Washington Post*, April 19, 2016.

178 Harry Enten, "The NFL Protests May Be Unpopular Now, but That Doesn't Mean They'll End That Way," FiveThirtyEight, September 25, 2017, www.fivethirtyeight.com (quoting a 1966 Gallup survey on King).

179 *See* Jason Reid, "NFL Fans and the Racial Divide," Undefeated, February 1, 2019, www.theundefeated.com (finding strong support among African Americans, in contrast to whites, for NFL players protests).

180 John Pavlovitz, "How People of Color Can Protest 'The Right Way' for White America" (blog post), September 3, 2016, www.johnpavlovitz.com; *see* Bryant, *The Heritage*, 12 ("It was a charade of platitudes to democracy, the old lines of 'You can speak out, but there are other ways to protest,' which naturally was shorthand for the white mainstream still making the rules, of telling the players what they could do and when they could do it, which naturally defeated the entire purpose of protest. Protest didn't ask permission"); Ta-Nehisi Coates, "Civil-Rights Protests Have Never Been Popular," Atlantic, October 3, 2017 ("If young people attempting to board a bus are unacceptable, if gathering on the National Mall is verboten, if preaching nonviolence gets you harassed by your own government and then killed, if a protest founded in consultation with military veterans is offensive, then what specific manner of protest is white America willing to endure? It's almost as if the manner of protest isn't the real problem").

181 Kareem Abdul-Jabbar, "Why the NFL Player Protests Still Matter," *Guardian*, February 3, 2018.

182 *Id.*

183 Bryant, *The Heritage*, xi.

184 A number of editorials and other opinion pieces took the position that the protests were patriotic. *See, e.g.,* Nancy Armour, "Trump Has No Right Questioning Patriotism of NFL Players" (op-ed), *USA Today*, July 20, 2018; "The N.F.L. Kneels to Trump" (editorial), *New York Times*, May 23, 2018; "This Is What the Flag Stands For, Mr. President" (editorial), *Washington Post*, September 24, 2017.

185 John Legend, "The NFL Protests Are Patriotic," Slate, September 24, 2017, www. slate.com.

186 Reid, "Why Colin Kaepernick."

187 See Evan Hill, Ainara Tiefenthaler, Christiaan Triebert, Drew Jordan, Haley Willis, and Robin Stein, "How George Floyd Was Killed in Police Custody," *New York Times*, May 31, 2020.

188 *See* Dan Wetzel, "Poll on Opinion Shift of Colin Kaepernick Could Explain NFL's About-Face on Players Protesting during Anthem," Yahoo Sports, June 11, 2020, www.sports.yahoo.com (Yahoo News/YouGov poll found "Fifty-two percent of people said it was 'OK' for 'NFL players to kneel during the national anthem to protest police killings of African-Americans,'" up from 35 percent in 2018); Michael Rosenberg, "What Do You Think of Colin Kaepernick Now?," *Sports Illustrated*, June 1, 2020; *see also* Derrick Bryson Taylor, "George Floyd Protests: A Timeline," *New York Times*, June 22, 2020.

189 NFL (@NFL), Twitter, June 5, 2020, www.twitter.com (quoting Goodell video statement included with tweet that said, in part, "We, the NFL, believe Black Lives Matter"). Ten days later, Goodell said that if Kaepernick "wants to resume his career in the NFL, then obviously it's going to take a team to make that decision. But I welcome that, support a club making that decision and encourage them to do that." "NFL Commissioner Roger Goodell: I 'Encourage a Team to Sign Colin Kaepernick,'" ESPN.com, June 15, 2020, www.espn.com.

190 Howard Bryant, "Why It Matters That Roger Goodell Didn't Say Colin Kaepernick's Name," ESPN.com, June 6, 2020, www.espn.com.

191 *Barnette*, 319 U.S. at 641.

192 *Id.* at 642.

Chapter 3. Libel, Actual Malice, and the Civil Rights Movement

1 Ian Schwartz, "Trump Promises to Open Up Libel Laws to Take On New York Times, Washington Post," RealClearPolitics, February 26, 2016, www.realclearpolitics.com.

2 Ted Johnson, "Trump Vows 'to Take a Strong Look' at Libel Laws in Wake of 'Fire and Fury' Release," *Variety*, January 10, 2018; Michael M. Grynbaum, "Trump Renews Pledge to 'Take a Strong Look' at Libel Laws," *New York Times*, January 10, 2018. *See also* Bob Woodward, *Fear: Trump in the White House* (New York: Simon & Schuster, 2018), 318–19 (Woodward reports this exchange took place between Trump and Senator Lindsey Graham during a phone call in January 2018: "'Can we change the libel laws?' Trump asked, rapidly shifting the tenor of the conversation to one of his pet peeves. 'No,' Graham, the lawyer, said. 'Why?' We are not England, Graham said, where the libel laws were stricter. People were writing 'bullshit,' Trump said. 'I don't doubt it,' Graham agreed. 'But no, we can't change the libel laws and don't worry about it.' . . . 'Well, I don't intend to become like England,' Trump said").

3 Jessica Levinson, "Trump Can't Sue Bob Woodward for Libel, So He's Going After Free Speech Instead," NBC News, September 11, 2018, www. nbcnews.com (opinion piece by professor at Loyola Law School). In 2019, Trump tweeted again about changing libel laws: "Really, the libel laws should be changed to hold Fake News Media accountable!" *See* Donald J. Trump (@realDonaldTrump), Twitter, May 27, 2019, www.twitter.com.

4 *McKee v. Cosby*, 586 U.S. ____ (2019) (Justice Thomas concurring in the denial of certiorari). *See* Adam Liptak, "Justice Clarence Thomas Calls for Reconsideration of Landmark Libel Ruling," *New York Times*, February 19, 2019.

5 Proponents of originalism, like its chief champion, Justice Scalia, believe the Constitution should be interpreted based largely on its original meaning at the time of enactment. In contrast, to take one leading example, Justice Thurgood Marshall viewed the Constitution as a "living document" that was intended to evolve with society. *See* Lyle Denniston, "Justice Thomas, Originalism and the First Amendment," National Constitution Center, February 20, 2019, www.constitution-center.org; Aaron Blake, "Neil Gorsuch, Antonin Scalia and Originalism, Explained," *Washington Post*, February 1, 2017; Stuart Taylor Jr., "Marshall Sounds Critical Note on Bicentennial," *New York Times*, May 7, 1987 (describing Justice Marshall's speech titled "The Constitution: A Living Document").

6 *See* David J. Garrow, *Bearing the Cross: Martin Luther King, Jr., and the Southern Christian Leadership Conference* (New York: HarperCollins 1986), 127–31.

7 *See id.* at 129; Anthony Lewis, *Make No Law: The Sullivan Case and the First Amendment* (New York: Vintage Books, 1991), 5–6. Martin Luther King called the perjury indictment "a new attempt on the part of the State of Alabama to harass me for the role that I have played in the civil rights struggle." *See* Civil Rights Digital Library, "WSB-TV Newsfilm Clip of Dr. Martin Luther King, Jr., Speaks to a Reporter after Being Indicted and Arrested for Tax Fraud in Alabama in Atlanta, Georgia, 1960 February 17," www.crdl.usg.edu. He would be acquitted later that May by an all-white jury. *See* Garrow, *Bearing the Cross*, 136–37; Stanford University, Martin Luther King, Jr. Research and Education Institute, "State of Alabama v. M. L. King, Jr., Nos. 7399 and 9593," https://kinginstitute.stanford.edu.

8 *See* Garrow, *Bearing the Cross*, 130.

9 *See* Lewis, *Make No Law*, 5–6 (an advertisement of that size cost about $4,800 in 1960).

10 For the original layout of the ad and a full transcript, *see* National Archives, "Advertisement, 'Heed Their Rising Voices,' New York Times, March 29, 1960," www.archives.gov.

11 The committee would soon raise "contributions totaling many times the cost of the ad" (Lewis, *Make No Law*, 7); it ultimately took in and spent $86,000 (Garrow, *Bearing the Cross*, 654 n.8).

12 *See New York Times Co. v. Sullivan*, 376 U.S. 254, 260 n.3 (1964).

13 Lewis, *Make No Law*, 11–12.

14 *Id.* at 12.

15 The role of these civil rights icons has often been underemphasized in discussing the heroes of the *Sullivan* case. *See, e.g.,* Garrett Epps, "The Civil Rights Heroes the Court Ignored in *New York Times v. Sullivan*: Celebrations of This Landmark Case Are Incomplete without Any Mention of Ralph David Abernathy, S. S. Seay Sr., Fred L. Shuttlesworth, and J. E. Lowery," *Atlantic*, March 20, 2014.

16 The full retraction letter from Governor Patterson to the *New York Times* can be found online at Stanford University's Martin Luther King, Jr. Papers Project, Martin Luther King, Jr. Research and Education Institute, "From John Malcolm Patterson," https://kinginstitute.stanford.edu.

17 *See* Lewis, *Make No Law*, 13; Kermit L. Hall and Melvin I. Urofsky, *New York Times v. Sullivan: Civil Rights, Libel Law and the Free Press* (Lawrence: University Press of Kansas, 2011), 32–33.

18 *See* Bureau of Labor Statistics, "CPI Inflation Calculator," www.bls.gov.

19 Harrison E. Salisbury, *Without Fear or Favor: An Uncompromising Look at the New York Times* (New York: Times Books, 1980), 382.

20 Hall and Urofsky, *New York Times v. Sullivan*, 12–13.

21 *See* Branch, *Parting the Waters*, 186–87.

22 *See* Hall and Urofsky, *New York Times v. Sullivan*, 14; Randall Kennedy, "The Forgotten Origins of the Constitution on Campus," *American Prospect*, December 28, 2017 (discussing the Alabama State College sit-in, and the groundbreaking *St. John Dixon v. Alabama State Board of Education* decision by the Fifth Circuit holding due process before expulsion was constitutionally required).

23 *See* Hall and Urofsky, *New York Times v. Sullivan*, 45.

24 *See* Garrow, *Bearing the Cross*, 90, 120.

25 *See* Taylor Branch, *Parting the Waters: America in the King Years 1954–63* (New York: Simon & Schuster, 1988), 158. For brief biographical entries on the minister defendants, *see also* Stanford University, Martin Luther King, Jr. Research and Education Institute, "Martin Luther King, Jr. Encyclopedia," https://kinginstitute.stanford.edu.

26 *New York Times Company v. Sullivan*, Oyez, www.oyez.org (Samuel R. Pierce Jr. quoting Judge Jones, at oral argument on behalf of the minister defendants). All oral argument quotations are taken from Oyez transcripts unless otherwise noted.

27 The ministers' Black lawyers—Fred Gray, Vernon Z. Crawford, and S. S. Seay Jr.—are referred to in the trial transcript as "Lawyer Gray," "Lawyer Crawford," and "Lawyer Seay," whereas the white lawyers on both sides are referred to as "Mr. Nachman" or "Mr. Embry." Lewis, *Make No Law*, 27. *See New York Times v. Sullivan*, Oyez (Samuel R. Pierce Jr., in his oral argument on behalf of the minister defendants, pointed out this racist terminology, calling it "a shame in this day in time").

28 Since libel law is primarily a matter of state law, the elements of libel can vary somewhat from state to state. To establish libel, the statement at issue must also be a

factual one, and not an opinion. Post-*Sullivan* there is the additional requirement that the plaintiff show fault on the part of the person making the statements. This fault standard depends on the *plaintiff's* status—for public figures it is actual malice (knowing falsity or reckless disregard for the truth), and for private individuals it the lesser standard of negligence (lacking reasonable care under the circumstances).

29 *See* Lewis, *Make No Law*, 28–30. Nachman, a top libel lawyer in Alabama, has been called the "chief architect" of Sullivan's lawsuit, having delivered the advertisement to Sullivan and the commissioners along with the suggestion that Sullivan could sue the *Times*, even if he was not named. *See* Ronald K. L. Collins and Sam Chaltain, *We Must Not Be Afraid to Be Free: Stories of Free Expression in America* (New York: Oxford University Press, 2011), 152–53, 163.

30 *See New York Times v. Sullivan*, 376 U.S. at 258–59 ("It is uncontroverted that some of the statements contained in the two paragraphs were not accurate descriptions of events which occurred in Montgomery. Although Negro students staged a demonstration on the State Capitol steps, they sang the National Anthem and not 'My Country, 'Tis of Thee.' Although nine students were expelled by the State Board of Education, this was not for leading the demonstration at the Capitol, but for demanding service at a lunch counter in the Montgomery County Courthouse on another day. Not the entire student body, but most of it, had protested the expulsion, not by refusing to register, but by boycotting classes on a single day; virtually all the students did register for the ensuing semester. . . . Although the police were deployed near the campus in large numbers on three occasions, they did not at any time 'ring' the campus, and they were not called to the campus in connection with the demonstration on the State Capitol steps, as the third paragraph implied"). Fred Gray would later write that "[i]f a copy of the advertisement had been sent to me for verification, the errors probably would have been avoided. Of course, then we might not have had a major advance in the nation's libel law. . . . God and the law work in mysterious ways." Fred Gray, *Bus Ride to Justice: Changing the System by the System—the Life and Works of Fred Gray* (Montgomery, AL: NewSouth Books, 2013), 159.

31 Fred D. Gray, "The Sullivan Case: A Direct Product of the Civil Rights Movement," 42 *Case Western Reserve Law Review* 1223, 1227 (1992). Among his many other groundbreaking accomplishments, Fred Gray was only twenty-four years old when he became the lawyer for Rosa Parks, Martin Luther King, Jr., and the Montgomery Bus Boycott. His lawsuit challenging the segregated bus system as an unconstitutional denial of equal protection was affirmed by the United States Supreme Court in the seminal case of *Gayle v. Browder*, 352 U.S. 903 (1956). *See* Leonard S. Rubinowitz, "The Courage of Civil Rights Lawyers: Fred Gray and His Colleagues," 67 *Case Western Reserve Law Review* 1227, 1235–37 (2017).

32 *See* Lewis, *Make No Law*, 32.

33 *See id.* at 33.

34 *Id.* at 34–35 (quoting *Alabama Journal* editorial).

35 Rex Thomas, "State Finds Formidable Legal Club to Swing at Out-of-State Press," *Montgomery Advertiser*, September 25, 1960, page 7 (accessible at www.newspapers. com) ("When they print deliberately or through carelessness libels against individuals and communities, untrue stories about men and people they must expect to answer for them in the courts").

36 Hall and Urofsky, *New York Times v. Sullivan*, 70.

37 Lewis, *Make No Law*, 35.

38 Branch, *Parting the Waters*, 44–45.

39 Gray, *Bus Ride to Justice*, 162–63.

40 The prevalence of civil rights advertising is noted in Susan Dente Ross and R. Kenton Bird, "The Ad That Changed Libel Law: Judicial Realism and Social Activism in New York Times Co. v. Sullivan," 9 *Communication Law and Policy* 489, 492 (2004) ("Between 1945 and 1964, a variety of civil rights groups sponsored at least fourteen advertisements in the Times promoting racial equality"). When *Sullivan* reached the Supreme Court, the ACLU would file an amicus brief noting the free speech importance of protecting paid advertisements, particularly when dealing with political matters since political organizations "did not have the resources to publish a newspaper or operate a radio or television station, but they could raise the money for advertisements such as 'Heed Their Rising Voices.'" Hall and Urofsky, *New York Times v. Sullivan*, 135.

41 Branch, *Parting the Waters*, 296, 771–72 (in May 1963, Stanley Levinson, on behalf of the Southern Christian Leadership Conference, "worked to place the first newspaper fund-raiser since the 1960 ad that had brought the crippling *Sullivan v. New York Times* libel suit [but was told] 'the bastards at the Times wouldn't print the ad. . . . [T]hey want to take out references to brutality and all strong references to segregation and discrimination in Birmingham.' Although the deletions included headlines and copy that had been published in the Times' own news stories [he worked on a compromise given] that the Times was fearful of being sued again over a controversial King ad").

42 *See* Gray, "The Sullivan Case," 1226 ("The manner in which *The New York Times* and other outside news organizations covered the racial events in Montgomery and in the State of Alabama displeased Mr. Sullivan and the Montgomery County power structure. By obtaining a large monetary judgment, Mr. Sullivan and the others expected that the media would be intimidated and would shy away from covering the civil rights struggle in Alabama. . . . Collectively, these suits were part of a concerted strategy to rid Alabama of outside news coverage").

43 Mary-Rose Papandrea, "The Story of *New York Times Co. v. Sullivan*," in *First Amendment Stories*, edited by Richard W. Garnett and Andrew Koppelman (New York: Foundation Press, 2012), 256–57 (citing Hon. Andrew Young, "Address at Presentation of Freedom Award to Justice Brennan: His Opinion in Sullivan Made Possible a Peaceful Revolution in This Country and around the World" [November 4, 1992]).

44 *New York Times Company v. Sullivan*, 144 So. 2d 25, 51 (Alabama Supreme Court, 1962). *See* Lewis, *Make No Law*, 43; Hall and Urofsky, *New York Times v. Sullivan*, 84.

45 Gene Roberts and Hank Klibanoff, *The Race Beat: The Press, the Civil Rights Struggle, and the Awakening of a Nation* (New York: Random House, 2006), 357. *See also* Hall and Urofsky, *New York Times v. Sullivan*, 85 (a sheriff in Alabama sued the publisher of *Ladies' Home Journal* "for $3 million, following an article in the Ladies Home Journal by Lillian Hellman that accused [the sheriff] and his deputies of police brutality during racial demonstrations in the summer of 1963"); Salisbury, *Without Fear or Favor*, 388–89 ("By March of 1964 the total of libel actions outstanding against newspapers, news magazines, television networks and other public media had reached nearly $300 million. Actions had been filed in southern states from Florida to Texas. Editors and publishers could not send a reporter or a photographer into these states without putting themselves at risk").

46 *See* Carlo A. Pedrioli, "*New York Times v. Sullivan* and the Rhetorics of Race: A Look at the Briefs, Oral Arguments, and Opinions," 7 *Georgetown Journal of Law & Modern Critical Race Perspectives* 109, 135 (2015) ("In terms of the attorneys' advocacy, counsel for the Times focused on the First Amendment instead of race. Meanwhile, counsel for the ministers, as well as making the First Amendment arguments, presented a vision of a case saturated with multiple acts of racism best understood from a perspective that considered the longstanding history of racial discrimination in the South").

47 Wechsler's views on race and constitutional theory have rightly been challenged as highly problematic. *See* Stanley Fish, "When Principles Get In the Way," *New York Times*, December 26, 1996 (criticizing Wechsler's highly influential 1959 *Harvard Law Review* article "Toward Neutral Principles," in which Wechsler posited that the Supreme Court's decision in *Brown v. Board of Education*, holding segregated schools unconstitutional, was not justified by appropriate neutral principles. Fish writes, "Once the historical specificity of that issue is lost, there no longer seems to be any moral difference between the two sides, although the difference was perfectly clear before Wechsler began his tortured analysis").

48 Brief for Petitioners at 53, *Abernathy v. Sullivan*, 376 U.S. 254 (1964) (No. 40).

49 Taylor Branch, *Pillar of Fire: America in the King Years, 1963–65* (New York: Simon & Schuster, 1998), 44.

50 *Id.*

51 *New York Times v. Sullivan*, Oyez.

52 *Id.*

53 *See* Philip Shenon, "Samuel R. Pierce Jr., Ex-Housing Secretary, Dies at 78," *New York Times*, November 3, 2000.

54 *New York Times v. Sullivan*, Oyez (Pierce also made a pure free speech argument that "a fair reading of the entire advertisement involved in this case discloses simply an attempt to speak on a crucial public issue. It is not an attack upon any specific individual therefore it's protected by the First Amendment").

55 *New York Times v. Sullivan*, Oyez.

56 "Justice White and some of the others found this statement disturbing. It is one thing to publish allegations that are known to be false; it is quite another to publish something that a reporter or editor has every reason to believe true and later discovers it is in error." Hall and Urofsky, *New York Times v. Sullivan*, 157.

57 Bruce Weber, "M. Roland Nachman, Lawyer in Times v. Sullivan Libel Case, Dies at 91," *New York Times*, December 4, 2015 (quoting his daughter's eulogy).

58 *See* Lee Levine and Stephen Wermiel, *The Progeny: Justice William J. Brennan's Fight to Preserve the Legacy of New York Times v. Sullivan* (Chicago: ABA Publishing, 2014), 18.

59 In a footnote, Brennan wrote that since they had decided the case on freedom of speech and press grounds, the Court did not decide the ministers' claims of equal protection violations "by racial segregation and racial bias in the courtroom." *Sullivan*, 376 U.S. at 293 n.4.

60 *Sullivan*, 376 U.S. at 256.

61 *Id.* at 270.

62 *Id.* at 271–72.

63 *Id.* at 278–79.

64 *Id.* at 279–80. The Court would later provide guidance on what constitutes "reckless disregard," clarifying that there must be evidence that the defendant "entertained serious doubts as to the truth of his publication," or "where there are obvious reasons to doubt the veracity of the informant or the accuracy of his reports." *St. Amant v. Thompson*, 390 U.S. 727, 731–32 (1968).

65 *See Sullivan*, 376 U.S. at 285–88.

66 *Id.* at 288, 292.

67 *Id.* at 295 (emphasis added), 297 (Black, concurring) ("This Nation, I suspect, can live in peace without libel suits based on public discussions of public affairs and public officials. But I doubt that a country can live in freedom where its people can be made to suffer physically or financially for criticizing their government, its actions, or its officials"); *Sullivan*, 376 U.S. at 304 (Goldberg, concurring) ("the citizen and the press should . . . be immune from libel actions for their criticism of official conduct").

68 Lewis, *Make No Law*, 155 (quoting Brennan at his 1965 Meiklejohn Lecture at Brown University).

69 Another common misunderstanding regarding the actual malice standard is the term "absence of malice," which has no legal meaning, but is most famously (and inaccurately) used in the 1981 Sydney Pollack film *Absence of Malice* starring Sally Field and Paul Newman.

70 Three years after *Sullivan*, the Court extended the "actual malice" standard beyond just public officials to also include public figures. *See Curtis Publishing Co. v. Butts*, 388 U.S. 130 (1967). Seven years later, however, the Court refused to stretch the "actual malice" requirement further to encompass private figures, and held that states may define libel for such private individuals as they wish so long as there is at

least a fault (or reasonableness) requirement. This "less demanding showing" means that private individuals do not have to prove actual malice. It makes sense that as a result, it is easier for private citizens to win libel judgments than for public figures, the Court reasoned, since "private individuals are not only more vulnerable to injury than public officials and public figures; they are also more deserving of recovery." *Gertz v. Robert Welch, Inc.*, 418 U.S. 323, 345–48 (1974).

71 Harry Kalven, Jr., "The New York Times Case: A Note on 'The Central Meaning of the First Amendment,'" 1964 *Supreme Court Review* 191, 221 n.125 (1964) (quoting Alexander Meiklejohn).

72 Christopher W. Schmidt, "New York Times v. Sullivan and the Legal Attack," 66 *Alabama Law Review* 293, 332–33 (2014) (citing "Good News for the Press," *Pittsburgh Courier*, March 21, 1964, at 14) (but note this author also writes critically about the decision and that "scholars have surely overestimated the impact of the South's libel-law offensive against the Civil Rights Movement—and hence the impact of the *Sullivan* decision").

73 *See* Anthony Lewis, *Freedom for the Thought That We Hate: A Biography of the First Amendment* (New York: Basic Books, 2007), 55.

74 Elena Kagan, "Sullivan Then and Now (reviewing Anthony Lewis, Make No Law: The Sullivan Case and the First Amendment (1991))," 18 *Law and Social Inquiry* 197, 216 (1993).

75 Andrew Cohen, "Today Is the 50th Anniversary of the (Re-)Birth of the First Amendment," *Atlantic*, March 9, 2014.

76 *See* Douglas Martin, "Thomas A. Johnson, Pioneering Black Journalist, Dies at 79," *New York Times*, June 5, 2008 ("Arthur Gelb, a former managing editor for The New York Times, wrote . . . that when Mr. [Thomas A.] Johnson joined the paper in February 1966, he was the only black reporter at The Times").

77 Catherine A. MacKinnon, "The First Amendment: An Equality Reading," in *The Free Speech Century*, ed. by Lee C. Bollinger and Geoffrey R. Stone (New York: Oxford University Press 2019), 144–45.

78 Gray, *The Sullivan Case*, 1228.

79 Collins and Chaltain, *We Must Not Be Afraid to Be Free*, 223–24 (quoting *Abuse of Power: The New Nixon Tapes* [Stanley I. Cutler, ed., 1997], 164).

80 Collins and Chaltain, *We Must Not Be Afraid to Be Free*, 225 (quoting John P. MacKenzie, "Libel Changes; Nixon Urges Changes in Libel Laws," *Washington Post*, March 9, 1974).

81 *See* Collins and Chaltain, *We Must Not Be Afraid to Be Free*, 225.

82 Erwin Chemerinsky, "Two Recent Opinions by Justice Clarence Thomas Should Alarm Us All," *Los Angeles Times*, op-ed, March 5, 2019 (Chemerinksy is dean of the UC Berkeley School of Law).

83 Al Kamen, "Marshall Blasts Celebration of Constitution Bicentennial," *Washington Post*, May 7, 1987 ("Marshall yesterday sharply attacked the Founding Fathers and the planned celebration of the Constitution's bicentennial, urging Americans not to

go overboard in praising a document that sanctioned slavery and denied women the right to vote"); Stuart Taylor Jr., "Marshall Sounds Critical Note on Bicentennial," *New York Times*, May 7, 1987 (Marshall's "remarks contrasted sharply with the lavish praise of the Framers' wisdom and devotion to liberty and justice by figures including President Reagan").

84 Thurgood Marshall, "Commentary: Reflections on the Bicentennial of the United States Constitution," 26 *Valparaiso University Law Review* 21 (1991).

Chapter 4. Student Speech from the Vietnam War to the National School Walkout

1 *See* Arian Campo-Flores, "Gun-Violence Protests Drew an Estimated 1 Million Students," *Wall Street Journal*, March 15, 2018.

2 *See* Dave Cullen, *Parkland* (New York: HarperCollins 2019), 146; Sarah Gray, "Thousands of Students Walked Out of School Today in Nationwide Protests. Here's Why," *Time*, March 14, 2018. *See also* Kathryn Schumaker, *Troublemakers: Students' Rights and Racial Justice in the Long 1960s* (New York: New York University Press, 2019), 213 ("The youngest speaker [at the March for Our Lives] was eleven-year-old Naomi [Wadler], who led a walkout at her elementary school. The protest lasted for eighteen silent minutes: seventeen minutes for the students murdered at Douglas and an extra minute for a black teenager who died after being shot at an Alabama high school in early March").

3 *See* Women's March Youth Empower, "Enough: National School Walkout," www. actionnetwork.org. Women's March Youth Empower were the organizers of this mass protest, who called it the #Enough National School Walkout, and were supported by the March for Our Lives students. *See* National School Walkout (@schoolwalkoutUS), Twitter, February 18, 2018, www.twitter.com (commenting, "There may be different dates but this is one movement!" on a retweet of @AMarch4OurLives, saying it was "in solidarity" with other gun violence protests).

4 *See* David Hogg and Lauren Hogg, *#Never Again* (New York: Random House, 2018), 17 ("David was just so determined. He said, 'Dad, I need to do this. If they don't get any stories, this will just fade away. I have to make sure this stays in the news'"); March for Our Lives Founders, *Glimmer of Hope: How Tragedy Sparked a Movement* (New York: Penguin Random House, 2018), 7 ("I had to change the narrative as quickly as possible and let the country know that our generation—the school shooting generation—wasn't going to stand for this anymore," quoting Cameron Kasky's chapter, "How It All Began: February 14"). *See also* Jen Kirby, "The National School Walkout, Explained," Vox, March 14, 2018, www.vox.com ("The Parkland survivors ignited a new gun control movement by finding a platform in their tragedy").

5 Vivian Yee and Alan Blinder, "National School Walkout: Thousands Protest against Gun Violence across the U.S.," *New York Times*, March 14, 2018. For a Marjory Stoneman Douglas student journalist perspective on the Walkout, *see* Christy Ma, "Not Just a Walk to the Park: Covering Civil Disobedience," in *We Say #NeverAgain:*

Reporting by the Parkland Student Journalists, edited by Melissa Falkowski and Eric Garner (New York: Crown Books, 2018), 62–65. For a moving and intimate look at some of the Parkland students and their families in the aftermath of the shooting, *see* the documentary *After Parkland* (ABC Documentaries, 2019), directed by Emily Taguchi and Jake Lefferman, www.afterparklandmovie.com.

6   *See* Cullen, *Parkland*, 146 ("Every school had to deal with its administration, and the responses ran the gamut across the country. Many administrators threatened detentions or suspensions for the insubordination"); David Williams, "Schools Threaten to Punish Students Who Join Walkouts over Gun Control," CNN.com, February 21, 2018, www.cnn.com.

7   Williams, "Schools Threaten to Punish Students." The post was later taken down from the district's Facebook page, after it received national media attention. *See* Blake Montgomery, "Students Face Suspension If They Walk Out in Support of the Pro Gun Control Movement 'Never Again,'" BuzzFeedNews, February 23, 2018, www.buzzfeednews.com.

8   *See* Olivia B. Waxman, "Student Walkouts Have Changed American History Before. Here's How," *Time*, March 15, 2018.

9   *See* John W. Johnson, *The Struggle for Student Rights: Tinker v. Des Moines and the 1960s* (Lawrence: University Press of Kansas, 1997), 13.

10 *See Amicus with Dahlia Lithwick*, "Back to School Protest Special" (podcast), Slate, September 1, 2018, www.slate.com (Mary Beth Tinker describing in interview that she was "really nervous" on the day she wore the armband); Johnson, *The Struggle for Student Rights*, 19.

11 *See* Susan Dudley Gold, *Tinker v. Des Moines: Free Speech for Students* (Tarrytown, NY: Marshall Cavendish Benchmark, 2007), 19; Johnson, *The Struggle for Student Rights*, 19.

12 *So to Speak: The Free Speech Podcast*, "From Black Armbands to the U.S. Supreme Court," January 10, 2019, www.sotospeak.libsyn.com (quoting Mary Beth Tinker in an interview on the podcast: "The black armbands were for mourning the dead in Vietnam on both sides of the war. And that's what made it so controversial"); Mary Beth Tinker, "'I'm Going to *Kill* You!,'" in *The Courage of Their Convictions*, edited by Peter Irons (New York: Free Press, 1988), 247 (quoting Mary Beth Tinker on RFK's "call for a Christmas truce in '65").

13 Irons, *The Courage of Their Convictions*, 246 (quoting Mary Beth Tinker). *See also* Johnson, *The Struggle for Student Rights*, 3–4; "Frequently Asked Questions," Tinker Tour USA, www.tinkertourusa.org (Mary Beth Tinker answers the question "How did you get the idea to wear the armbands?").

14 *See* "Frequently Asked Questions," Tinker Tour USA (Tinker answers, "Why black armbands?").

15 *See id.* (Tinker answers "Were you interested in civil rights before the armband controversy started?"). Tinker also has said that the issues of civil rights and anti-war protests "were so linked" in her mind and at the Supreme Court. *Amicus with Dahlia Lithwick*, "Back to School Protest Special."

16 *See* Johnson, *The Struggle for Student Rights*, 5–7.

17 *See So to Speak*, "From Black Armbands" (after the school district ban, Tinker said, "most of the . . . 50 kids who were going to wear armbands dropped off").

18 Irons, *The Courage of Their Convictions*, 246 (quoting Mary Beth Tinker).

19 *See* "Frequently Asked Questions," Tinker Tour USA.

20 *Amicus with Dahlia Lithwick*, "Back to School Protest Special" (quoting from Mary Beth Tinker's interview).

21 *Id.; Trumpcast*, "High School Revolutionaries Are Changing the Gun Debate" (podcast), February 22, 2018, https://podcasts.apple.com (Lithwick interviews Mary Beth Tinker).

22 *See* Irons, *The Courage of Their Convictions*, 247 (quoting Mary Beth Tinker); Johnson, *The Struggle for Student Rights*, 19–20.

23 *See* Johnson, *The Struggle for Student Rights*, 9, 16.

24 Marcia Amidon Lusted, *Tinker v. Des Moines: The Right to Protest in Schools* (Minneapolis: Abdo Publishing, 2013), 12 (quoting Eckhardt).

25 *See* Johnson, *The Struggle for Student Rights*, 17.

26 *Id.* (quoting Eckhardt).

27 *Id.* (quoting Eckhardt).

28 *Id.* at 18.

29 *See* Johnson, *The Struggle for Student Rights*, 2; Irons, *The Courage of Their Convictions*, 246 (quoting Mary Beth Tinker: "The two little kids in the family. . . . Hope was in the fifth grade and Paul was in the second grade. They wore black armbands [too], but nothing happened to them").

30 *See* Johnson, *The Struggle for Student Rights*, 24.

31 *Id.* at 24–25.

32 Richard Panchyk, *Our Supreme Court: A History with 14 Activities* (Chicago: Chicago Review Press, 2007), 58 (quoting John Tinker in an interview with the author).

33 *See* Johnson, *The Struggle for Student Rights*, 27.

34 *See id.*

35 *See id.* at 49.

36 *See id.* at 29, 45.

37 *See id.* at 56.

38 Irons, *The Courage of Their Convictions*, 248 (quoting Mary Beth Tinker).

39 Joseph Russomanno, *Speaking Our Minds: Conversations with the People Behind Landmark First Amendment Cases* (Mahwah, NJ: Lawrence Erlbaum Associates, 2002), 9 (quoting Dan Johnston). *See also* Ronald K. L. Collins and Sam Chaltain, *We Must Not Be Afraid to Be Free: Stories of Free Expression in America* (New York: Oxford University Press, 2011), 275; Johnson, *The Struggle for Student Rights*, 62–63, 66–68.

40 *See* Johnson, *The Struggle for Student Rights*, 37.

41 *Id.* at 37, 57.

42 David L. Hudson Jr., *Let the Students Speak!: A History of the Fight for Free Expression in American Schools* (Boston: Beacon Press, 2011), 61 (quoting John Tinker in 2009).

43 Irons, *The Courage of Their Convictions*, 248 (quoting Mary Beth Tinker).

44 *See* "CBS News Poll: U.S. Involvement in Vietnam," January 28, 2018, cbsnews.com, (citing Gallup polling data from 1965–1971).

45 *See* Collins and Chaltain, *We Must Not Be Afraid to Be Free*, 271; Abe Fortas, *Concerning Dissent and Civil Disobedience* (New York: Signet Books, 1968), 85 ("The revolt of the young people, on and off the campus, is a fairly new phenomenon in this country").

46 *See* Maggie Astor, "7 Times in History When Students Turned to Activism," *New York Times*, March 5, 2018 (discussing impact of the 1960 Greensboro sit-ins); Townsend Davis, *Weary Feat, Rested Souls: A Guided History of the Civil Rights Movement* (New York: W. W. Norton & Company, 1998), 309–12; Taylor Branch, *Parting the Waters: America in the King Years 1954–63* (New York: Simon & Schuster, 1988), 272–75.

47 Schumaker, *Troublemakers*, 4.

48 *See Tinker v. Des Moines Independent Community School District*, 258 F. Supp. 971, 973 (S. D. Iowa, 1966).

49 *Id.* at 972.

50 *Id.* at 973.

51 *See* Scott A. Moss, "The Story of Tinker v. Des Moines to Morse v. Frederick: Similar Stories of Different Student Speech with Different Results," in *First Amendment Stories*, edited by Richard W. Garnett and Andrew Koppelman (New York: Foundation Press, 2012), 406 ("After argument to the usual three-judge panel, the judges took the unusual step of ordering reargument to the entire eight judge Circuit sitting en banc").

52 *See Tinker*, 383 F.2d 988 (1967).

53 *See Burnside v. Byars*, 363 F.2d 744 (5th Cir. 1966).

54 *See* Hudson, *Let the Students Speak!*, 50–51.

55 *Burnside*, 363 F.2d 744; *see* Astor, "7 Times in History" ("The actions of the so-called Greensboro Four led directly to the creation of the Student Nonviolent Coordinating Committee, which the civil rights organizer Ella Baker urged students to form in April 1960 to coordinate the continuing sit-ins. Later, SNCC would play a major role in the Freedom Rides and in voter registration efforts across the South").

56 *Burnside*, 363 F.2d 744.

57 *Id.*

58 On the same day that the Fifth Circuit decided in *favor* of student speech rights in *Burnside*, the court also ruled *against* students wearing the same type of buttons in *Blackwell v. Issaquena County Board of Education*, because in the latter case there was evidence of significant disruption in the school. *See Blackwell*, 363 F.2d 749 (5th Cir. 1966); *see also* Schumaker, *Troublemakers*, 50 ("In *Blackwell* and *Burnside*, the court effectively brought the politics of respectability into the classroom, making it crucial that students engaging in symbolic protest at school be quietly deferential to school

officials ... In the end, the button cases laid the groundwork ... [and] smoothed the path to *Tinker*").

59 Legal definition of "circuit split": a circuit split occurs when at least two circuits in the United States court of appeals rule differently on the same federal issue. Resolving a circuit split is often an important factor in the Supreme Court justices' decision to grant review of a case.

60 Professor Randall Kennedy makes clear how the foundation of student speech rights, including those in *Tinker*, were made possible through the efforts of the civil rights movement, in cases such as *Burnside*. *See* Randall Kennedy, "The Forgotten Origins of the Constitution on Campus," *American Prospect*, December 28, 2017 ("Because of the efforts of activists who demanded rights of due process and freedom of expression as they fought to dismantle Jim Crow pigmentocracy, all students and teachers at public institutions came to enjoy an elevated legal status.... Here, as elsewhere, brave souls committed to battling racial oppression widened the circle of freedoms to which all in America can properly lay claim").

61 *See* Hudson, *Let the Students Speak!*, 63–64 (quoting Eckhardt in 1999).

62 *See* National Archives, "Military Records, Vietnam War U.S. Military Fatal Casualty Statistics," www.archives.gov.

63 *See* "CBS News Poll" (citing Gallup polling data from February 1968 that 46 percent viewed the war as "a mistake" and 42 percent as "not a mistake"; by January 1970, 57 percent called the Vietnam War a mistake and only 32 percent did not).

64 *See* Daniel S. Levy, "Behind the Anti-War Protests That Swept America in 1968," *Time*, January 19, 2018 ("Agitation spread to hundreds of schools. A Milwaukee Journal survey found that 75 percent of students supported organized protest as a 'legitimate means of expressing student grievances'"). For a riveting look at the student-led antiwar movement at the University of Wisconsin–Madison, *see* the Academy Award–nominated documentary *The War at Home* (Glenn Silber and Barry Alexander Brown, dirs.; First Run Features, 1979).

65 *See* Clara Bingham, "'The Whole World Is Watching': An Oral History of the 1968 Columbia Uprising," *Vanity Fair*, April 2018; Jennifer Schuessler, "At Columbia, Revisiting the Revolutionary Students of 1968," *New York Times*, March 21, 2018.

66 *See* Fortas, *Concerning Dissent and Civil Disobedience*, 87 ("refusal to accept the existing pattern of life and thought merely because it exists is, I think, the common element in the revolt of the youth-generation," from "Part 3: The Revolt of Youth").

67 Russomanno, *Speaking Our Minds*, 16; Johnson, *The Struggle for Student Rights*, 143.

68 Justin Driver, *The Schoolhouse Gate: Public Education, the Supreme Court, and the Battle for the American Mind* (New York: Pantheon Books, 2018), 72 (Driver's book provides a masterfully comprehensive analysis of constitutional issues in public education).

69 *See* Russomanno, *Speaking Our Minds*, 16–18 (quoting Johnston).

70 *Tinker v. Des Moines Independent Community School District*, Oyez, www.oyez.org.

71 *Id.*

72 *Id.*

73 *Id.* Justice Fortas is apparently referring to Tom Wolfe's *The Electric Kool-Aid Acid Test* (New York: Farrar, Straus & Giroux, 1968), his New Journalism nonfiction classic about Ken Kesey, LSD, and hippie culture.

74 *Tinker*, Oyez; *see also* Russomanno, *Speaking Our Minds*, 18 (Johnston said in this interview: "To the extent that I was nervous, I felt that Earl Warren would protect me from anything that could happen. He was sort of a large, grandfatherly, white-haired figure").

75 *Tinker*, Oyez.

76 *See* Johnson, *The Struggle for Student Rights*, 64–65.

77 *Id.* (describing Herrick's attitude toward anti-war protests).

78 *See* "Rise Up, Be Heard," *dsm*, January/February 2019, https://dsmmagazine.com (John Tinker recalled that "Herrick had a gravelly voice").

79 *Tinker*, Oyez.

80 *Id.*

81 *Id.*

82 *Id.* (emphasis added).

83 *Id.*

84 Justice Stewart referred to this point as "an equal protection argument." It also can be seen as "viewpoint discrimination," which the Supreme Court usually strongly disfavors. *See* Catherine J. Ross, *Lessons in Censorship: How Schools and Courts Subvert Students' First Amendment Rights* (Cambridge, MA: Harvard University Press, 2015), 22 (after *Barnette*, the Supreme Court "established that restrictions on speech based on either its content (that is, subject matter) or its viewpoint (the position a speaker takes with respect to a subject) are presumptively unconstitutional").

85 *Tinker*, Oyez.

86 *Id.*

87 Russomanno, *Speaking Our Minds*, 18 (quoting Johnston). *See also* Johnson, *The Struggle for Student Rights*, 161.

88 Russomanno, *Speaking Our Minds*, 21 (quoting Eckhardt).

89 *Tinker v. Des Moines Independent Community School District*, 393 U.S. 503, 505–6 (1969).

90 *Id.* at 506.

91 *See* Driver, *The Schoolhouse Gate*, 75 ("If *Tinker* were memorable only for containing that sentence, the opinion would nevertheless rank high on the list of the Court's momentous defenses of students' constitutional rights, as that language established the fundamental terms of debate for subsequent cases").

92 *Tinker*, 393 U.S. at 508.

93 *Id.* at 508–9.

94 *Id.* at 513–14 (citing *Burnside*). *See* Ross, *Lessons in Censorship*, 29–30 (describing "*Tinker* test" and *Burnside* adoption); Hudson, *Let the Students Speak!*, 55 ("Fortas

articulated what came to be known as the 'reasonable forecast of substantial disruption test,' acknowledging that schools do not have to wait for an actual riot before censoring student expression").

95 *Tinker,* 393 U.S. at 510.

96 *Id.*

97 *See* Driver, *The Schoolhouse Gate,* 75 ("The state—through its public schools—could not prevent students from expressing particular ideas simply because their message may run contrary to the state's own preferred message"); John E. Taylor, "Tinker and Viewpoint Discrimination," 77 *University of Missouri-Kansas City Law Review* 569 (2009).

98 *Tinker,* 393 U.S. at 511.

99 *Id.* at 511; *see* Anne Proffitt Dupre, *Speaking Up: The Unintended Costs of Free Speech in Public Schools* (Cambridge, MA: Harvard University Press, 2009), 19 ("This solemn declaration that schools 'may not be enclaves of totalitarianism' insinuated that this was exactly what was going on in Des Moines. These would be biting words at any time, but they were especially caustic when the country was in the midst of the Cold War against these oppressive regimes").

100 Less than three months after the *Tinker* decision was issued, Fortas resigned in the wake of a financial scandal. *See* "Fortas Is First Justice to Resign under Fire," *New York Times,* May 16, 1969; *see also* Linda Greenhouse, "Ex-Justice Abe Fortas Dies at 71; Shaped Historic Rulings on Rights," *New York Times,* April 7, 1982 ("Mr. Fortas resigned from the Court amid an uproar over disclosures that he had accepted a $20,000 fee from a foundation controlled by Louis E. Wolfson, a friend and former client who at the time of the payment was under Federal investigation for violating securities laws. His resignation ended a stormy three-and-a-half-year tenure on the Court, which included an abortive effort by President Johnson to name him Chief Justice, and made Mr. Fortas the only Justice in the history of the Supreme Court to resign under the pressure of public criticism").

101 *See* Andrew Lowy, "Reading a Dissent from the Supreme Court Bench," National Constitution Center, July 18, 2014, www.constitutioncenter.org.

102 Johnson, *The Struggle for Student Rights,* 176.

103 *Tinker,* 393 U.S. at 518.

104 *Id.* at 522.

105 *Id.* at 524–26.

106 *See* Ross, *Lessons in Censorship,* 30 ("Black has staunchly defended speech rights for adults even before a reliable majority coalesced around that stance. In a 1941 dissent, he proclaimed . . . the First Amendment 'is as important in the life of our government as is the heart to the human body'").

107 *See* Roger K. Newman, *Hugo Black: A Biography* (New York: Fordham University Press, 1997), 592.

108 *See* Ross, *Lessons in Censorship,* 32; Newman, *Hugo Black,* 592.

109 Newman, *Hugo Black*, 392. This focus on the possible personal motives of Justice Black, rather than his legal analysis, is a telling example of the legal realist approach to judicial understanding. *See* William H. Rehnquist, "Remarks on the Process of Judging," 49 *Washington and Lee Law Review* 263 (1992) ("Legal Realists—so called because they were said to believe that what a judge had for breakfast made more difference in how he would decide a case than what he knew about existing precedents").

110 *See* Newman, *Hugo Black*, 593 ("Black wrote his opinion with Sterling's children [his grandchildren] directly in mind").

111 *See* Driver, *The Schoolhouse Gate*, 84 (citing Harris poll).

112 *Id. See also* Laura Kalman, *Abe Fortas: A Biography* (New Haven, CT: Yale University Press, 1990), 292.

113 *See Bethel School District. v. Fraser*, 478 U.S. 675, 746 (1986) ("The First Amendment does not prevent the school officials from determining that to permit a vulgar and lewd speech . . . would undermine the school's basic educational mission"); *Hazelwood School District v. Kuhlmeier*, 484 U.S. 260, 273 (1988) ("We hold that educators do not offend the First Amendment by exercising editorial control over the style and content of student speech in school-sponsored expressive activities, so long as their actions are reasonably related to legitimate pedagogical concerns"); *Morse v. Frederick*, 551 U.S. 393, 397 (2007) ("We hold that schools may take steps to safeguard those entrusted to their care from speech that can reasonably be regarded as encouraging illegal drug use"). For a comparison of *Tinker, Bethel*, and *Cohen v. California, see Bethel*, 478 U.S. at 682 ("the First Amendment gives a high school student the classroom right to wear Tinker's armband, but not Cohen's jacket" [quotation omitted]).

114 Driver, *The Schoolhouse Gate*, 125. For a contrasting view on the current strength of *Tinker, see* Steven H. Shiffrin, *What's Wrong with the First Amendment* (Cambridge, UK: Cambridge University Press, 2017), 124 ("*Morse* simply backed away from *Tinker's* perspective that students should be free to dissent from authoritarian dictates, and *Morse* is part of a pattern in which the Court has bent over backward to uphold censorship by school authorities of student speeches and the student press").

115 *See* David L. Hudson Jr., "Court Grants Preliminary Relief to Student Wearing T-Shirts about Gun Ownership," Freedom Forum Institute, November 18, 2018, www.freedomforuminstitute.org.

116 *See* Umair Irfan, "Greta Thunberg Is Leading Kids and Adults from 150 countries in a Massive Friday Climate Strike," Vox, September 20, 2019, www.vox.com.

117 Even if skipping school is not constitutionally protected, one of the largest public school districts in the country has decided to grant seventh through twelfth grade students one excused absence a year to attend a protest. *See* Hannah Natanson, "One of the Nation's Biggest School Systems Will Let Students Take Time Off to Protest. The Conservative Backlash Has Begun," *Washington Post*, December 26, 2019.

118 *See* Vera Eidelman, "Can Schools Discipline Students for Protesting," ACLU, February 22, 2018, www.aclu.org.

119 Dahlia Lithwick, "They Were Trained for This Moment: How the Student Activists of Marjory Stoneman Douglas High Demonstrate the Power of a Comprehensive Education," *Slate*, February 28, 2018, www.slate.com.

120 *See* "On Tour: Stoneman Douglas High School in Ft. Lauderdale, Florida," Tinker Tour USA, www.tinkertourusa.org.

121 "About the Tinker Tour," Tinker Tour USA, www.tinkertourusa.org.

122 Mackenzie Ryan, "Tinker: School Walkouts Mark 'Turning Point' for Gun Violence, Teen Activism," *Des Moines Register*, March 14, 2018.

123 *Id.*

124 Elliot Fremont-Smith, "Freedom and Procedure," *New York Times*, May 27, 1968 (quoting from book review of *Concerning Dissent and Civil Disobedience*).

125 *See* Fortas, *Concerning Dissent and Civil Disobedience*, vii.

126 *Id.* at 85.

127 *Id.* at 93.

Chapter 5. Stormy Daniels, Prior Restraints, and the Pentagon Papers

1 *See* Michael Avenatti (@MichaelAvenatti), Twitter, March 8, 2018, www.twitter.com.

2 *See* Michael Rothfeld and Joe Palazzolo, "Trump Lawyer Arranged $130,000 Payment for Adult-Film Star's Silence," *Wall Street Journal*, January 12, 2018.

3 *See* Chris Geidner, "Trump Lawyers Are Considering a Challenge to Stop '60 Minutes' from Airing a Stormy Daniels Interview," Buzzfeed, March 11, 2018, www.buzzfeednews.com.

4 *See* Lloyd Grove, "Can Team Trump Stop Stormy Daniels' '60 Minutes' Interview?," Daily Beast, March 15, 2018, www.thedailybeast.com; Dawn C. Chmielewski, "Stormy Daniels Interviewed for '60 Minutes' Amid Reports Of Possible Legal Challenge," Deadline, March 11, 2018, www.deadline.com; Frances Stead Sellers, "Stormy Daniels Uncertain about Fate of Her '60 Minutes' Segment," *Washington Post*, March 11, 2018.

5 Scott Roxborough, "CBS News President David Rhodes on Stormy Daniels's '60 Minutes' Interview," *Hollywood Reporter*, March 13, 2018. Legal definition of "injunction": an injunction is a court order to stop, or sometimes continue, a particular action.

6 403 U.S. 713 (1971).

7 Only *Bush v. Gore* had a faster Supreme Court review—a stay was granted on December 9 (after the Florida Supreme Court ordered a recount), oral argument was heard on the 11th, and the decision was issued the next day. *See Bush v. Gore*, 531 U.S. 98 (2000), Oyez, www.oyez.org.

8 Leslie H. Gelb, "Foreign Affairs; 100 Questions," *New York Times*, June 16, 1991.

9 *See New York Times Company v. United States*, 403 U.S. 713 (1971), Oyez, www.oyez.org (Erwin N. Griswold citing Section 1(a) of Executive Order 10501 (1953) in his oral argument).

10 *See* "Pentagon Papers," National Archives, www.archives.gov.

11 Daniel Ellsberg, "Lying about Vietnam," *New York Times,* June 29, 2001.

12 *See* Sam Schwarz, "What Are the Pentagon Papers," *Newsweek,* December 26, 2017.

13 Floyd Abrams, *Friend of the Court: On the Front Lines with the First Amendment* (New Haven, CT: Yale University Press, 2013), 138. Full disclosure: it was my privilege to work for Mr. Abrams as an associate at the law firm Cahill Gordon & Reindel at the beginning of my career.

14 *See* Judith Ehrlich and Rick Goldsmith, dirs., *The Most Dangerous Man in America: Daniel Ellsberg and the Pentagon Papers* (ITVS/POV, 2009).

15 Daniel Ellsberg, *Secrets: A Memoir of Vietnam and the Pentagon Papers* (New York: Penguin, 2002), xii.

16 *Id.*

17 *See id.* at 270–71.

18 *Id.* at 272.

19 *See id.,* xi. Ellsberg's less famous compatriot in the leaking of the Pentagon Papers was Anthony J. Russo. *See* Barbara Myers, "The Forgotten Pentagon Papers Conspirator," *Mother Jones,* June 2, 2015; Douglas Martinaug, "Anthony J. Russo, 71, Pentagon Papers Figure, Dies," *New York Times,* August 8, 2008.

20 *See* Ellsberg, *Secrets,* 356–68.

21 *See* David Rudenstine, *The Day the Presses Stopped* (Berkeley: University of California Press, 1996), 52 (Ellsberg withheld from Sheehan volumes concerning then recent diplomatic efforts to end the war). *See also* Floyd Abrams, *Speaking Freely: Trials of the First Amendment* (New York: Viking, 2005), 10.

22 *See* Niraj Chokshi, "Behind the Race to Publish the Top-Secret Pentagon Papers," *New York Times,* December 20, 2017; James L. Greenfield, *The Pentagon Papers: The Secret History of the Vietnam War* (New York: Racehorse Publishing, 2017), foreword; Abrams, *Speaking Freely,* 10.

23 *See* Abrams, *Speaking Freely,* 11 (*New York Times* general counsel James Goodale took the opposite view from that of his former law firm and "at considerable personal risk, urged the *Times* to publish").

24 Neil Sheehan, "Vietnam Archive: Pentagon Study Traces 3 Decades of Growing U.S. Involvement," *New York Times,* June 13, 1971.

25 *See id.*

26 *See* the *New York Times* front page as it was published on June 13, 1971, www. timesmachine.nytimes.com.

27 *See* "Richard Nixon and Alexander M. Haig Jr. on 13 June 1971," Conversation 005–050, *Presidential Recordings Digital Edition* [Nixon Telephone Tapes 1971, ed. Ken Hughes] (Charlottesville: University of Virginia Press, 2014), www.prde.upress. virginia.edu.

28 "Richard Nixon and Henry A. Kissinger on 13 June 1971," Conversation 005–059, *Presidential Recordings Digital Edition* [Nixon Telephone Tapes 1971, ed. Ken Hughes] (Charlottesville: University of Virginia Press, 2014), www.prde.upress.virginia.edu.

29 *Id.*

30 *See id.*

31 *See* "Richard Nixon, Henry A. Kissinger, and John N. Mitchell on 14 June 1971," Conversation 005–070, *Presidential Recordings Digital Edition* [Nixon Telephone Tapes 1971, ed. Ken Hughes] (Charlottesville: University of Virginia Press, 2014), www.prde.upress.virginia.edu.

32 *Id.*

33 *Id.*

34 *See id.*

35 Chokshi, "Behind the Race."

36 *Id.*

37 Neil Sheehan, "Mitchell Seeks to Halt Series on Vietnam, but Times Refuses," *New York Times,* June 15, 1971.

38 *Id.*

39 *See* Abrams, *Speaking Freely,* 17–18.

40 *See id.* at 13.

41 *See id.* at 7.

42 *Id.; see also* James L. Greenfield, "How the New York Times Published the Pentagon Papers," Salon, December 17, 2017, www.salon.com.

43 Abrams, *Speaking Freely,* 18.

44 *See* Abrams, *Speaking Freely,* 18.

45 *See* James D. Zirin, *The Mother Court: Tales of Cases That Mattered in America's Greatest Trial Court* (Chicago: ABA Publishing 2014), 113; Abrams, *Speaking Freely,* 18.

46 *See* "Judge Gurfein's First Case" (editorial), *New York Times,* December 18, 1979; Rudenstine, *The Day the Presses Stopped,* 105.

47 *See* Abrams, *Speaking Freely,* 19–20; Fred P. Graham, "Judge, at Request of U.S., Halts Times Vietnam Series Four Days Pending Hearing on Injunction," *New York Times,* July 16, 1971. Legal definition of "temporary restraining order": a temporary restraining order is a short-term order that is granted when the party seeking it successfully demonstrates that immediate and irreparable harm will occur if no action is taken.

48 *See* Abrams, *Speaking Freely,* 25 (Abrams also discussed Bickel's position in a seminar at his law firm, Cahill Gordon & Reindel, on February 14, 2018).

49 Bickel and Abrams also heavily emphasized a statutory argument that the Espionage Act's Section 793, which the government claimed was the specific federal law violated by the *New York Times,* did not directly authorize the government to bring a prior restraint action. *See id.* at 14–16, 23.

50 *Id.* at 15–16; *see Near v. Minnesota,* 283 U.S. 697, 718 (1931) ("The fact that, for approximately one hundred and fifty years, there has been almost an entire absence of attempts to impose previous restraints upon publications . . . is significant of the deep-seated conviction that such restraints would violate constitutional right").

51 *See id.* at 16.

52 "Text of Gurfein Opinion Upholding the Times and Kaufman Order Extending Ban," *New York Times,* June 20, 1971.

53 *Id.*

54 *See id.*

55 *See* Benjamin C. Bradlee, "Big Ben: The Pentagon Papers," *Washington Post,* September 17, 1995.

56 *See id.* The *Washington Post* headline on June 18, 1971, would read: "Documents Reveal U.S. Effort in '54 to Delay Viet Election." *See* www.apps.washingtonpost.com.

57 *See* Ben Bradlee, *A Good Life: Newspapering and Other Adventures* (New York: Simon & Schuster, 1996), 308.

58 *See id.*

59 Chokshi, "Behind the Race"; Ronald K. L. Collins and Sam Chaltain, *We Must Not Be Afraid to Be Free: Stories of Free Expression in America* (New York: Oxford University Press 2011), 337 n.56 ("Although nineteen newspapers published parts of the Pentagon Papers, the government only pursued TROs for The New York Times, The Washington Post, The Boston Globe, and The St. Louis Post-Dispatch"); Ellsberg, *Secrets,* 403.

60 *See* Abrams, *Speaking Freely,* 34–35.

61 *See id.* at 35–36.

62 *See* Supreme Court of the United States, "Oral Arguments," www.supremecourt.gov; C-SPAN, "Chief Justice Roberts on Oral Argument" (video), October 6, 2009, www.c-span.org (Roberts discussing Supreme Court oral argument from his perspective as a former litigator and now as a member of the Court).

63 *See* Amanda Frost, "Academic Highlight: Does Oral Argument Matter?," *SCOTUSblog,* March 24, 2016, www.scotusblog.com.

64 Legal definition of "solicitor general": the solicitor general is the fourth-highest-ranking person in the US attorney general's office, whose primary role is to argue on behalf of the United States government in cases before the Supreme Court. *See* US Department of Justice, Office of the Solicitor General, www.justice.gov.

65 *See* Bob Woodward and Scott Armstrong, *The Brethren: Inside the Supreme Court* (New York: Simon & Schuster, 1979), 143.

66 *New York Times Company v. United States,* Oyez, 1964, www.oyez.org.

67 *Id.*

68 *See id.*

69 *Id.* (internal quotation marks omitted).

70 *See* Rudenstine, *The Day the Presses Stopped,* 259; *see also Speaking Freely,* 17, 36–37, 42 ("But what of Justices Stewart and White, the center of the Court in those days?").

71 *See New York Times v. United States,* Oyez.

72 *Id.*

73 *Id.*

74 *See* Abrams, *Speaking Freely,* at 43.

75 *See* Woodward and Armstrong, *The Brethren*, 145.

76 *New York Times*, 403 U.S. at 714. The Court's three paragraph ruling was issued as an unusual *per curiam* decision. Legal definition of "per curiam": a *per curiam* (in Latin meaning "by the court") opinion is issued on behalf of the court, as opposed to a named individual judge as is typical.

77 *New York Times*, 403 U.S. at 714.

78 Fred P. Graham, "First Amendment Rule Held to Block Most Prior Restraints," *New York Times*, July 1, 1971.

79 *New York Times*, 403 U.S. at 763 (internal citations omitted).

80 Graham, "First Amendment Rule."

81 *New York Times*, 403 U.S. at 715.

82 *Id*. at 717.

83 *See id*. at 730.

84 *Id*.

85 *See* Abrams, *Speaking Freely*, 57.

86 *See id*. at 43–44.

87 Justice White's opinion (joined by Justice Stewart) seemed to support prosecution. *See New York Times*, 403 U.S. at 733. *See also* Abrams, *Speaking Freely*, 58 ("A majority of the Supreme Court left open the possibility . . . of criminal sanctions being imposed upon the press following publication of the Papers themselves"); Rudenstein, *The Day the Presses Stopped*, 343.

88 *See* Rudenstein, *The Day the Presses Stopped*, 341–42; Collins and Chaltain, *We Must Not Be Afraid to Be Free* (Ellsberg "faced twelve felony charges and a possible total of 115 years in prison"); Ellsberg, *Secrets*, 414, 430.

89 *See* Rudenstein, *The Day the Presses Stopped*, at 323; "The 1972 Pulitzer Prizes," www.pulitzer.org.

90 *See* Dana Priest, "Did the Pentagon Papers Matter?," *Columbia Journalism Review*, Spring 2016 ("The Pentagon Papers decision tilted the power balance between the government and the media to the media's side"); Abrams, *Speaking Freely*, 53 ("There are many who hold that, for better or worse, publication of the Pentagon Papers marked the beginning of a new period of press militancy").

91 Abrams, *Speaking Freely*, 53 (quoting Harvard law professor Charles Nesson).

92 *See* Jordan Moran, "Nixon and the Pentagon Papers," University of Virginia, Miller Center, www.millercenter.org.

93 *See* Priest, "Did the Pentagon Papers Matter?" ("The Plumbers also inadvertently helped Ellsberg and Russo. The judge dropped charges against the men in 1973 after learning Ellsberg's psychiatrist's office had been burglarized"); Abrams, *Speaking Freely*, 53; Rudenstein, *The Day the Presses Stopped*, 342; Martin Arnold, "Pentagon Papers Charges Are Dismissed; Judge Byrne Frees Ellsberg and Russo, Assails 'Improper Governemnt Conduct,'" *New York Times*, May 12, 1973 (describing granting motion to dismiss on its eighty-ninth day of trial).

94 Floyd Abrams made this comment in a seminar on the Pentagon Papers and *The Post* film at his law firm, Cahill Gordon & Reindel, on February 14, 2018.

95 *See* Brian Farkas, "Donald Trump and Stormy Daniels: An Arbitration Case Study," *ABA Dispute Resolution Magazine*, Summer 2018, 14.

96 *Id.; see also* Callum Borchers, "Has Trump's Legal Battle with Stormy Daniels 'Already Been Won in Arbitration'?," *Washington Post*, March 8, 2018.

97 For a clarifying discussion of the highly complicated procedural nature of these legal maneuvers, which included actions in arbitration, state, and federal courts, *see* Farkas, "Donald Trump and Stormy Daniels," 14–15.

98 *See* Brian Stelter, "Stormy Daniels Gave Big Boost to '60 Minutes' Ratings," CNNMoney, March 26, 2018, www.money.cnn.com ("Anderson Cooper's interview with Stormy Daniels . . . averaged 22.1 million viewers for Sunday's show . . . more than twice as many viewers than a typical edition of the show").

99 Charlie Savage, "'A Simple Private Transaction': Trump Lays Out a Defense in a Campaign-Finance Case," *New York Times*, December 10, 2018.

100 *See* Benjamin Weiser and William K. Rashbaum, "Cohen Gets 3 Years in Prison for 'Smorgasbord of Fraudulent Conduct,'" *New York Times*, December 13, 2018. Cohen also admitted to working with the tabloid publisher American Media (owner of the *National Enquirer*) to pay former *Playboy* model Karen McDougal $150,000 to prevent her story of an alleged ten-month affair with Trump from becoming public. *See* Mike McIntire, Charlie Savage, and Jim Rutenberg, "Tabloid Publisher's Deal in Hush-Money Inquiry Adds to Trump's Danger," *New York Times*, December 13, 2018.

101 Jim Rutenberg, "It's a Tawdry Tabloid Saga, but It's More," *New York Times*, December 10, 2018.

102 "His Dirty Deeds" (editorial), *New York Times*, December 13, 2018.

103 *See* Philip Bump, "The Evidence Undercutting Trump's Insistence He Didn't Know about the Stormy Daniels Payment," *Washington Post*, March 1, 2019; Joe Palazzolo, Nicole Hong, Michael Rothfeld, Rebecca Davis O'Brien, and Rebecca Ballhaus, "Donald Trump Played Central Role in Hush Payoffs to Stormy Daniels and Karen McDougal," *Wall Street Journal*, November 9, 2018.

104 *See, e.g., Nebraska Press Association v. Stuart*, 427 US 539, 558 (1976) (in the Pentagon Papers case, "Each of the six concurring Justices and the three dissenting Justices expressed his views separately, but every member of the Court, tacitly or explicitly accepted . . . prior restraint as presumptively unconstitutional" [internal quotations omitted]); Abrams, *Speaking Freely*, 55 ("The practical effect of the Nebraska ruling, built in turn upon that in the Pentagon Papers case, has been virtually to end the issuance of prior restraints on publication").

105 *New York Times*, 403 U.S. at 730.

106 *See* Susan E. Seager, "Donald J. Trump Is a Libel Bully but Also a Libel Loser," Media Law Resource Center, October 2016, www.medialaw.org ("Trump and his companies have been involved in a mind-boggling 4,000 lawsuits over the last 30 years and sent countless threatening cease-and-desist letters to journalists and critics").

107 *See* Katelyn Polantz, "Trump Administration Asks Court to Stop Release of Bolton's Book by Claiming It Would Reveal Government Secrets," CNN Politics, June 17, 2020, www.cnn.com.

108 *See* Charlie Savage, "Judge Rejects Trump Request for Order Blocking Bolton's Memoir," *New York Times*, June 20, 2020. Judge Royce C. Lamberth of the Federal District Court of the District of Columbia's primary reason for refusing to grant an injunctive order was that in advance of publication "thousands of copies" of the book had already been sent around the globe to the press and booksellers: "the horse is already out of the barn." Distressingly, the judge did not then address First Amendment concerns or emphasize that prior restraints are presumptively unconstitutional. He did however warn that Bolton could face "civil (and potentially criminal) liability" for allegedly breaching pre-publication review agreements. *See United States v. Bolton*, Memorandum Order, June 20, 2020.

109 *See* Maggie Haberman, "Trump Family Asks Court to Stop Publication of Tell-All by President's Niece," *New York Times*, June 23, 2020.

110 *See* Maggie Haberman and Alan Feuer, "Tell-All Book on Trump Can Move Forward Pending Hearing, Judge Rules," *New York Times*, July 1, 2020 (a New York appellate judge reversed a lower court's order that would have stopped publication, allowing Simon & Schuster to proceed with the release of Mary Trump's book).

111 *See id.*; Savage, "Judge Rejects Trump Request for Order."

112 *See, e.g., Robert S. Trump v. Mary L Trump and Simon & Schuster*, Defendant Mary L. Trump's Memorandum of Law in Opposition to Plaintiff's Motion for a Preliminary Injunction and Temporary Restraining Order, July 2, 2020, www.gibsondunn.com (Mary Trump's lawyers cite *New York Times v. United States* on page 1 of their brief): John Bolton (@AmbJohnBolton), Twitter, June 16, 2020, www.twitter.com (Bolton retweeting an @ACLU statement: "50 years ago, SCOTUS rejected the Nixon administration's attempt to block the publication of the Pentagon Papers, establishing that government censorship is unconstitutional. Any Trump administration efforts to stop John Bolton's book from being published are doomed to fail").

Chapter 6. Flipping Off the President and Fuck the Draft

1 Christine Hauser, "Cyclist Lost Her Job after Raising Middle Finger at Trump's Motorcade," *New York Times*, November 6, 2017.

2 Lily Herman, "This Woman Flipped Off Donald Trump's Motorcade Last Year. She's Still Paying for It," Refinery29, June 29, 2018, www.refinery29.com.

3 Steve Herman (@W7VOA), Twitter, October 28, 2017, www.twitter.com.

4 Petula Dvorak, "She Flipped Off President Trump—and Got Fired from Her Government Contracting Job," *Washington Post*, November 6, 2017.

5 *Late Show with Stephen Colbert*, "Hire the Woman Who Was Fired for Flipping Off Trump," CBS, November 6, 2017, www.cbs.com.

6 Dvorak, "She Flipped Off President Trump"; Hauser, "Cyclist Lost Her Job."

7 *Id.*

8   See Debra Cassens Weiss, "Woman Who Flipped the Bird at Trump Motorcade Sues over Forced Resignation," *ABA Journal*, April 5, 2018.

9   See Petula Dvorak, "The Woman Who Got Fired for Flipping Off the President Trump Just Sued her Former Employer," *Washington Post*, April 4, 2018; Debra Cassens Weiss, "Woman Is Fired after Flipping the Bird at Trump Motorcade; Does She Have a Case?," *ABA Journal*, November 8, 2017.

10 See *Cohen v. California*, 403 U.S. 15, 23 (1971) (referring to the word "fuck" as "this unseemly expletive"). It may go without saying, but giving someone the middle finger, or flipping someone the bird, generally means the same as "fuck you." See Slang by Dictionary.com, "What Does Middle Finger Mean?," www.dictionary.com ("giving someone the middle finger, an offensive gesture in which a person flips up their middle finger in a fist to show contempt or defiance" means "fuck you"); Melissa Mohr, *Holy Shit: A Brief History of Swearing* (New York: Oxford University Press, 2013), 36 (in ancient Rome, the middle finger, or "*digitus impudicus*, [was] already known as a sign of aggression and disrespect, from its resemblance to the erect penis"); Lauren Rosewarne, *American Taboo: The Forbidden Words, Unspoken Rules, and Secret Morality of Popular Culture* (Santa Barbara, CA: Praeger, 2013) ("Described using a variety of names—including *digitus impudicus* (impudent finger), the one finger salute, flipping the bird, or flicking someone off—the erect middle finger translates as *up yours* at the innocent end of the spectrum, and *fuck you* or *fuck off* at the more aggressive extreme").

11 See *Cohen*, 403 U.S. at 16; Daniel A. Farber, "Civilizing Public Discourse: An Essay on Professor Bickel, Justice Harlan, and the Enduring Significance of Cohen v. California," 1980 *Duke Law Journal* 283, 286 (1980).

12 See Susan J. Balter-Reitz, "*Cohen v. California*," in *Free Speech on Trial: Communication Perspectives on Landmark Supreme Court Decisions*, edited by Richard A. Parker (Tuscaloosa: University of Alabama Press, 2003), 160; Richard C. Cortner, *The Supreme Court and Civil Liberties Policy* (Palo Alto, CA: Mayfield, 1975), 123.

13 *Cohen*, 403 U.S. at 16; see Balter-Reitz, "*Cohen v. California*," 160.

14 See Farber, "Civilizing Public Discourse," 286.

15 See David L. Hudson, Jr., "Paul Robert Cohen and 'His' Famous Free-Speech Case," Freedom Forum Institute, May 4, 2016, www.freedomforuminstitute.org.

16 *Cohen*, 403 U.S. at 27 n.3.

17 *Id.*; Cortner, *The Supreme Court*, 123.

18 *Id.*

19 *Id.* at 16. Forty-five years later, Cohen would tell a somewhat different story about how the stenciling had been done by a woman he encountered the night before his trip to the courthouse. "I had a Ph.D. in partying back in those days," he said in an interview. "I wasn't trying to make a political statement." Hudson, "Paul Robert Cohen" (quoting Cohen, who no longer goes by that last name after having "adopted a family surname").

20 *Cohen*, 403 U.S. at 16–17.

21 *Id.* at 16 (citing California Penal Code § 415).

22 *People v. Cohen*, 1 Cal. App. 3d 94, 99 (Cal. Ct. App. 1969).

23 *Id.* at 103. "The California Supreme Court declined review by a divided vote." *Cohen,* 403 U.S. at 17.

24 *See* Farber, "Civilizing Public Discourse," 287. *See also* Nadine Strossen, "Justice Harlan's Enduring Importance for Current Civil Liberties Issues, from Marriage Equality to Dragnet NSA Surveillance," 61 *New York Law School Law Review* 331, 337 (2016–2017) ("Back then, the so-called 'F-word' was analogous to the so-called 'N-word' today: so taboo that polite people were loath to utter it for any purpose").

25 "Fuck the Draft" as a slogan would also gain popularity on a poster, designed and distributed in 1968 by activist Kiyoshi Kuromiya. *See* Victoria and Albert Museum, "Fuck the Draft," www.collections.vam.ac.uk ("The language Kuromiya used in the poster was designed to shock the establishment and resonates with the ways in which 1960s American youth culture sought to challenge authority through alternative politics, lifestyles, fashion and music").

26 *See* Tom Bowman, "Military Victory but Political Defeat: The Tet Offensive 50 Years Later," NPR, January 29, 2018, www.npr.org; Julian E. Zelizer, "How the Tet Offensive Undermined American Faith in Government," *Atlantic,* January 15, 2018; Barbara Crossette, "Tet Offensive: Turning Point in Vietnam War," *New York Times,* January 31, 1988; *see also* Daniel S. Levy, "Behind the Anti-War Protests That Swept America in 1968," *Time,* January 19, 2018 ("While a March 1967 poll had shown that more than half of Americans supported the way Johnson was handling the war, by early 1968 that proportion was down to about a third").

27 Joel Achenbach, "Did the News Media, Led by Walter Cronkite, Lose the War in Vietnam," *Washington Post,* May 25, 2018 (quoting Cronkite's February 27, 1968, program, "Report from Vietnam: Who, What, When Where, Why?," and noting that in response President Johnson has been attributed as saying, "If I've lost Cronkite, I've lost Middle America"); *All Things Considered,* "Final Words: Cronkite's Vietnam Commentary," NPR, July 18, 2009, www.npr.org.

28 *See* Ron Elving, "Remembering 1968: LBJ Surprises Nation with Announcement He Won't Seek Re-election," NPR, March 25, 2018, www.npr.org.

29 Christopher M. Fairman, *FUCK: Word Taboo and Protecting Our First Amendment Liberties* (Naperville, IL: Sphinx Publishing, 2009), 109.

30 Hudson, "Paul Robert Cohen" (quoting Cohen).

31 *Cohen v. California,* Oyez, 1971, www.oyez.org. The chief justice "may have been particularly sensitive because a group of nuns were there that day." Anthony Lewis, *Freedom for the Thought That We Hate: A Biography of the First Amendment* (New York: Basic Books, 2007), 131.

32 *See* Bob Woodward and Scott Armstrong, *The Brethren: Inside the Supreme Court* (New York: Simon & Schuster, 1979), 129; *see also* Adam Liptak, "A Word Heard Often, except at the Supreme Court," *New York Times,* April 30, 2012 ("By repeating

the word in court, the protester's lawyer showed that it could have a role in public discourse").

33 *Cohen v. California*, Oyez.

34 *See* Thomas G. Krattenmaker, "Looking Back at *Cohen v. California: A 40 Year Retrospective from Inside the Court*," 20 *William & Mary Bill of Rights Journal* 651, 654–55 n.17 (2012).

35 Strossen, "Justice Harlan's Enduring Importance," at 337 n.42 (quoting Professor Joel Gora of Brooklyn Law School, who was in the court during the *Cohen* argument).

36 *See* Fairman, *FUCK: Word Taboo*, 109 (discussing how Cohen's lawyer had "to convince nine judges, who were not young, to be comfortable with the youth culture of the sixties").

37 *Cohen v. California*, Oyez.

38 *Id.*

39 *Id.*

40 *See* Associated Press, "Judge in Paris Hilton Case Praised as Unflappable, Fair," *Houston Chronicle*, June 9, 2007.

41 *Cohen v. California*, Oyez.

42 *Id.*

43 *Id.*

44 *Id.*

45 *Id.*

46 *Id.*

47 Legal definition of "law clerk": law clerks are generally newly graduated law students who work for a judge during a one-year clerkship. The clerks assist the judges in researching and writing their decisions, as well as other court matters.

48 *See* Administrative Office of the US Courts, "Supreme Court Procedures," United States Courts, www.uscourts.gov.

49 *See* Woodward and Armstrong, *The Brethren*, 131.

50 Legal definition of "free speech absolutist": a free speech absolutist is someone who believes in the theory, often championed by Justice Black, that the government should literally "make no law" that restricts free speech rights.

51 *See* Woodward and Armstrong, *The Brethren*, 131–32; Strossen, "Justice Harlan's Enduring Importance," 332.

52 *See* Woodward and Armstrong, *The Brethren*, 131.

53 *Id.*

54 *Id.*; *see* Krattenmaker, "Looking Back at *Cohen v. California*," 655.

55 *See* Woodward and Armstrong, *The Brethren*, 131.

56 The chief justice or the senior justice in the majority assigns who will write the majority opinion. According to Woodward and Armstrong's reporting in *The Brethren*, "Douglas, the senior member of the new 5-to-4 majority, realized that Harlan was the shakiest vote. Over the course of thirty-two years on the Court, he

had learned that the best way to hold a swing vote was to assign that Justice to write the decision." *Id.* at 132.

57 *Id.* at 131.

58 *See* C-SPAN, "Process: Supreme Court Robing Room" (video), June 13, 2018, www.c-span.org (providing a view of the robing room and a description of the robing process).

59 Woodward and Armstrong, *The Brethren*, 133; *see* Krattenmaker, "Looking Back at *Cohen v. California*," 655-56.

60 *See* Woodward and Armstrong, *The Brethren*, 133.

61 *See* Farber, "Civilizing Public Discourse," 290 n.47 ("A LEXIS search indicates that the *Cohen* opinion contains the first appearance of the word 'fuck' or its derivatives in the United States Reports").

62 *See Cohen*, 403 U.S. at 18.

63 *Cohen*, 403 U.S. at 18.

64 *Id.*

65 *Id.* at 19–20.

66 *See id.* at 19–22. For further discussion of obscenity, see chapter 7. The complex and arguably inconsistent "fighting words" doctrine concerns permitted restrictions on speech involving "those personally abusive epithets which, when addressed to the ordinary citizen, are, as a matter of common knowledge, inherently likely to provoke violent reaction." *Cohen*, 403 U.S. at 20; *see* David L. Hudson, Jr., "Fighting Words," Freedom Forum Institute, July 2009, www.freedomforuminstitute.org (overview of fighting words cases and context).

67 *See* Krattenmaker, "Looking Back at *Cohen v. California*," 665.

68 *Cohen*, 403 U.S. at 23.

69 *Id.* at 22.

70 *Id.* at 23. *See* chapter 4 for a full discussion of *Tinker v. Des Moines*.

71 *Cohen*, 403 U.S. at 22.

72 *Id.* at 24–25 (internal citation omitted).

73 *Id.* at 25.

74 *Id.*

75 The poetic quality of this phrase and a number of other important passages in the opinion may have been inspired by Harlan's instruction to his clerk to make the draft "Elizabethan." *See* Krattenmaker, "Looking Back at *Cohen v. California*," 652–53 n.8.

76 *Cohen*, 403 U.S. at 26.

77 *Id.*

78 *Id.* The Orwellian overtones of this warning still feel contemporary. *See* George Orwell, *Nineteen Eighty-Four* (New York: Alfred A. Knopf, 1949), 313 (from the "Principles of Newspeak" appendix: "Newspeak was designed not to extend but to diminish the range of thought, and this purpose was indirectly assisted by cutting the choice of words down to a minimum").

79 *Cohen*, 403 U.S. at 26.

80 White joined only the second paragraph of Black's dissent, which discussed a California Supreme Court case that construed the statue at issue in *Cohen*, but was decided after *Cohen*, and therefore recommended reconsideration by the California courts. *See id.* at 27–28.

81 *Id.* at 27. Blackmun, joined by Burger and Black, also wrote in a single sentence that the case was "well within" the fighting words exception. *Id.*

82 *Id.*

83 *See* Krattenmaker, "Looking Back at *Cohen v. California*," 684 ("Undoubtedly, a more powerful dissent than the pithy little Blackmun note could have been written. Indeed, one might ask whether *Cohen* has withstood the test of time and the judgment of history fairly well in part because it was not squarely challenged when written").

84 Lewis, *Freedom for the Thought That We Hate*, 132; *see* Krattenmaker, "Looking Back at *Cohen v. California*," 682 ("*Snyder* [v. *Phelps*, discussed in chapter 9] shows that *Cohen*, forty years after its release, is alive and well in the opinion's conclusions that the picketing at issue 'cannot be restricted simply because it is upsetting or arouses contempt' and that '[s]peech is powerful. . . . [W]e cannot react, to [the] pain [it inflicted] by punishing the speaker'").

85 *See* Farber, "Civilizing Public Discourse," 203 ("offensiveness is often an important part of the speaker's message. . . . Suppressing this language violates a cardinal principle of a free society, that truths are better confronted than repressed. As long as we live in an ugly world, ugly speech must have its forum. We cannot expect to have, nor should we require, true civility in discourse until we achieve civility in society"). Although in *Cohen* the Supreme Court protected the use of curse words in general, it did not overrule its past decision in *Chaplinsky v. New Hampshire*, 315 U.S. 568 (1942), which allowed the state to prohibit the use of curse words *directed at* someone. *See Cohen*, 403 U.S. at 20 (citing *Chaplinsky*, holding "fighting words," which are "those personally abusive epithets, which, when addressed to the ordinary citizen, are . . . inherently likely to provoke violent reaction," were unprotected by the First Amendment); *see also* David L. Hudson, Jr., "Fighting Words Case Still Making Waves in First Amendment Jurisprudence," Freedom Forum Institute, March 9, 2012, www.freedomforuminstitute.org.

86 Strossen, "Justice Harlan's Enduring Importance," 336–37 (Nadine Strossen is the John Marshall Harlan II Professor of Law at New York Law School and the past president of the American Civil Liberties Union, 1991–2008).

87 *See* Balter-Reitz, "*Cohen v. California*," 160 (*Cohen* "is perhaps the Court's finest articulation of the importance of protecting the ability of protesters to use the language they find most appropriate to their message"). Thanks to my son Leo for his help talking through with me this meaning of *Cohen*, particularly in comparison to *Tinker* (discussed in chapter 4).

88 Hudson, "Paul Robert Cohen" (quoting Cohen).

89 *See* Debra Cassens Weiss, "Judge Tosses Wrongful Termination Claim by Woman Forced to Resign after Flipping Off Trump Motorcade," *ABA Journal*, July 2, 2018. The judge did allow another claim, that Briskman was not given two of the four weeks of severance she says she was promised, to move forward. *Id*. It appears that Briskman eventually won her severance claim. *See* Hayley Miller, "She Famously Flipped Off Trump's Motorcade. Now She's Running for Office," HuffPost, September 12, 2018, www.huffpost.com; Jenna Portnoy, "The Cyclist Who Flipped Off Trump's Motorcade Is Running for Public Office," *Washington Post*, September 12, 2018.

90 *See* Matthew S. Schwartz, "Police Officer Can't Pull Over Driver for Giving Him the Finger, Court Rules," NPR, March 15, 2019, www.npr.org (describing a Sixth Circuit decision from 2019, *Cruise-Gulyas v. Minard*, that held, "Any reasonable officer would know that a citizen who raises her middle finger engages in speech protected by the First Amendment," and citing *Cohen*).

91 *See* Passman & Kaplan, P.C., "Woman Who 'Flipped Off President Loses Termination Lawsuit," July 10, 2018, www.passmanandkaplan.com; Braden Campbell, "Woman Who Flipped Trump Off Loses Unfair Firing Claim," Law360, June 29, 2018, www.law360.com; Lata Nott and Melemaikalani Moniz, "Government Employees & First Amendment Overview," Freedom Forum Institute, April 24, 2017, www.freedomforuminstitute.org.

92 *See* Petula Dvorak, "She Famously Flipped Off the President. Now Juli Briskman Is Running for Office," *Washington Post*, July 18, 2019.

93 *Id*.

94 *See* Loudoun Now, "Ballot Set: Primaries Settle 6 Races; 70 Candidates in Running for November," June 11, 2019, www.loudounnow.com.

95 *See* Dvorak, "She Famously Flipped Off the President."

96 Portnoy, "The Cyclist Who Flipped Off Trump's Motorcade" (quoting Briskman).

97 *See* Nicholas Bogel-Burroughs, "The Woman Who Flipped Off Trump Has Won an Election in Virginia," *New York Times*, November 6, 2019.

Chapter 7. Samantha Bee, Seven Dirty Words, and Indecency

1 *See, e.g., Full Frontal with Samantha Bee* (TBS), "Is Tucker Carlson a White Supremacist?," YouTube, March 13, 2019, www.youtube.com (over one million views on YouTube).

2 *See* Sonia Rao, "Samantha Bee Apologizes for Calling Ivanka Trump a Vulgar Word after White House Condemnation," *Washington Post*, March 31, 2018.

3 *See* Ivanka Trump (@IvankaTrump), Twitter, May 27, 2018, www.twitter.com.

4 Megh Wright, "Samantha Bee to Ivanka Trump: 'Do Something about Your Dad's Immigration Practices, You Feckless C*nt!," Vulture, May 31, 2018, www.vulture. com (video clip included at link, with Bee's unbleeped use of the word).

5 John Koblin, "Slur toward Ivanka Trump Brings an Apology from Samantha Bee," *New York Times*, March 31, 2018.

6 Samantha Bee (@iamsambee), Twitter, May 31, 2018, www.twitter.com.

7 Donald J. Trump (@realDonaldTrump), Twitter, June 1, 2018, www.twitter.com.

8 *Full Frontal with Samantha Bee* (TBS), "A Message from Sam," YouTube, June 6, 2018, www.youtube.com.

9 On reclaiming the C-word, *see* Samantha Schmidt, "Why the C-Word Is So Taboo, and Why Some Women Want to Reclaim It," *Washington Post*, June 1, 2018; Katy Waldman, "Ivanka Trump, Samantha Bee, and the Strange Path of an Ancient Epithet," *New Yorker*, June 1, 2018 (providing a history of the word, and scathingly supporting the Bee word choice: "'Cunt' makes of womanhood something repugnant, and so does Ivanka, who embraces the shine and the softness of femininity at the same time that she rejects its bravery, love, and power").

10 George Carlin with Tony Hendra, *Last Words* (New York: Simon & Schuster, 2009), 162. For the full audio of the recording, *see* "George Carlin—Seven Words You Can Never Say on Television," YouTube, April 10, 2011, www.youtube.com.

11 James Sullivan, *Seven Dirty Words: The Life and Crimes of George Carlin* (New York: Da Capo Press, 2010), 142 ("For Carlin, the symbolic seven words changed everything. From then on, he would forever be known as the comic who shattered the language barrier, for better and worse"). For more on Lenny Bruce's free speech trials, *see* Ronald K. L. Collins and David M. Skover, *The Trials of Lenny Bruce: The Fall and Rise of an American Icon* (Naperville, IL: Sourcebooks, 2002).

12 Carlin, *Last Words*, 167.

13 *See* Sullivan, *Seven Dirty Words*, 132.

14 *See* Mark Goff, "Summerfest 50: George Carlin's Big Gig Act for the Ages," On Milwaukee, June 13, 2017, www.onmilwaukee.com; Matthew J. Prigge, "You Can't Say That at Summerfest: The City of Milwaukee v. George Carlin," *Shepherd Express*, June 18, 2013, www.shepherdexpress.com.

15 *Id.*

16 Carlin, *Last Words*, 168; Sullivan, *Seven Dirty Words*, 137.

17 Carlin, *Last Words*, 169.

18 *FCC v. Pacifica Foundation*, 438 U.S. 726, 751–55 (1978) (an appendix to the Supreme Court's decision includes "a verbatim transcript of the 'Filthy Words' prepared by the Federal Communications Commission"). The full audio of the recording is available to listen to at George Carlin—Topic, "Filthy Words," YouTube, April 29, 2016, www.youtube.com.

19 Pacifica had been investigated by the FCC over content issues almost a decade before the Carlin incident. *See* Adam M. Samaha, "Story of FCC v. Pacifica Foundation," in *First Amendment Stories*, edited by Richard W. Garnett and Andrew Koppelman (New York: Foundation Press, 2012), 381 ("FCC licensing proceeding scrutinized Pacifica broadcasts of gay men discussing homosexuality and a reading of Edward Albee's *Zoo Story*").

20 Samaha, "Story of FCC v. Pacifica Foundation," 382.

21 FCC, "Citizen's Complaint against Pacifica Foundation Station WBAI (FM), New York, NY—Declaratory Order," February 12, 1975, www.FCC.gov (quoting from WBAI response to complaint).

22 *FCC v. Pacifica Foundation*, 438 U.S. 726, 730 (1978).

23 FCC, "Citizen's Complaint against Pacifica."

24 *See FCC v. Pacifica Foundation*, 438 U.S. 726, 730 (1978) ("Pacifica stated that it was not aware of any other complaints about the broadcast"); *FCC v. Pacifica*, Oyez, 1978, www.oyez.org (the FCC's counsel, Joseph A. Marino, acknowledged during oral argument, "We only received one complaint").

25 Samaha, "Story of FCC v. Pacifica Foundation," 384 (quoting Douglas interview).

26 *See id.* at 383.

27 Carlin, *Last Words*, 172 (quoting journalist Nat Hentoff).

28 *See* FCC, "The Public and Broadcasting," March 25, 2019, www.FCC.gov.

29 *See* FCC, "Obscenity, Indecency, Profanity—Complaint Process," www.FCC.gov.

30 *See* FCC, "Obscene, Indecent and Profane Broadcasts," September 13, 2017, www.FCC.gov.

31 FCC, "Citizen's Complaint against Pacifica."

32 *Id.*

33 FCC, "Citizen's Complaint against Pacifica." Legal definition of "declaratory order": a declaratory order is a government agency decision that legally binds the parties and is intended to clarify agency regulations, but does not impose a penalty.

34 *FCC v. Pacifica*, 438 U.S. at 732.

35 *Id.* at 755 n.23.

36 *Id.* at 731 (internal quotes omitted).

37 *Pacifica Foundation v. FCC*, 556 F.2d 9, 13 (D.C. Cir. 1977).

38 *Id.* at 17.

39 *Id.* at 30.

40 *See* Adam Samaha, "The Story of FCC v. Pacifica Foundation (and Its Second Life)" (University of Chicago Public Law & Legal Theory Working Paper No. 314, 2010), 14.

41 *See FCC v. Pacifica*, 438 U.S. at 729.

42 *Miller v. California*, 413 U.S. 15, 24 (1973).

43 *FCC v. Pacifica*, Oyez.

44 Collins and Skover, *The Trials of Lenny Bruce*, 435.

45 *See* Adam Liptak, "A Word Heard Often, except at the Supreme Court," *New York Times*, April 30, 2012 (pointing out that when the lawyer took the hint and declined to say the actual "seven dirty words" in his oral argument, he lost the case; but when the lawyer in *Cohen v. California* said the word "fuck" at oral argument, he won).

46 *FCC v. Pacifica*, 438 U.S. at 745–46.

47 *Id.* at 748.

48 *Id.* at 748–49.

49 *Id.* at 749.

50 *Id.*

51 *Id.*

52 *Id.* (internal quotation omitted).

53 *Id.* at 750–51.

54 *Id.* at 762.

55 *Id.* at 765–66.

56 *FCC v. Pacifica*, 438 U.S. at 769 (internal quotation omitted).

57 *Id.* at 747. Stevens distinguished *Cohen* in terms of the speech penalties at issue ("It should be noted that the Commission imposed a far more moderate penalty on Pacifica than the state court imposed on Cohen. Even the strongest civil penalty at the Commission's command does not include criminal prosecution"). *Id.* at n.25.

58 *Id.* at 765.

59 *Id.* at 773.

60 *Id.* at 777.

61 Carlin later praised Justice Brennan's dissent in his own amusing way: "All right, Bill Brennan! We Irish stick together. And he got it right. Words were the issue. The Court was banning not just words but ways of thinking, acting, speaking, communicating with one another." Carlin, *Last Words*, 172. *See also* R. Wilfred Tremblay, *"FCC v. Pacifica Foundation"* in *Free Speech on Trial: Communication Perspectives on Landmark Supreme Court Decisions*, edited by Richard A. Parker (Tuscaloosa: University of Alabama Press, 2003), 230 ("Subsequent court rulings failed to apply *Pacifica* directly to other media, including the mail (*Bolger v. Youngs Drug Products Corporation*, 1983) . . . telephone (*Sable Communications v. FCC*, 1989), or the Internet (*Reno v. ACLU*, 1997)").

62 FCC, "Obscenity, Indecency, Profanity."

63 FCC, "Obscene, Indecent and Profane Broadcasts."

64 *See* Cynthia Chris, *The Indecent Screen: Regulating Television in the Twenty-First Century* (New Brunswick, NJ: Rutgers University Press, 2018), 49 ("Seeking to recognize that children are more likely to form a portion of the TV audience during some parts of the day than others, the commission established a 'safe harbor' for indecent broadcast speech. (The term safe harbor itself may invite confusion: it does not refer to the period that is safe for children to watch but rather to the period in which indecent programming is safe from regulatory action.)").

65 *See FCC v. Fox Television Stations*, 132 S. Ct. 2307, 2313 (2012) ("From 1978 to 1987, the Commission . . . brought no indecency enforcement actions").

66 *See In the Matter of Infinity Broadcasting Corporation of Pennsylvania*, 2 F.C.C. Rcd. 2705, 2706 (1987) (finding Stern's material "actionable under the indecency standard as clarified today"); *see also* Associated Press, "F.C.C. Fine Prompts Clear Channel to Drop Stern," *New York Times*, April 8, 2004 ("The Center for Public Integrity, a watchdog group, said fines against Stern accounted for almost half of the $4 million in penalties proposed by the FCC" between 1990 and 2004).

67 Robert L. Hilliard and Michael C. Keith, *Dirty Discourse: Sex and Indecency in Broadcasting* (Malden, MA: Blackwell Publishing, 2007), 66; Paul Farhi, "Stern Indecency Case Settled," *Washington Post*, September 2, 1995.

68 Hilliard and Keith, *Dirty Discourse*, 69; Farhi, "Stern Indecency Case Settled." The fight between the FCC and Howard Stern would continue for another decade. In June 2004, Clear Channel Communications settled with the FCC over indecency claims for a new record of $1.75 million in fines, which included a $495,000 fine against Stern. Clear Channel, the largest radio broadcasting company in the country at the time, had permanently dropped Stern's program in response to the FCC's fines. *See* Reporters Committee for Freedom of the Press, "Clear Channel Reaches $1.75 Million Settlement with FCC," June 11, 2004, www.rcfp.org. A few months later Stern made major news by leaving broadcast radio for Sirius Satellite Radio, finally taking himself beyond the reach of the FCC. *See* Krysten Crawford, "Howard Stern Jumps to Satellite," CNN Money, October 6, 2004, www.money.cnn.com.

69 *See FCC v. Fox*, 132 S. Ct. at 2314. In the Court's decision, the words "fuck" and "shit" are written out as "f***" and "s***." This is not how the court wrote the words in either the *Cohen* or *Pacifica* opinions (in both cases spelling out all the curse words fully). *See* Geoffrey R. Stone, "What the F***?," HuffPost, June 21, 2012, www.huffpost.com.

70 *See FCC v. Fox*, 132 S. Ct. at 2314.

71 *Id.*

72 *Id.* at 2314 (quoting the FCC *Golden Globes* order).

73 *Id.* at 2315.

74 *Id.* at 2314, 2319.

75 Jackson's breast was not fully exposed, since her nipple remained covered by jewelry. *See* Jon Pareles, "Justin Timberlake, Back at the Super Bowl. What about Janet?," *New York Times*, February 1, 2018 (also noting: "More than a decade later, particularly in the context of the #MeToo movement, the situation comes across as a demonstration of the victim-blaming that sustains male privilege. He grabbed, she was vulnerable—yet she faced the consequences"); Bethonie Butler and Elahe Izadi, "Everything You Forgot about Janet Jackson and Justin Timberlake's 2004 Super Bowl Controversy," *Washington Post*, February 1, 2018 (including a link to video of the incident).

76 *See* Butler and Izadi, "Everything You Forgot"; Reporters Committee for Freedom of the Press, "CBS Fined $550,000 for Superbowl Incident," September 22, 2004, www.rcfp.org.

77 *See* Associated Press, "Fines to Rise for Indecency in Broadcasts," *New York Times*, June 8, 2006 ("Congress gave notice to broadcasters on Wednesday that they would pay dearly for showing material like Janet Jackson's 2004 Super Bowl 'wardrobe malfunction,' passing legislation that would multiply indecency fines 10 times").

78 *See* Pub. L. No. 109–235; Broadcast Decency Act Enforcement Act of 2005, S. 193, 109th Cong. (2006). Since 2016, the FCC's indecency fines rose even higher, and will

continue to do so, based on the 2015 Inflation Adjustment Act, which "directs federal agencies to adjust their penalties for inflation each year." Eve K. Reed, "Beware: Higher Fines for FCC Violations Coming July 1, 2016," Wiley Rein LLP, June 30, 2016, www.wileyonmedia.com.

79 In 2009 the Supreme Court reversed decisions in the Fox and CBS cases on Administrative Procedure Act grounds, and remanded them for further consideration by the Second and Third Circuit courts. The cases would not return to the Supreme Court for review again until 2012. *See* Lili Levi, "'Smut and Nothing But': The FCC, Indecency, and Regulatory Transformations in the Shadows," 65 *Administrative Law Review* 509, 530–32 (2013) (citing *FCC v. Fox*, 556 U.S. 502 (2009); *FCC v. CBS*, 556 U.S. 1218 (2009)).

80 *See FCC v. Fox*, 132 S. Ct. at 2320.

81 *Id.*

82 *Id.* Only Justice Ginsburg, concurring, would also write to say that in her view *Pacifica* "was wrong when it issued. Time, technological advances, and the Commission's untenable rulings in the cases now before the Court show why Pacifica bears reconsideration." *Id.* at 2321.

83 *See FCC v. CBS*, 132 S. Ct. 2677 (2012); *see, e.g.,* Brian Feldman, "Looking Back at Nipplegate, the Last Great Pre-YouTube Scandal," *New York*, February 1, 2018. Legal definition of "certiorari": when the Supreme Court declines to review a case, it is denying certiorari. When the Supreme Court agrees to hear a case, it is granting certiorari. The term is frequently abbreviated as "cert." Four Supreme Court justices must agree to review a case in order for cert to be granted.

84 *See CBS v. FCC*, 633 F.3d 122, 124 (3d Cir. 2011) (FCC acted arbitrarily when it "improperly imposed a penalty on CBS for violating a previously unannounced policy").

85 *FCC v. CBS*, 132 S. Ct. 2677, 2678 (2012); *see* James Vicini, "High Court Agrees No Indecency Fine for CBS 'Wardrobe Malfunction,'" Reuters, June 29, 2012, www. reuters.com; Mike Sacks, "Janet Jackson 'Wardrobe Malfunction' Case Declined by Supreme Court, Erasing CBS Fine," HuffPost, June 29, 2012, www.hufpost.com.

86 One troubling irony resulting from the FCC's indecency policy occurred in 2007, when WBAI feared broadcasting a recording of Allen Ginsberg reading his poem "Howl" on the fiftieth anniversary of the state-court ruling holding that his work was not obscene. Given the threat of FCC fines, the Pacifica station felt compelled to play the recording only on its website, which is not subject to the agency's regulation. *See* Ronald K. L. Collins and David M. Skover, *The People v. Ferlinghetti: The Fight to Publish Allen Ginsberg's "Howl"* (Lanham, MD: Rowman & Littlefield, 2019), 96–98.

87 *See* FCC, "Obscene, Indecent and Profane Broadcasts" ("the same rules for indecency and profanity do not apply to cable, satellite TV and satellite radio because they are subscription services"). *See also* FCC, "Various Complaints against the Cable/Satellite Television Program 'Nip/Tuck,'" 20 FCC Rcd 4255 (2005) ("The Commission does not regulate cable indecency. In this regard, the Commission

recently stated: 'Indecency regulation is only applied to broadcast services,' not cable").

88 *Id; see* FCC, "'Nip/Tuck.'"

89 *See* Brendan Koerner, "Can the FCC Regulate HBO?: Michael Powell Promises to Crack Down on Cable. Can He?," Slate, February 12, 2004, www.slate.com.

90 *See* Bethonie Butler, "Is There Anything You Can't Say on TV Anymore? It's Complicated," *Washington Post*, March 29, 2016; Paul Levinson, "Naked Bodies, Three Showings a Week, No Commercials: The Sopranos as a Nuts-and-Bolts Triumph of Non-Network TV" in *This Thing of Ours: Investigating the Sopranos*, edited by David Lavery (New York: Columbia University Press, 2002), 28. *See also* Whitney Friedlander, "FCC Censorship Rules Vary for Broadcast, Cable, and Streaming," *Variety*, August 15, 2017.

91 Bee, and for that matter any cable performer, need only worry about the fallout from any potential indecent content in terms of the reactions from their advertisers and network bosses. *See* John Koblin, "Slur toward Ivanka Trump Brings an Apology from Samantha Bee," *New York Times*, March 31, 2018 (noting that the TBS network "issued an apology, but took no disciplinary action against the late night host").

92 *See* Alison Brower and Marisa Guthrie, eds., "The 35 Most Powerful People in New York Media 2019," *Hollywood Reporter*, April 11, 2019; Laura Bradey, "Full Frontal's Emmy Nominations Seem Like a Big Middle Finger to the G.O.P.," *Vanity Fair*, July 12, 2018.

93 Carlin, *Last Words*, 173.

94 Tony Hendra, Carlin's friend and the co-author of his memoir *Last Words*, described the "Seven Dirty Words" as "rebellious on a sort of profound level and it also had a kind of jubilance to it." *See* Timothy Bella, "The '7 Dirty Words' Turn 40, but They're Still Dirty," *Atlantic*, May 24, 2012.

95 Bradley, "Samantha Bee Apologizes One Last Time," *Vanity Fair*, June 7, 2018.

96 Mohr, *Holy Shit*, 15.

Chapter 8. *Saturday Night Live*, *Hustler*, and the Power of Parody

1 *See* Kevin Uhrmacher and Kevin Schaul, "Trump Is Going on SNL. Here Are the Other Appearances by Politicians on the Show," *Washington Post*, November 6, 2015; Ben Geier, "Here's What Happened the Last Time Donald Trump Hosted SNL," *Fortune*, October 27, 2015.

2 Donald J. Trump (@realDonaldTrump), Twitter, November 8, 2015, www.twitter.com. *See* James Hibberd, "Donald Trump Gives 'SNL' Biggest Ratings in Years," *Entertainment Weekly*, November 8, 2015.

3 Donald J. Trump (@realDonaldTrump), Twitter, October 16, 2016, www.twitter.com. *See* Dean Obeidallah, "Trump's Beef with SNL Is No Laughing Matter," CNN.com, October 17, 2016, www.cnn.com.

4 Donald J. Trump (@realDonaldTrump), Twitter, November 20, 2016, www.twitter.com.

5   Donald J. Trump (@realDonaldTrump), Twitter, December 3, 2016; January 15, 2017; and September 30, 2018, www.twitter.com.

6   Donald J. Trump (@realDonaldTrump), Twitter, December 16, 2018, www.twitter.com. *See Saturday Night Live* (NBC), "White House Tree Trimming Cold Open—SNL," YouTube, December 16, 2017, www.youtube.com (sketch that triggered Trump's call for SNL to be "tested in courts").

7   Donald J. Trump (@realDonaldTrump), Twitter, February 17, 2019, www.twitter.com. *See Saturday Night Live* (NBC), "Trump Press Conference Cold Open—SNL," YouTube, February 16, 2019, www.youtube.com (sketch that triggered Trump's call for "retribution").

8   Donald J. Trump (@realDonaldTrump), Twitter, March 17, 2019, 4:59 and 5:13 a.m., www.twitter.com. *See* James Hibberd, "Trump Threatens *SNL* with Federal Investigation for Mocking Him," *Entertainment Weekly*, March 17, 2019 ("Oddly, SNL didn't even air a new episode last night, but rather a repeat that featured at least one Trump sketch (with Alec Baldwin reprising his role as Trump)").

9   *See* William T. Horner and M. Heather Carver, *Saturday Night Live and the 1976 Presidential Election* (Jefferson, NC: McFarland & Company, 2018), 14, 135, 143 (analyzing how *SNL*'s jokes about Ford "contributed to a long-lasting impression of Gerald Ford on the America public as a stumbling, bumbling dolt" which may have contributed to his election loss); *see also* Steve Hendrix, "SNL Has Skewered Every President since Ford. All of Them Reacted the Same Way—until Now," *Washington Post*, December 17, 2018; Josef Adalian, "How Each Era of *SNL* Has Ridiculed American Presidents," Vulture, June 2, 2017, www.vulture.com.

10 William Cummings, "'It's Called the First Amendment': Pundits Decry Trump Call for 'Retribution' against 'SNL,'" *USA Today*, February 17, 2019.

11 Joseph Russomanno, *Speaking Our Minds: Conversations with the People Behind Landmark First Amendment Cases* (Mahwah, NJ: Lawrence Erlbaum Associates, 2002), 189 (quoting Larry Flynt).

12 Rodney A. Smolla, *Jerry Falwell v. Larry Flynt: The First Amendment on Trial* (New York: St. Martin's Press, 1988), 22.

13 To hear Jill St. John reading her Campari ad, *see Unprecedented*, "Terry Abrahamson's Dirty Joke" (podcast), WAMU, November 6, 2019, www.wamu.org (interviewing the writer of the *Hustler* parody ad, Terry Abrahamson).

14 Smolla, *Jerry Falwell v. Larry Flynt*, 1–2 (quoting *Hustler* parody ad).

15 *Id.* at 3. The difference between satire and parody is often confusing. Generally, parody is a subset of satire that imitates the form of the parodied work.

16 *See Hustler Magazine, Inc. v. Falwell*, 485 U.S. 46, 48 (1988).

17 Smolla, *Jerry Falwell v. Larry Flynt*, 7–8. Flynt brought a copyright infringement lawsuit against Falwell for including copies of the ad parody in his fundraising letters. Falwell won the case in 1986 when the Ninth Circuit upheld the copying as "fair use." *See Hustler Magazine, Inc. v. Moral Majority, Inc.*, 796 F.2d 1148 (9th Cir. 1986).

18 Smolla, *Jerry Falwell v. Larry Flynt*, 7–8 (the fundraising amounts requested differed in the targeted mailings).

19 *Id.* at 9.

20 United Press International, "Flynt Cleared of Libel but Must Pay $200,000," *New York Times*, December 9, 1984 (quoting Falwell).

21 *See Hustler v. Falwell*, 485 U.S. at 49 n.1.

22 *See* "Rev. Jerry Falwell Dies at Age 73," CNN.com, May 17, 2007, www.cnn.com.

23 *See id.*; Walt Harrington, "What Hath Falwell Wrought? Fundamentalism's Superstar Has Won Power and Respect for His Religion. In the Process, He Is Risking Fundamentalism's Soul," *Washington Post*, July 24, 1988; Jerry Falwell, *Strength for the Journey* (New York: Simon & Schuster, 1987), 179, 183.

24 *See* Peter Applebome, "Jerry Falwell, Moral Majority Founder, Dies at 73," *New York Times*, May 16, 2007; Frances FitzGerald, "A Disciplined, Charging Army," *New Yorker*, May 18, 1981; Liberty University, "About Liberty," www.liberty.edu.

25 "Rev. Jerry Falwell Dies," CNN.com; Falwell, *Strength for the Journey*, 202–7; FitzGerald, "A Disciplined, Charging Army"; *see also* Smolla, *Jerry Falwell v. Larry Flynt*, 96.

26 *See* FitzGerald, "A Disciplined, Charging Army"; *see also* Smolla, *Jerry Falwell v. Larry Flynt*, 131 ("The *Washington Star* called Falwell the 'second most watched TV personality in the country, surpassed only by Johnny Carson'").

27 *See* FitzGerald, "A Disciplined, Charging Army."

28 Falwell, *Strength for the Journey*, 361.

29 *See* FitzGerald, "A Disciplined, Charging Army."

30 Falwell, *Strength for the Journey*, 364–65. Falwell disbanded the Moral Majority in 1989, asserting that "our mission is accomplished." *See* Applebome, "Jerry Falwell, Moral Majority Founder, Dies."

31 Smolla, *Jerry Falwell v. Larry Flynt*, 102–3 (quoting Falwell in trial transcript).

32 *See* FitzGerald, "A Disciplined, Charging Army."

33 *Id.*; Robert Pear, "Falwell Denounces Tutu as a 'Phony,'" *New York Times*, August 21, 1985.

34 Hans Johnson and William Eskridge, "The Legacy of Falwell's Bully Pulpit," *Washington Post*, May 19, 2007; Christopher Reed, "The Rev Jerry Falwell: Rabid Evangelical Leader of America's 'Moral Majority,'" *Guardian*, May 17, 2007. Falwell also called Ellen DeGeneres "Ellen DeGenerate" after she publicly came out in 2001. *See* Bruce Handy, "He Called Me Ellen DeGenerate?," *Time*, June 24, 2001.

35 FitzGerald, "A Disciplined, Charging Army" (quoting Falwell speaking to a crowd "on the steps of the Virginia state capitol").

36 Harrington, "What Hath Falwell Wrought?"; Mark Feeney, "Rev. Jerry Falwell Dies at 73," *Boston Globe*, May 15, 2007.

37 "Falwell Apologizes to Gays, Feminists, Lesbians," CNN.com, September 14, 2001, www.cnn.com (Falwell later told CNN "that only the hijackers and terrorists were

responsible for the deadly attacks," but at the same time still maintained that the ACLU and other groups "created an environment which possibly has caused God to lift the veil of protection which has allowed no one to attack America on our soil since 1812").

38 Larry Flynt, "Larry Flynt: My Friend, Jerry Falwell," *Los Angeles Times*, May 20, 2007.

39 Larry Flynt, *An Unseemly Man: My Life as Pornographer, Pundit, and Social Outcast* (Los Angeles: Dove Books, 1996), 69–71.

40 *Id.* at 82, 88.

41 *Id.* at 91.

42 *Id.* at 98–103.

43 *Id.*

44 *Id.* at 102 (quoting a December 1975 *Wall Street Journal* article by Frederick Klein).

45 *Id.* at 103 (claiming revenue of over $1 million in 1975); David Z. Morris, "How Porn Publisher Larry Flynt Hustled—and Wound Up Richer than Hugh Hefner," *Fortune*, October 15, 2017; Smolla, *Jerry Falwell v. Larry Flynt*, 37 ("When Flynt took the magazine to major league status, its circulation skyrocketed in just four years to over two million, with annual profits of over $13 million").

46 Flynt, *An Unseemly Man*, 122, 169 (describing obscenity trials in Cincinnati, Ohio, and Lawrenceville, Georgia); *see also* Dirk Johnson, "Flynt Pleads Guilty in Ohio Obscenity Case," *New York Times*, May 13, 1999 (*Hustler* corporation plead guilty to pandering obscenity charges in a deal to avoid jail time for Flynt and his brother/partner); David L. Hudson, Jr., "Larry Flynt Primed to Battle Obscenity Charges in Cincinnati," Freedom Forum Institute, May 22, 1998, www.freedomforuminstitute.com (noting that Flynt served only six days of a twenty-five-year sentence, with the obscenity conviction overturned on appeal).

47 Flynt, *An Unseemly Man*, 169–71.

48 *See id.* at 174–77, 187.

49 Michael Musakl, "Joseph Paul Franklin, Serial Killer and Larry Flynt Shooter, Executed," *Los Angeles Times*, November 20, 2013.

50 Kyung Lah, "Serial Killer Joseph Paul Franklin Prepares to Die," CNN.com, November 19, 2013, www.cnn.com.

51 *See* IMDb, "The People vs. Larry Flynt (1996) Awards," www.imdb.com.

52 *See* Cheryl Lavin, "The Redemption of Larry Flynt," *Chicago Tribune*, December 27, 1996.

53 Nina Bernstein, "A Free Speech Hero? It's Not That Simple," *New York Times*, December 22, 1996.

54 *Id.*

55 Gloria Steinem, "Hollywood Cleans Up *Hustler*" (op-ed), *New York Times*, January 7, 1997. Steinem also notes that Flynt had been accused by one his daughters of sexually molesting her when she was a child. Flynt denies the accusations. *See, e.g.*, Johann Hari, "Larry Flynt: Freedom Fighter, Pornographer, Monster?,"

Independent, May 27, 2011 (also taking a critical look at Flynt being "lauded as a crusader for free speech [while getting] rich by depicting women being raped in concentration camps").

56 Steinem, "Hollywood Cleans Up *Hustler*." *See also* Hanna Rosin, "*Hustler*," *New Republic*, January 6, 1997 (criticizing the film's depiction of the magazine: "in the movie, *Hustler* is almost accidentally in the nudie business (which is, by the way, presented as pretty innocent). Its real mission is social progress").

57 United Press International, "Flynt Cleared of Libel but Must Pay $200,000," *New York Times*, December 9, 1984.

58 Smolla, *Jerry Falwell v. Larry Flynt*, 11; Nat Hentoff, "Larry Flynt Bowdlerized," Washington Post, March 8, 1997.

59 Smolla, *Jerry Falwell v. Larry Flynt*, 18.

60 *See* Clay Calvert and Robert D. Richards, "Alan Isaacman and the First Amendment: A Candid Interview with Larry Flynt's Attorney," 19 *Cardozo Arts & Entertainment Law Journal* 313, 346 (2001).

61 *See Hustler v. Falwell*, 485 U.S. at 47–48 (the district court judge ruled against Falwell on an additional invasion of privacy claim, which was not sent to the jury for consideration).

62 *See* Recording Academy, "Artist: Beyoncé Knowles," www.grammy.com.

63 *Hustler v. Falwell*, 485 U.S. at 52–53.

64 *See* Mike Hudson, "Falwell vs. Flynt," *Roanoke Times*, January 8, 1999.

65 Flynt, *An Unseemly Man*, 164; *see* Hudson, "Falwell vs. Flynt."

66 *See* Flynt, *An Unseemly Man*, 225; Hudson, "Falwell vs. Flynt."

67 Smolla, *Jerry Falwell v. Larry Flynt*, 92 (quoting from the trial transcript).

68 *Id*. at 94, 100.

69 *Id*. at 101.

70 *Id*.

71 *Id*. at 105.

72 *Id*. at 120.

73 *Id*. at 116–17.

74 *Id*. at 134.

75 *Id*. at 137.

76 Martha White, *In the Words of E. B. White: Quotations from America's Most Companionable of Writers* (Ithaca, NY: Cornell University Press, 2011), 129 (quoting E. B. White, "Some Remarks on Humor," adapted from *A Subtreasury of American Humor*, 1941).

77 Linder, *Famous Trials*, "Excerpts from the Testimony of Larry Flynt," www.famous-trials.com.

78 *Id*.

79 *See* Smolla, *Jerry Falwell v. Larry Flynt*, 139.

80 Hudson, "Falwell vs. Flynt."

81 *Id*.

82 Mary Battiata, "Jury Awards Falwell $200,000 Damages," *Washington Post*, December 9, 1984.

83 Flynt, *An Unseemly Man*, 232.

84 Hudson, "Falwell vs. Flynt"; Battiata, "Jury Awards Falwell"; United Press International, "Flynt Cleared of Libel."

85 *Hustler v. Falwell*, 485 U.S. at 49.

86 *See* Hudson, "Falwell vs. Flynt"; Battiata, "Jury Awards Falwell." The split decision was greeted with alarm by some free speech commentators, *see* Ellen Goodman, "Flynt Was Wronged," *Washington Post*, December 15, 1984 ("You can't have it both ways. If it's not libel, *Hustler* wasn't liable"); David Margolick, "Some See Threat in Non-libel Verdict in Falwell Parody Case," *New York Times*, December 10, 1984.

87 *Hustler v. Falwell*, 485 U.S. at 49–50 (citing *Falwell v. Flynt*, 797 F.2d 1270 (4th Cir. 1986)).

88 *See* Smolla, *Jerry Falwell v. Larry Flynt*, 168.

89 *See* Russomanno, *Speaking Our Minds*, 182. Flynt commented, "The mainstream press lacked moral courage and was afraid that the justices would only affirm the lower court's decision, establishing a new precedent. And they all thought I was too unseemly to associate with." Flynt, *An Unseemly Man*, 236.

90 *Hustler v. Falwell*, 485 U.S. at 50.

91 *See* Linda Greenhouse, "High Court Focuses on 3 Libel Cases," *New York Times*, November 9, 1983.

92 *Id.*; Flynt, *An Unseemly Man*, 191. Legal definition of "jurisdictional questions": jurisdictional questions involve whether a court has the power to hear a case, based often on geographic limitations or subject matter issues.

93 Lee Levine and Stephen Wermiel, *The Progeny: Justice William J. Brennan's Fight to Preserve the Legacy of New York Times v. Sullivan* (Chicago: ABA Publishing, 2014), 216.

94 Levine and Wermiel, *The Progeny*, 217. Flynt's own accounting of the incident differs somewhat in the details. He wrote that he shouted *after* the argument was over as the justices were rising to leave, "You're nothing but eight assholes and a token cunt!" Flynt, *An Unseemly Man*, 192.

95 *Id.* Flynt claimed that "in the end the charges were dismissed," but the AP reported that he plead guilty to "charges that he used threatening and abusive language before the United States Supreme Court." Flynt, *An Unseemly Man*, 195; Associated Press, "Larry Flynt Pleads Guilty," *New York Times*, February 13, 1985.

96 *See* Smolla, *Jerry Falwell v. Larry Flynt*, 261.

97 *See* "Larry Flynt Wins First Amendment Case," ABC News, February 24, 1988, www.abcnews.go.com.

98 *Hustler Magazine, Inc. v. Falwell*, Oyez, 1988, www.oyez.org.

99 *Id.*

100 *Id.*

101 *Id.* (emphasis added).

102 *Id.*

103 *Id.*

104 *Id.*

105 *Id.*

106 Russomanno, *Speaking Our Minds*, 187 (quoting Isaacman).

107 *Hustler v. Falwell*, Oyez.

108 *Id.* For the *Hustler* case, the Supreme Court, as usual, "received a host of amicus submissions, but one, filed on behalf of the Association of American Editorial Cartoonists, appeared to have been particularly effective. It included an appendix containing examples of the kinds of cartoons that, throughout history, had almost certainly inflicted emotional distress on the public officials and figures depicted in them." Levine and Wermiel, *The Progeny*, 301.

109 *Id.*

110 *See* Supreme Court, "Visitor's Guide to Oral Argument at the Supreme Court of the United States," www.supremecourt.gov ("On the [attorneys'] lectern there are two lights. When the white light goes on, the attorney has five minutes remaining to argue. The red light indicates that the attorney has used all the allotted time").

111 *Hustler v. Falwell*, Oyez.

112 *Id.*

113 *See* Flynt, *An Unseemly Man*, 243.

114 *Hustler v. Falwell*, Oyez.

115 *Id.*

116 *Id.* Like Grutman, Gary Hart also used the term "character assassination," in response to reporting on his alleged affair. *See* James R. Dickenson and Paul Taylor, "Gary Hart's Fall: How the Washington Post Covered the Affair That Derailed His Presidential Bid," *Washington Post*, November 17, 2018 (showing *Washington Post* May 4, 1987, cover story on Hart with the subheading, "Report on Female House Guest Called 'Character Assassination'").

117 *Hustler v. Falwell*, Oyez.

118 *Id.*

119 *Id.*

120 *Id.*

121 *Id.*

122 *Id.*

123 *Id.*

124 Flynt, *An Unseemly Man*, 245. The ruling was 8–0, with only Justice White writing a separate two-sentence concurring opinion. Justice Kennedy did not participate in the case as he not yet joined the Court (to replace the retiring Justice Lewis Powell) at the time of the argument. *See* Stuart Taylor, Jr., "Court, 8–0, Extends Right to Criticize Those in Public Eye," *New York Times*, February 25, 1988.

125 *See* Smolla, *Jerry Falwell v. Larry Flynt*, 298 ("Given Rehnquist's strongly conservative anti-press record, and the strong emotional temptation to side with Falwell,

Rehnquist's eloquent endorsement of freedom of speech ranks as one of the most striking events in his career"); Alex S. Jones, "Double-Barrel Judgement; The Hustler Decision Bolsters Protections of Frist Amendment and the Sullivan Rule," *New York Times*, February 25, 1988 ("And the decision was not only unanimous but also written by Chief Justice William H. Rehnquist, who has generally been unsympathetic to arguments made by First Amendment advocates that have come before the Court").

126 *Hustler v. Falwell*, 485 U.S. at 51 (internal quotations omitted).

127 *Id.* at 50.

128 *Id.* at 56 (emphasis added).

129 *Id.*

130 *Id.* at 53.

131 *Id.* at 54 (internal quotation omitted).

132 *Id.* at 55.

133 *See* Al Kamen, "Court Bars Damages to Falwell," *Washington Post*, February 25, 1988.

134 *Hustler v. Falwell*, 485 U.S. at 51

135 *Id.* at 55.

136 *See* Taylor, "Court, 8–0, Extends Right."

137 *See* Jones, "Double-Barrel Judgement" ("'That the opinion relies to such a significant degree on Sullivan makes it unlikely that tomorrow or next year the Court will reconsider Sullivan,' said Floyd Abrams, a lawyer who specializes in First Amendment issues").

138 *See* Rodney A. Smolla, "First Amendment Martyr, First Amendment Opportunist," 9 *First Amend. Law Review* 1, 10 (2010) ("It really is fair to say that Larry Flynt's crusades were very powerful in bringing into First Amendment doctrine the notion that we're all in this together").

139 *Hustler v. Falwell*, 485 U.S. at 50–51 (internal quotation omitted).

140 *See* Kamen, "Court Bars Damages to Falwell."

141 *See* Flynt, "Larry Flynt: My Friend, Jerry Falwell"; Carl M. Cannon, "Flynt & Falwell: A First Amendment Odd Couple," RealClearPolitics, February 24, 2014, www.realclearpolitics.com.

142 Flynt, "Larry Flynt: My Friend, Jerry Falwell"; *see* Cannon, "Flynt & Falwell."

143 *See* Associated Press, "The Preacher and the Porn King; Flynt, Falwell Make Joint Appearance in Virginia to Discuss Free Speech Case," *Spokesman-Review*, November 3, 1997 (quoting Falwell, "We're good friends. We just have strong disagreements," and Flynt, "In recent months, Jerry and I have established a relationship. I like him very much").

144 *See* Russomanno, *Speaking Our Minds*, 192 (quoting Flynt in an interview).

145 Flynt, "Larry Flynt: My Friend, Jerry Falwell." In 2019, Flynt celebrated the forty-fifth anniversary of *Hustler*, "the only adult publication in America still published every four weeks." Globe Newswire, "Hustler Magazine Celebrates 45 Years in Print," Yahoo Finance, July 2, 2019, www.finance.yahoo.com (quoting *Hustler* press release).

Chapter 9. Nazis in Charlottesville, Funeral Protests, and Speakers We Hate

1 *See* Michael Signer, *Cry Havoc: Charlottesville and American Democracy Under Siege* (New York: PublicAffairs, 2020), 205–6 (Charlottesville mayor Signer's thoughtful, candid, and detailed analysis of the events leading up to the Unite the Right rally, through the crisis, and its aftermath.); Timothy J. Heaphy, "Final Report: Independent Review of the 2017 Protest Events in Charlottesville, Virginia," November 24, 2017, www.charlottesvilleindependentreview.com, 9, 110 (the City of Charlottesville commissioned this 207-page report by a former United States attorney in Virginia to provide "an independent evaluation of the City's handling of the summer protest events"); Joe Heim, "Recounting a Day of Rage, Hate, Violence and Death," *Washington Post*, August 14, 2017; Hawes Spencer and Sheryl Gay Stolberg, "White Nationalists March on University of Virginia," *New York Times*, August 11, 2017.

2 *See* Sarah Rankin (Associated Press), "Chaos and Violence Rock Charlottesville as White Nationalists Rally; 3 Dead," *Virginian-Pilot*, August 12, 2017.

3 *See* Heaphy, "Final Report," 1; Spencer and Stolberg, "White Nationalists."

4 Heaphy, "Final Report," 69.

5 *See* Signer, *Cry Havoc*, 105–8; Heaphy, "Final Report," 24–25, 69; Spencer and Stolberg, "White Nationalists March."

6 Spencer and Stolberg, "White Nationalists March" (quoting Kessler).

7 *See* Heaphy, "Final Report," 83.

8 *Id.* (quoting letter from the city manager to Kessler).

9 Signer, *Cry Havoc*, 197 (quoting pre-litigation ACLU email to Mayor Signer). *See also* Heaphy, "Final Report," 84. For a historical precursor to the ACLU action in Charlottesville, *see* ACLU, "ACLU History: Taking a Stand for Free Speech in Skokie," 2019, www.aclu.org ("In 1978, the ACLU took a controversial stand for free speech by defending a neo-Nazi group that wanted to march through the Chicago suburb of Skokie, where many Holocaust survivors lived"). *See also* Professor Donald Alexander Downs's authoritative, discerning, and in-depth analysis of the Skokie controversy, *Nazis in Skokie: Freedom, Community and the First Amendment* (Notre Dame, IN: University of Notre Dame Press, 1985), 153.

10 *Kessler v. City of Charlottesville* (W.D. Va. 2017), Justia.com, August 11, 2017, page 4, www.law.justia.com.

11 *See* Terry McAuliffe, *Beyond Charlottesville: Taking a Stand against White Nationalism* (New York: St. Martin's Press, 2019), 90; Rankin, "Chaos and Violence Rock Charlottesville."

12 *See* Signer, *Cry Havoc*, 208 ("I watched video of alt-right members bearing Confederate and neo-fascist flags beating up counterprotesters on Market Street, in open view of hundreds"); Heaphy, "Final Report," 6 ("Because of their misalignment and lack of accessible protective gear, officers failed to intervene in physical altercations that took place in areas adjacent to Emancipation Park"); Heim,

"Recounting a Day of Rage"; Hawes Spencer, "A Far-Right Gathering Bursts into Brawls," *New York Times*, August 13, 2017.

13 *See* Heaphy, "Final Report," 133; Heim, "Recounting a Day of Rage."

14 *See id.*

15 *Id.*

16 Heaphy, "Final Report," 6.

17 *See* Paul Duggan and Justin Jouvenal, "Neo-Nazi Sympathizer Pleads Guilty to Federal Hate Crimes for Plowing Car into Protesters at Charlottesville Rally," *Washington Post*, April 1, 2019; Jonathan M. Katz and Farah Stockman, "James Fields Guilty of First-Degree Murder in Death of Heather Heyer," *New York Times*, December 7, 2018; Heaphy, "Final Report," 144.

18 Charles Bethea, "A Witness to Terrorism in Charlottesville," *New Yorker*, August 13, 2017 (quoting the account of Kristin Adolfson, a local counterprotestor at the rally).

19 *See id.*

20 *See* Katz and Stockman, "James Fields Guilty"; Heaphy, "Final Report," 144.

21 *See* Ellie Silverman, "From Wary Observer to Justice Warrior: How Heather Heyer's Death Gave Her Mom a Voice," *Washington Post*, February 1, 2018; Christina Caron, "Heather Heyer, Charlottesville Victim, Is Recalled as 'a Strong Woman,'" *New York Times*, August 13, 2017. Two state troopers, Lieutenant H. Jay Cullen and Trooper Berke M. M. Baters, who were surveying the protests by helicopter and relaying "video of the rally to officers on the ground," also died that day when their helicopter crashed. The cause of the accident had not been determined two years after the crash. *See* Mark Bowes, "Final Decision Still Elusive in Federal Probe of State Police Helicopter Crash That Killed 2 Troopers during Charlottesville Rally," *Richmond Times-Dispatch*, August 11, 2019.

22 *See* Jenna Johnson and John Wagner, "Trump Condemns Charlottesville Violence but Doesn't Single Out White Nationalists," *Washington Post*, August 12, 2017 (containing video of statement). *See also* McAuliffe, *Beyond Charlottesville*, ix–x (Congressman John Lewis's criticism of Trump's "on many sides" remarks, in the foreword: "That was very surprising to me, that any person in a position of leadership would equate the actions of violent white nationalists with those of peaceful protesters").

23 *See* Aaron Blake, "Trump Tries to Re-write His Own History on Charlottesville and 'Both Sides,'" *Washington Post*, April 26, 2019; Bob Woodward, *Fear: Trump in the White House* (New York: Simon & Schuster, 2018), 239–40; Glenn Thrush and Maggie Haberman, "Trump Gives White Supremacists an Unequivocal Boost," *New York Times*, August 15 2017.

24 *See* David Nakamura and Sari Horwitz, "'Racism Is Evil,' Trump Says, Condemning 'White Supremacists' and Hate Groups," *Washington Post*, August 14, 2017 (Trump said, "Racism is evil, and those who cause violence in its name are criminals and thugs, including the KKK, neo-Nazis, white supremacists and other hate groups").

25 Woodward, *Fear*, 245–46; "Remarks by President Trump on Infrastructure," White House, August 15, 2017, www.whitehouse.gov.

26 *See* Signer, *Cry Havoc*, 215; *see also* Kristine Phillips, "'Look at the Campaign He Ran': Charlottesville Mayor Is Becoming One of Trump's Strongest Critics," *Washington Post*, August 13, 2017.

27 *See* Adrian Chen, "Unfollow: How a Prized Daughter of the Westboro Baptist Church Came to Question Its Beliefs," *New Yorker*, November 23, 2015; John Swaine, "Westboro Baptist Church Founder Fred Phelps Dies Aged 84," *Guardian*, March 20, 2014; Michael Paulson, "Fred Phelps, Anti-gay Preacher Who Targeted Military Funerals, Dies at 84," *New York Times*, March 20, 2014.

28 *See* Chen, "Unfollow." Two of Phelps's children, Nathan and Mark, who left the church, accuse their father of physical abuse. *See* Swaine, "Fred Phelps Dies"; Chris Bury and Claire Pedersen, "Son Turns on Church That Pickets Soldiers' Funerals," ABC News, May 4, 2010, www.abcnews.go.com.

29 *See* Chen, "Unfollow"; Paulson, "Fred Phelps, Anti-gay Preacher." Along with gay people, the Westboro Baptist Church also hated Jews and Catholics, among others. *See* Dahlia Lithwick, "Up in Their Grill," Slate, October 6, 2010, www.slate.com.

30 *See id.*; Steven Petrow, "Fred Phelps Preached Hate, but His Death Is No Reason to Celebrate," *Washington Post*, March 20, 2014; Swaine, "Fred Phelps Dies."

31 *See* Petrow, "Fred Phelps Preached Hate." In 2003, Phelps, perhaps one of the most hated men in America, also protested outside of the memorial for Fred Rogers, one of the most beloved. *See* Amy Davidson Sorkin, "The Two Freds: When Phelps Protested Mr. Rogers's Memorial," *New Yorker*, March 20, 2014. *See also* Michael Paulson, "For Antigay Church, Losing Its Cause before Its Founder," *New York Times*, March 22, 2014 (the church's outrageous tactics may have backfired on them and actually helped the gay rights movement: "Mark R. Silk, a professor of religion in public life at Trinity College in Hartford, suggested in a blog post that Fred Phelps 'made religious hostility to homosexuality repulsive'").

32 *See* Megan Phelps-Roper, *Unfollow: A Memoir of Loving and Leaving the Westboro Baptist Church* (New York: Farrar, Straus and Giroux, 2019), 80–82; Chen, "Unfollow."

33 *See Snyder v. Phelps*, 562 U.S. 443, 448 (2011).

34 *See Unprecedented*, "Middle Finger to God" (podcast), WAMU, November 13, 2019, www.wamu.org.

35 *See id.*

36 *See id.*; Michael Smerconish, "He Looked Hate in the Eye," Politico, March 7, 2014, www.politico.com.

37 *See Unprecedented*, "Middle Finger to God."

38 *See id.*; Smerconish, "He Looked Hate in the Eye."

39 *See id.*

40 *See Snyder*, 562 U.S. at 449; *see also* Phelps-Roper, *Unfollow*, 89.

41 See Snyder, 562 U.S. at 448, 454.

42 See id. at 449.

43 See Unprecedented, "Middle Finger to God."

44 See id.; Snyder, 562 U.S. at 449; Snyder v. Phelps, Oyez, www.oyez.org.

45 See Unprecedented, "Middle Finger to God."

46 See id.; Smerconish, "He Looked Hate in the Eye."

47 See id.

48 See Unprecedented, "Middle Finger to God."

49 See Snyder, 562 U.S. at 449–50. Snyder also sued Phelps's daughters and alleged four
    other "state tort law claims: defamation, publicity given to private life . . . intrusion
    upon seclusion, and civil conspiracy." The judge dismissed the defamation and
    publicity-given-to-private-life claims before trial. See id.

50 See Snyder v. Phelps, 533 F.Supp.2d 567, 573, 588–89 (D. Md., 2008).

51 Smerconish, "He Looked Hate in the Eye" (quoting Snyder's attorney, Sean
    Summers).

52 See Snyder, 562 U.S. at 450. The jury found Phelps liable for intentional infliction of
    emotional distress, as well as intrusion upon seclusion (a privacy violation claim)
    and civil conspiracy. See id. The defendants filed a posttrial motion claiming that the
    damages were "grossly excessive." The district court then reduced the jury's punitive
    damages award to $2.1 million. See id. Legal definition of "compensatory damages":
    compensatory damages, or "actual damages" are those awarded to a plaintiff for
    quantifiable injuries suffered, intended to restore the person financially to the place
    they were before the injury. Punitive damages are those awarded to punish the
    defendant for their intentional wrongdoing and/or to deter anyone from committing
    such wrongful action.

53 Phelps-Roper, Unfollow, 92.

54 See Unprecedented, "Middle Finger to God."

55 Phelps-Roper, Unfollow, 92.

56 See Snyder v. Phelps, 580 F.3d 206, 222–23 (4th Cir., 2009); see also Snyder, 562 U.S. at
    451–56, 1215–18 (discussing greater protections for speech on issues of public concern
    rather than private concern, and the "guiding principles" for distinguishing between
    the two).

57 Snyder, 580 F.3d at 226.

58 Id. (internal quotation omitted).

59 See id. at 267.

60 See Garrett Epps, "Westboro Baptist Church's Surreal Day in Court," Atlantic,
    October 6, 2010 ("The most logical course for the Court would have been to leave
    this stinker alone"); Snyder v. Phelps, Brief of Amicus Curiae Anti-Defamation League
    in Support of Neither Party, May 2010, page 5, www.americanbar.org ("the central
    point is that the facts at issue and the decision below offer an extremely poor vehicle
    for rendering the type of expansive ruling . . . [the Supreme Court review] appears to
    invite").

61 *See* Devin Dwyer, "States Line Up against Funeral Hecklers in Supreme Court Brief," ABC News, May 28, 2010, www.abcnews.go.com ("all but two state attorneys general have signed a 'friend of the court' brief . . . that argues the First Amendment should not apply to some 'intrusive and harassing' forms of expression"); *Snyder v. Phelps*, Brief of Senators Harry Reid, Mitch McConnell, and 40 Other Members of the U.S. Senate as *Amici Curiae* in Support of Petitioner, May 28, 2010, page 4, www. americanbar.org ("In recent years, Congress and forty-six state legislatures have enacted laws to minimize picketing and other forms of disruptive activity in or near cemeteries during a funeral. Those laws are not challenged here, but they evidence the significant governmental interest in protecting the dignity of private funerals").

62 *See Snyder v. Phelps*, Brief of the State of Kansas, 47 Other States, and the District of Columbia as *Amici Curiae* in Support of Petitioner, June 2010, pages 2–5, www. americanbar.org.

63 *See Snyder v. Phelps*, Brief of *Amici Curiae* of the Foundation for Individual Rights in Education and Law Professors Ash Bhagwat, David Post, Martin Redish, Nadine Strossen, and Eugene Volokh in Support of Respondent, July 14, 2010, page 3, www.americanbar.org ("If the government acting as sovereign may impose liability on allegedly outrageous and severely distressing speech, even when it relates to matters of public concern, then public universities would be equally able to discipline their students for allegedly outrageous commentary. . . . This would dramatically endanger free discussion at academic institutions"); *Snyder v. Phelps*, Brief of *Amici Curiae* of the Reporters Committee for Freedom of the Press and Twenty-One News Media Organizations in Support of Respondent, pages 1–3, www.americanbar.org.

64 *See* "Lamentable Speech" (editorial), *New York Times*, October 6, 2010.

65 *See* Sean Gregory, "Inside the Supreme Court's Free-Speech Showdown," *Time*, October 6, 2010.

66 *See* Phelps-Roper, *Unfollow*, 93; Gregory, "Inside the Supreme Court."

67 *See* Jena Lowe, "Supreme Court Sets Stage for Latest from Phelps," Medill News Service, October 6, 2010, https://dc.medill.northwestern.edu.

68 *See id.*; Gregory, "Inside the Supreme Court."

69 *See* Smerconish, "He Looked Hate in the Eye."

70 *See id.*; *Snyder v. Phelps*, Oyez. Legal definition of "pro bono": pro bono, which comes from a Latin term that means "for the public good," describes the practice of lawyers representing a client free of charge for their time.

71 *See Snyder v. Phelps*, Oyez.

72 *See* Bill Mears, "Justice Kagan Makes Her Mark on Day One, Then Has to Go," CNN.com, October 4, 2010, www.cnn.com.

73 *See Snyder v. Phelps*, Oyez.

74 *See id.*

75 *See id.*

76 *See id.*

77 *See id.*

78 *See* Lithwick, "Up in Their Grill" (the justices "express just how much they hate the Phelps tactics . . . [by] 'posing hypotheticals.' Counsel [Phelps] spends the remainder of the day refusing to answer the hypotheticals. It's rapidly become a hate stalemate").

79 *See* Epps, "Westboro Baptist Church's Surreal Day" (criticizing the performance of both lawyers, and saying the result was an oral argument that "sometimes resembles the 1945 World Series, between two teams so war-depleted that sportswriter Warren Brown said, 'I don't think either one of them can win it'"); "Lamentable Speech," *New York Times* ("During the oral arguments, there were persistent questions from every justice but Clarence Thomas, seeking help in striking a balance between privacy and protest in the Internet age, and often unhelpful answers from the overmatched lawyers for each side").

80 Jess Bravin, "Court Weighs Limits on Speech," *Wall Street Journal*, October 7, 2010 (quoting Snyder).

81 Phelps-Roper, *Unfollow*, 93.

82 *Id.*

83 ALM Media, "Roberts Declares Himself First Amendment's 'Most Aggressive Defender' at SCOTUS," Yahoo Finance, February 12, 2019, www.finance.yahoo.com.

84 *See id.* (quoting First Amendment scholars' reactions to Roberts's comments); Amelia Thomson-DeVeaux, "Chief Justice Roberts Is Reshaping the First Amendment," FiveThirtyEight, March 20, 2018, www.fivethirtyeight.com; Ronald Collins, "The Roberts Court and the First Amendment," *SCOTUSblog*, July 9, 2013, www.scotusblog.com.

85 *See* Thomson-DeVeaux, "Chief Justice Roberts"; Collins, "The Roberts Court."

86 *See Snyder,* 562 U.S. at 457–60.

87 *Id.* at 451.

88 *Id.* at 452 (internal quotations and citations omitted).

89 *Id.* at 452.

90 *Id.* at 453 (internal quotations and citations omitted).

91 *See id.*

92 *Id.* at 454.

93 *Id.*

94 *See Snyder v. Phelps,* Oyez (Justice Kagan, asking Summers for an approach if otherwise-protected speech includes personal, targeted attacks: "So does that mean that now we have to start reading each sign, and saying 'war is wrong' falls on one side of the line but 'you are a war criminal' falls on another side of the line?").

95 *Snyder,* 562 U.S. at 455.

96 *Id.* at 456 (internal quotation marks and citation omitted).

97 The Court declined to expand the "few limited situations where the location of targeted picketing can be regulated under provisions that the Court has determined to be content neutral," which has included prohibiting picketing at a residence or "requiring a buffer zone between protesters and an abortion clinic

entrance." *Id.* at 457 (citing *Frisby v. Schultz* and *Madsen v. Women's Health Center*, respectively).

98 *Id.* at 456–57 (quotation and citation omitted). Roberts mentions that forty-four states and the federal government had laws at the time of the decision "imposing restrictions on funeral picketing," but that the constitutionality of such laws were not part of the case because the Maryland law "was not in effect at the time" the Phelpses were picketing Snyder's funeral. *See id.*

99 *See* David L. Hudson, Jr., "Content Neutral," First Amendment Encyclopedia, www.mtsu.edu (providing an overview of the principle with links to representative cases); Catherine J. Ross, *Lessons in Censorship: How School and Courts Subvert Students' First Amendment Rights* (Cambridge, MA: Harvard University Press, 2015), 22 ("In the decades after *Barnette*, the Supreme Court added to its cannon of free speech principles beyond the presumption against prior restraint. Most critically, it established that restrictions on speech based on either its content (that is, subject matter) or its viewpoint (the position of a speaker takes with respect to aa subject) are presumptively unconstitutional"); Geoffrey Stone, "Content Regulation and the First Amendment," 25 *William & Mary Law Review* 189, 189–90 (1983).

100 *Snyder*, 562 U.S. at 457.

101 *Id.* at 458.

102 *Id.* (internal quotations and citations omitted).

103 *Id.* at 460–61. The majority also held that since "the First Amendment bars Snyder from recovery for . . . intrusion upon seclusion . . . Snyder cannot recover for civil conspiracy based on those [privacy] torts." *Id.* at 460.

104 *Id.* at 461.

105 *See* Duke Law, "First Amendment Legend Abrams Urges Broad Protections for Free Speech," October 24, 2019, www.law.duke.edu. (Commenting on Snyder, Floyd Abrams said, "The theme of the First Amendment as it has been applied through the years in the courts is that we're ready to take, and to inflict, a lot of pain for the— hopefully—greater good of living in a freer society and avoiding the risks of governmental involvement in what people say").

106 *See* Garrett Epps, "The Free Speech Jurisprudence of Justice Alito," Knight First Amendment Institute at Columbia University, May 1, 2018, www.knightcolumbia. org ("Alito envisions an American social center occupied by holders of power, wealth, and traditional values. The closer to this 'center' the speaker lies, in his analysis, the more robustly the speaker's speech should be protected"); Jeffrey Toobin, *The Oath: The Obama White House and the Supreme Court* (New York: Doubleday, 2012), 254–55 (discussing Alito's different approach to free speech, in contrast to how "under Roberts, the Court reached a consensus that the government had little or no power to regulate" hateful speech, and stating "Alito was . . . outraged by his colleagues' decision" in *Snyder*).

107 *Snyder*, 562 U.S. at 463.

108 Alito does refer positively to part of Justice Breyer's concurrence. *See id.* at 471. Justice Breyer wrote a concurrence to qualify that in his view the "State can sometimes regulate picketing, even picketing on matters of public concern," and in some circumstances may constitutionally be able to "provide private individuals with necessary protection" from such speech. *Id.* at 461–62. In essence, Breyer agreed with the decision in this particular case, but wanted to limit the reach of the opinion so as not to foreclose potential future regulations and remedies for extreme violations of personal privacy, even when speech on matters of public concern is involved.

109 *Id.* at 470.

110 *Id.* at 1226–27.

111 *Id.* at 471.

112 *Id.* at 472.

113 *Id.* at 456 n.4.

114 *Id.* at 475.

115 *See* Eugene Volokh, "No, There's No 'Hate Speech' Exception to the First Amendment," *Washington Post*, May 7, 2015 (discussing hate speech precedent and narrow exceptions).

116 *See* Richard Wolf, "From Cross Burning to Funeral Protests, Hate Speech Enjoys Broad Protection," *USA Today*, August 16, 2017.

117 *See* Noah Feldman, "Sorry, Charlottesville, but You Can't Stop the Protests," Bloomberg, December 14, 2017, www.bloomberg.com (Harvard Law professor Feldman explains that although "a city can't block peaceful protests just because it's worried about keeping them peaceful," it can regulate protesters and counterprotesters in other ways "to assure safety").

118 James Fields Jr. was convicted by a jury on state charges of first-degree murder, pled guilty to federal hate crimes, and was sentenced to life in prison. *See* Sasha Ingber, "Neo-Nazi James Fields Gets 2nd Life Sentence for Charlottesville Attack," NPR, July 15, 2019, www.npr.org. Attorney General William Barr described the hate crimes as "acts of domestic terrorism." *See* Mitch Smith, "James Fields Sentenced to Life in Prison for Death of Heather Heyer in Charlottesville," *New York Times*, June 28, 2019.

119 For some of the leading positions on hate speech law, *see* Mari J. Matsuda, "Dissent in a Crowded Theater," 72 *SMU Law Review* 441, 441–42 (2019) ("Critical race theorists argue for a distinction between dissent and hate speech. This approach sees two imperatives: (1) criticism of the government is required in a democracy, and (2) subordinated citizens whose participation in democracy does not carry presumptions of entitlement require protection from assaultive speech"); Richard Delgado and Jean Stefancic, *Must We Defend Nazis?: Why the First Amendment Should Not Protect Hate Speech and White Supremacy* (New York: New York University Press, 2018), 2 ("The First Amendment protects speech as a prime value and considers it democracy-enhancing instrument and protector of communal decision-making. Yet hateful speech, especially the racial kind, can shock and wound, rending its victims

speechless, afraid, and silent, less able to participate in public conversation than they were before being made to suffer it"); Steven H. Shiffrin, *What's Wrong with the First Amendment* (Cambridge, UK: Cambridge University Press, 2016), 10, 46 (advocating that we "recognize that stigmatized groups deserve protection from many forms of hateful speech"); Nadine Strossen, *Hate: Why We Should Resist It with Free Speech, Not Censorship* (New York: Oxford University Press, 2018) (Strossen's definitive contemporary analysis of the reasons to support the Supreme Court's current approach on hate speech); Henry Louis Gates, Jr., "War of Words: Critical Race Theory and the First Amendment," in *Speaking of Race, Speaking of Sex: Hate Speech, Civil Rights, and Civil Liberties*, edited by Henry Louis Gates, Jr., Anthony P. Griffin, Donald E. Lively, Robert C. Post, William B. Rubenstein, and Nadine Strossen (New York: New York University Press, 1994), 47 (in this insightful, nuanced review of critical race theory and hate speech, Professor Gates points out that "in American society today, the real power commanded by the racist is likely to vary inversely with the vulgarity with which it is expressed. . . . Unfortunately, those who pit the First Amendment against the Fourteenth invite us to spend more time worrying about speech codes than coded speech"); Mari J. Matsuda, Charles R. Lawrence III, Richard Delgado, and Kimberlé Williams Crenshaw, *Words That Wound: Critical Race Theory, Assaultive Speech, and the First Amendment* (Boulder, CO: Westview Press, 1993) (a seminal book with groundbreaking essays on critical race theory and the impacts of racist speech); Charles R. Lawrence III, "If He Hollers Let Him Go: Regulating Racist Speech on Campus," 1990 *Duke Law Journal*, 431, 474 (1990) ("If one asks why we always begin by asking whether we can afford to fight racism rather than asking whether we can afford not to, or if one asks why my colleagues who oppose all regulation of racist speech do not feel the burden is theirs (to justify a reading of the First Amendment that requires sacrificing rights guaranteed under the equal protection clause), then one sees an example of how unconscious racism operates in the marketplace of ideas").

120 Megan Phelps-Roper (@meganphelps), Twitter, March 2, 2011, www.twitter.com; Megan Phelps-Roper (@meganmpr), Instagram, March 2, 2011, www.instagram.com.

121 Jeff Chu, "What I Found at Westboro," Politico, March 7, 2014, (quoting Phelps-Roper). *See also* Ruth Padawer, "At 5, She Protested Homosexuality. Now She Protests the Church That Made Her Do It," *New York Times*, October 8, 2019 (book review, calling Phelps-Roper "the church's official voice on Twitter, where she expanded Westboro's reach by targeting influential users and baiting followers with her hateful posts"); Phelps-Roper, *Unfollow*, 98 ("I'd come to love the [Twitter] platform dearly: a place for me to spread our message in a way that didn't require the distorting lens of a journalist").

122 *See* Megan Phelps-Roper and Brittan Heller, "Conversion via Twitter" (video), Berkman Klein Center for Internet & Society at Harvard University, October 22, 2019, www.cyber.harvard.edu.

123 *See* Phelps-Roper, *Unfollow*, 160–62; Megan Phelps-Roper, "I Grew Up in the Westboro Baptist Church. Here's Why I Left" (video), TED, February, 2017, https://ed.ted.com; Chen, "Unfollow."

124 Phelps-Roper, *Unfollow*, 161.

125 *See* "Conversion via Twitter." These acts of effective counterspeech are the perfect embodiment of Justice Brandeis's guidance in his celebrated concurring opinion in *Whitney v. California*: "If there be time to expose through discussion the falsehood and fallacies, to avert the evil by the processes of education, the remedy to be applied is more speech, not enforced silence." *See Whitney*, 274 U.S. 357, 377 (1927).

126 Phelps-Roper, "I Grew Up in the Westboro Baptist Church."

127 Phelps-Roper, *Unfollow*, 161.

128 *See* Phelps-Roper, *Unfollow*, 194–203 (Phelps-Roper left with her younger sister Grace); Chen, "Unfollow."

129 Phelps-Roper, "I Grew Up in the Westboro Baptist Church."

130 *See* Phelps-Roper, *Unfollow*, 275–77.

131 *Id.* at 276.

132 *Id.* at 277.

133 *See* Tricia Bishop, "Justices Rule Anti-gay Church Can Protest at Military Funerals," *Baltimore Sun*, March 2, 2011.

134 *See id.*

135 *See* Sean Gregory, "Why the Supreme Court Ruled for Westboro," *Time*, March 3, 2011.

136 *See* Jolie Lee, "Phelps Deathbed Reports Spark Celebration from Foes," *USA Today*, March 18, 2014.

137 *Id.*

138 *See* Sarah Plake, "No Funeral for Westboro Founder," WIBW, March 20, 2014 (updated February 11, 2015), www.wibw.com.

139 *See Unprecedented*, "Middle Finger to God." To see how Snyder's position changed, note that in 2007 he said on NBC's *Today* show, "My son fought for freedom of speech. My son did not fight for freedom of hate speech." Mike Celizic, "'My Son Did Not Fight for Freedom of Hate Speech,'" *Today*, November 1, 2007, www.today.com.

Chapter 10. Social Media and the "Vast Democratic Forums of the Internet"

1 Sacha Baron Cohen, "Keynote Address at ADL's 2019 Never Is Now Summit on Anti-Semitism and Hate: Remarks by Recipient of ADL's International Leadership Award," ADL, November 21, 2019, www.adl.org.

2 *Id.*

3 *See id.*

4 *See, e.g.,* Andrew Marantz, "Free Speech Is Killing Us," *New York Times*, October 4, 2019 (opinion piece by the author of *Antisocial: Online Extremists, Techno-Utopians, and the Hijacking of the American Conversation*).

5 Lindy West, *Shrill: Notes from a Loud Woman* (New York: Hachette Books, 2016), 203 (from the chapter "It's about Free Speech, It's Not about Hating Women").

6 *Id.*

7 *See* Mike Isaac, "Twitter Bars Milo Yiannopoulos in Wake of Leslie Jones's Reports of Abuse," *New York Times*, July 20, 2016; *see also* Andrew Liptak, "Leslie Jones: 'Hate Speech and Freedom of Speech Are Two Different Things,'" Verge, July 22, 2016, www.theverge.com.

8 *See id.*

9 Robinson Meyer, "Twitter's Famous Racist Problem," *Atlantic*, July 21, 2016 (quoting Twitter's statement).

10 *See* Hamza Shaban, "Twitter Reveals Its Daily Active User Numbers for the First Time," *Washington Post*, February 7, 2019 (Twitter reported 321 million monthly users in 2019); Isaac, "Twitter Bars Milo Yiannopoulos" ("The move stops short of providing Twitter's 300-million-plus users with effective tools to combat trolls and abuse on a much larger scale, an issue that celebrities and everyday users alike deal with on a regular basis").

11 David Kaye, *Speech Police: The Global Struggle to Govern the Internet* (New York: Columbia Global Reports, 2019), 15. *See also* Alexandra Stevenson, "Facebook Admits It Was Used to Incite Violence in Myanmar," *New York Times*, November 6, 2018 ("Myanmar military officials were behind a systematic campaign on Facebook to target a mostly Muslim Rohingya minority, an investigation by The New York Times found. Human rights groups say this campaign has led to murder, rape and forced migration").

12 *See* Andrew Perrin and Monica Anderson, "Share of U.S. Adults Using Social Media, Including Facebook, Is Mostly Unchanged since 2018," Pew Research Center, April 10, 2019, www.pewresearch.org (the Pew survey found that 69% of adults "say they ever" use Facebook, and 73% of adults use YouTube).

13 *See* Kaye, *Speech Police*, 95 (expressing worry that in responding to "fake news" concerns, "democratic states might move so quickly that they would not pay adequate attention to the risks of speech regulation or the implications of making demands on companies that they act as arbiters of truth on their platforms"); Noah Feldman, "Fake News May Not Be Protected Speech," Bloomberg, November 23, 2016, www.bloomberg.com ("Under current First Amendment doctrine," regulation of fake news in the United States courts, "wouldn't be allowed. The Supreme Court has been expanding protections for knowingly false speech, not contracting it. And it would be extremely difficult to separate opinion from fact on a systematic basis").

14 In *Knight First Amendment Institute v. Trump*, a three-judge panel of the United States Court of Appeals for the Second Circuit held that President Trump's blocking of users from his Twitter account violates the First Amendment. *See* Charlie Savage, "Trump Can't Block Critics from His Twitter Account, Appeals Court Rules," *New York Times*, July 9, 2019; *but see* Noah Feldman, "The Courts Still Don't Understand

Trump's Twitter Feed," Bloomberg, July 9, 2019, www.bloomberg.com (disagreeing with the Second Circuit's reasoning, arguing "Trump's Twitter account isn't his private property or a government-controlled space. It's something else: property controlled by Twitter Inc"). *See also Davison v. Randall*, 912 F.3d 666 (4th Cir. 2019) (holding that local official's blocking of critic from her Facebook page was unconstitutional viewpoint discrimination).

15 *See Packingham v. North Carolina*, 137 S. Ct. 1730, 1736 (2017).

16 "IRL" is an acronym for "in real life," which is often used in social media communication to draw a contrast between real and online experiences.

17 *Packingham v. North Carolina*, 137 S. Ct. at 1734.

18 *See id.; State v. Packingham*, 777 S.E.2d 738, 742 (N.C. 2015) (North Carolina Supreme Court decision naming Durham Police Department officer Brian Schnee).

19 *See id.*

20 *See id.*

21 *See* Brent Kendall, "Supreme Court to Decide if North Carolina Can Bar Sex Offenders from Social Media," *Wall Street Journal*, October 28, 2016 (quoting from North Carolina brief opposing the Supreme Court granting certiorari).

22 *See State v. Packingham*, 777 S.E.2d at 742.

23 *See Packingham v. North Carolina*, 137 S. Ct. at 1734.

24 *See* Andrew Cohen, "The Man Arrested for Praising Jesus," Marshall Project, February 20, 2017, www.themarshallproject.org.

25 *See Packingham v. North Carolina*, 137 S. Ct. at 1734.

26 *See State v. Packingham*, 777 S.E.2d at 742.

27 *See Packingham v. North Carolina*, 137 S. Ct. at 1734.

28 *See id.* at 1735.

29 *See State v. Packingham*, 777 S.E.2d at 741, 747.

30 *See id.* at 747. The North Carolina Supreme Court described the Paula Deen Network as "a commercial social networking Web site that allows registered users to swap recipes and discuss cooking techniques." *See id.*

31 For an example of the unpredictability of what the Supreme Court will focus on in a case, *see Elonis v. United States*, 135 S. Ct. 2001 (2015). Before oral argument in *Elonis*, which involved a defendant who was convicted of making violent threats in rap lyrics on Facebook, the *Washington Post* billed the case as the Court's "first examination of the limits of free speech on social media." Ultimately however, Chief Justice Roberts's majority decision turned on the intent standard, and only glancingly referred to social media, while declining to address the First Amendment issues entirely. *See Elonis*, 135 S. Ct. at 2012; Robert Barnes, "Supreme Court Case Tests the Limits of Free Speech on Facebook and Other Social Media," *Washington Post*, November 23, 2014.

32 *See Packingham v. North Carolina*, Oyez, 2017, www.oyez.org.

33 *See id.; see also* Donhaue, Goldberg, Weaver & Littleton, "Attorneys: David T. Goldberg," https://donahuegoldberg.com.

34 *See Packingham*, Oyez. Trump himself ascribes enormous significance to the role of his own Twitter account, at least according to Bob Woodward. *See* Bob Woodward, *Fear: Trump in the White House* (New York: Simon & Schuster, 2018), 206 (attributing to Trump: "This is my megaphone. . . . This is who I am. This is how I communicate. It's the reason I got elected. It's the reason that I'm successful").

35 *See Packingham*, Oyez.

36 *Id.*

37 *See, e.g., Southeastern Promotions, Ltd. v. Conrad*, 420 U.S. 546, 552, 555 (1975) (finding municipal theaters "were public forums designed for and dedicated to expressive activities," and holding denial of a request to produce the musical *Hair* in such theaters was an unconstitutional prior restraint); *Hague v. Committee for Industrial Organization*, 307 U.S. 496, 515 (1939) ("Wherever the title of streets and parks may rest, they have immemorially been held in trust for the use of the public and, time out of mind, have been used for purposes of assembly, communicating thoughts between citizens, and discussing public questions. Such use of the streets and public places has, from ancient times, been a part of the privileges, immunities, rights, and liberties of citizens"); *see also* Aaron H. Caplan, "Invasion of the Public Forum Doctrine," 46 *Willamette Law Review* 647 (2010) (criticizing the spread of public forum references by courts as unhelpful and like "kudzu").

38 *See Packingham*, Oyez.

39 *Id.*

40 *See id.*

41 *See, e.g.,* Nadine Strossen, "Justice Anthony Kennedy's Free Speech Legacy," 70 *Hastings Law Journal* 1317 (2019) ("Justice Kennedy has been hailed by free speech advocates as a leading free speech champion. In contrast, other experts have not only criticized particular opinions and votes by Justice Kennedy that rejected free speech claims, but they also have maintained that Justice Kennedy specifically declined to protect speech that was at odds with his conservative political and religious views"); Floyd Abrams, "The First Amendment's Undisputed Champion," *Wall Street Journal*, June 28, 2018 (opinion by Abrams calling Kennedy "the Supreme Court's most dedicated, consistent and eloquent defender of the First Amendment"); Colin Dwyer, "A Brief History of Anthony Kennedy's Swing Vote—and the Landmark Cases It Swayed," NPR, June 27, 2018, www.npr.org.

42 *See* Erwin Chemerinsky, "Justice Kennedy: A Free Speech Justice? Only Sometimes," 70 *Hastings Law Journal* 1193 (2019); Ashutosh Bhagwat, "Candides and Cassandras: Technology and Free Speech on the Roberts Court," 95 *Washington University Law Review* 1327, 1329 (2018).

43 *Packingham*, 137 S. Ct. at 1735 (internal citations and quotation marks omitted).

44 *Id.* (internal citation and quotation marks omitted)

45 *Id.* at 1735–36 (internal citation and quotation marks omitted). The Court was quoting here from its decision in *Reno v. American Civil Liberties Union*, 521 U.S. 844, 849 (1997), which held that the 1996 Communications Decency Act, intended to

"protect minors from 'indecent' and 'patently offensive' communications on the Internet," violated the First Amendment for reasons of vagueness and overbreadth.

46 *Packingham*, 137 S. Ct. at 1736.

47 *Id.* (internal quotation marks omitted).

48 *Id.* (internal quotation marks omitted).

49 *Id.* at 1737.

50 *Id.*

51 *Id.* (internal quotation marks omitted).

52 *Id.* at 1738.

53 *See id.; see also* Brent Kendall, "Supreme Court Invalidates N.C. Law Barring Sex Offenders from Social Media," *Wall Street Journal,* June 19, 2017 ("Justice Neil Gorsuch didn't participate in the case, which was argued before he joined the high court").

54 *See Packingham*, 137 S. Ct. at 1738.

55 *See id.*

56 *See* Amy Howe, "Opinion Analysis: Court Invalidates Ban on Social Media for Sex Offenders," *SCOTUSblog,* June 19, 2017, www.scotusblog.com ("even though the justices all agreed on the result in [the *Packingham*] decision, it may be harder for them to find common ground in future cases involving the First Amendment and the Internet").

57 *See Packingham*, 137 S. Ct. at 1744 (citation omitted).

58 Zack Sharf, "Sacha Baron Cohen Uses Golden Globes to Slam Zuckerberg for 'Spreading Nazi Propaganda,'" IndieWire, January 5, 2020, www.indiewire.com (at the 2020 Golden Globes, Cohen introduced the Best Motion Picture Musical or Comedy nominee *Jojo Rabbit* by joking, "The hero of this next movie is a naive misguided child who spreads Nazi propaganda and only has imaginary friends. His name is Mark Zuckerberg").

59 Some scholars have advocated that state action requirements should be relaxed or reinterpreted in order to enable courts to apply First Amendment rules to private social media companies. *See, e.g.,* Tim Wu, "Is the First Amendment Obsolete?," in *The Free Speech Century,* edited by Lee C. Bollinger and Geoffrey R. Stone (New York: Oxford University Press, 2019), 274, 285–87 (suggesting accomplice liability could be used to hold "State or political leaders . . . constitutionally responsible for encouraging private parties to punish critics" online); David L. Hudson, Jr., "In the Age of Social Media, Expand the Reach of the First Amendment," *ABA Human Rights Magazine* 43.4 (October 20, 2018), www.americanbar.org ("The U.S. Supreme Court should . . . relax the state action doctrine. The Court should interpret the First Amendment to limit the 'unreasonably restrictive and oppressive conduct' by certain powerful, private entities—such as social media entities—that flagrantly censor freedom of expression"). This theoretical approach seems unlikely to be adopted by the Supreme Court in the near future. In 2019, the Court decided *Manhattan Community Access Center v. Halleck*, and declining to lossen state action

requirements held that private corporations running public access television channels were not state actors. *See Manhattan Community Access Center,* 139 S. Ct. 1921, 1930 (2019) ("merely hosting speech by others is not a traditional, exclusive public function and does not alone transform private entities into state actors subject to First Amendment constraints"); *see also* Susan E. Seager, "No, There Isn't a Double Standard for Conservatives and Liberals on Social Media" (op-ed), *Los Angeles Times,* July 12, 2019 (in *Manhattan Community Access Center,* "the Supreme Court shot a big hole in the argument that social media platforms were required by the 1st Amendment to provide neutral public forums for all users").

60 *See, e.g.,* Kate Conger, "Twitter Labels Trump Tweet about 'Racist Baby' as Manipulated Media," *New York Times,* June 18, 2020 (discussing how Twitter has started labeling some of Trump's tweets with critical disclaimers, and in retaliation Trump issued "an executive order designed to chip away at legal protections for Twitter and other internet companies that shield them from liability for what their users post").

61 *See* Eric Johnson, "Should the First Amendment Apply to Facebook? It's Complicated," Vox, November 19, 2018, www.vox.com ("'Facebook has its own First Amendment rights here,' [Jameel] Jaffer [director of the Knight First Amendment Institute] said. 'It expresses them by ejecting Alex Jones from the platform'").

62 Without First Amendment restrictions on government regulation of online speech, European countries have been able to take a different approach to regulating social media. "Europe has clamped down on violent content, hate speech and misinformation online through a thicket of new laws and regulations over the past five years. Now there are questions about whether the region is going too far, with the rules leading to accusations of censorship and potentially providing cover to some governments to stifle dissent." Adam Satariano, "Europe Is Reining in Tech Giants. But Some Say It's Going Too Far," *New York Times,* May 6, 2019.

63 *See* 47 U.S.C. § 230.

64 *See* Electronic Frontier Foundation, "Section 230 of the Communications Decency Act," www.eff.org. For more on the history of Section 230, *see* Jeff Kosseff, *The Twenty-Six Words That Created the Internet* (Ithaca, NY: Cornell University Press, 2019), 280 ("The modern Internet is the House That Is Built on Section 230. It isn't the nicest house on the block, but it's the house where we all live. We can't tear it down. We're stuck with it. So we must maintain our home and preserve it for the future").

65 For actions Facebook has taken to self-regulate speech on its platform, *see* Betsy Morris, "Facebook Bans Deepfakes but Permits Some Altered Content," *Wall Street Journal,* January 7, 2020 ("Facebook Inc. is banning videos that have been manipulated using advanced tools, though it won't remove most doctored content, as the social-media giant tries to combat disinformation without stifling speech"); Andrew Marantz, "Facebook and the 'Free Speech' Excuse," *New Yorker,* October 31, 2019 (criticizing Facebook policy regarding political ads allowing politicians to "say more

or less whatever they want," according to the author); Daphne Keller, "Facebook Restricts Speech by Popular Demand," *Atlantic*, September 22, 2019 (discussing Facebook announcing "its own version of the Supreme Court: a 40-member board that will make final decisions about user posts that Facebook has taken down").

66 After *Packingham*, Kennedy retired and Brett Kavanaugh was sworn in as the next Supreme Court justice. Given that Kavanaugh's and Gorsuch's positions on social media speech are unknown (since Gorsuch did not participate in *Packingham*), it is not clear whether there still is a majority of justices who would support the expansive language of Kennedy's opinion.

67 *See* Noah Feldman, "Supreme Court Doesn't Care What You Say on the Internet," Bloomberg, June 19, 2017, www.bloomberg.com (Harvard Law professor Noah Feldman writes that the post-*Packingham* impact on "the regulation of offensive speech on social media [is that the] government is not going to get involved. In practice, what that means is that the corporations that own and control social media are going to be squarely in charge of shaping the norms of speech").

68 *See* David Post, "Supreme Court Unanimously Overturns North Carolina's Ban on Social-Media Use by Sex Offenders," *Washington Post*, July 3, 2017 (Packingham reflects "one of the foundational issues in cyberlaw, 'Exceptionalism' vs. 'Unexceptionalism.' The majority takes the Unexceptionalist position. . . . The concurring justices are the Exceptionalists"); Paul Schiff Berman, *Law and Society Approaches to Cyberspace* (Burlington, VT: Ashgate, 2007), xiv ("[E]arly legal scholarship regarding online communication [was divided] into two camps. On one side were the cyberspace 'unexceptionalists' who argued in various contexts that the online medium did not significantly alter the legal framework to be applied. . . . On the other, cyberspace 'exceptionalists' argued that the medium itself created radically new problems requiring new analytical work to be done").

69 *See* Mark Tushnet, "Internet Exceptionalism: An Overview from General Constitutional Law," 56 *William & Mary Law Review* 1637, 1638 (2015) ("First Amendment Internet exceptionalism . . . refer[s] to question of whether the technological characteristics of the Internet . . . justify treating regulation of information dissemination through the Internet differently from regulation of such dissemination through nineteenth- and twentieth-century media such as print, radio and television").

70 *See Packingham*, 137 S. Ct. at 1739–40 (from Alito's concurrence: "the internet provides previously unavailable ways of communicating with, stalking, and ultimately abusing children").

71 *See* Floyd Abrams, "On Thinking about the First Amendment and the Internet," in *Friend of the Court: On the Front Lines with the First Amendment* (New Haven, CT: Yale University Press, 2013), 433 (I am pleased to note that I contributed research assistance to Abrams, as an associate at Cahill Gordon & Reindel, for the speech that was the basis for this chapter.)

72 *Id.* at 433–34 (internal quotation marks omitted).

73 *See* Stephen Budiansky, *Oliver Wendell Holmes: A Life in War, Law, and Ideas* (New York: W. W. Norton & Company, 2019), 460 ("A full century later [Holmes's] Abrams dissent continues to be invoked with admiration by conservative and liberal jurists alike").

Afterword

1 The Clash, "Know Your Rights," track 1 on *Combat Rock*, Sony Music, 1982.

2 This credo is inspired by Michael Pollan's remarkable ability to condense the "incredibly complicated and confusing question of what we humans should eat in order to be maximally healthy" down to just seven words: "Eat food. Not too much. Mostly plants." *See* Michael Pollan, "Unhappy Meals," *New York Times*, January 28, 2007.

3 George Orwell, "Freedom of the Park," *Tribune*, December 7, 1945 (accessible at www.orwellfoundation.com).

INDEX

Abdul-Jabbar, Kareem, 52

Abernathy, Ralph, 59, 60, 61–63

Abrams, Floyd: on Internet free speech, 194–95; as *New York Times* lawyer, 95, 98–100, 107

Abrams, Jacob: anarchist beliefs defended by, 12; as co-writer of anarchist journal, 7; guilty verdict for, 13; prison sentence for, 23–24

Abrams v. United States: Brandeis dissent in, 17, 22, 23; Clarke affirming convictions in, 18; common law nature reflected in, 23; Court ruling in, 23–24; in federal district court, 11–13, 206n50, 206n57; Holmes dissent in, 17–20, 22–23, 209n100; oral arguments in, 13–14; *Schenck v. United States* relevance to, 14–16, 207n79, 207n82, 208n93; Stewart representing government in, 14, 16

absence of malice, 230n69

ACLU. *See* American Civil Liberties Union

actual malice: absence of malice and, 230n69; changes to, 230n70; *Hustler v. Falwell* in relation to, 152, 156, 158; *New York Times Company v. Sullivan* as

test of, 56–57, 68; Thomas view of, 56; Trump, D., understanding of, 70

advertisements: Campari, 140, 148–49; Heed Their Rising Voices, 57–60, 228n40, 228n41; truth influenced by, 21–22. *See also* parody advertisement

affirm, 207n76

Albee, Edward, 253n19

Alito, Samuel: on *Packingham v. North Carolina*, 188–89, 191–92; on public concern, 169; *Snyder v. Phelps* dissent of, 176–77

American Civil Liberties Union (ACLU): Gardner of, 36–37; on Heed Their Rising Voices advertisement, 228n40; on *New York Times Company v. Sullivan*, 103; on religious persecution of Jehovah's Witnesses, 40; on students in Take a Knee protest, 222n172; on *Tinker v. Des Moines*, 89, 90; on Unite the Right rally, 161

American flag: Bennett and, 29; Flag Day, 44; Goodell and, 31; Kaepernick and, 26; as military symbol, 27; Reid and, 53; as symbol of national unity, 38; as symbol of personal liberty, 36; Trump, D., and, 29, 51. *See also* Pledge of Allegiance; Take a Knee protests

violent dissent, 115–16
vulgarity: as another's lyric, 121; on award shows, 133–34; of C-word, 124–25, 252n4, 253n9; of Fuck the Draft protest, 112–13, 247n19, 248n25; *Holy Shit* on, 137; marketplace of ideas and, 116; of seven dirty words, 125–27, 129. See also *Cohen v. California; FCC v. Pacifica Foundation*

Washington Post, 100–102, 104–5
Watergate, 106–7
wealth, 21–22
Wechsler, Herbert, 64–65, 229n47
Weinberger, Harry, 11, 12–14, 23–24
West, Lindy, 183
Westboro Baptist Church: funeral protests by, 163–65, 171; *Snyder v. Phelps* protesting by, 167–68; social media representation of, 179. *See also* Phelps, Fred; *Snyder v. Phelps*
West Virginia State Board of Education v. Barnette: federal district court ruling in, 42–43, 219n126; Frankfurter dissent in, 47–48; Jackson, R., on Court ruling in, 43–47; results from, 47, 48–49; Take a Knee protests in relation to, 50, 54; *Tinker v. Des Moines* support from, 81
Wetter, Donald M., 77

White, Byron: on armband protests, 82; *on Hustler v. Falwell*, 152, 155; on *New York Times Company v. Sullivan*, 230n56; *New York Times Company v. United States* position of, 105
white supremacists/nationalists: Flynt shot by, 144; KKK as, 59, 76, 160–62, 210n114; Trump, D., responses to, 162, 267n24; Unite the Right rally involving, 160–62, 178
Whitney v. California, 208n89, 275n125
Wilson, Woodrow, 7–10
Wolff, Michael, 56
Women's March (2017), 5–6, 25, 204n8
Woodward, Bob, 56, 224n2, 249n56, 278n34
"Workers-Wake Up!!" (Schwartz), 8–9
World War I, 7–10
World War II: *Minersville School District v. Gobitis* decision impacted by, 37–38; Pledge of Allegiance changes during, 43, 219n129, 219n131

Yiddish, 7–10, 12
Young, Andrew, 63, 228n43
youthful protest: antipathy toward, 79, 88; considered new cultural development, 79; rules for, 91–92. *See also* student activism

Zuckerberg, Mark, 182, 192, 279n58

ABOUT THE AUTHOR

Ian Rosenberg is Assistant Chief Counsel at ABC, Inc., where he has provided pre-broadcast counsel for ABC News clients on libel, newsgathering, intellectual property, and FCC regulatory issues since 2003. He graduated with distinction from the University of Wisconsin–Madison, and magna cum laude from Cornell Law School. Rosenberg began his legal career clerking in the Eastern District of New York, and then working as a litigation associate at Cahill Gordon & Reindel. He is also an Emmy-nominated documentary filmmaker and teaches media law at Brooklyn College.